Fighting to Speak

Rugby, Rage & Redemption

'You may as well hang for a sheep as hang for a lamb!'
One of my father's favourite sayings

Fighting to Speak

Rugby, Rage & Redemption

Mark Jones
With Anthony Bunko

Cardiff

Published in Wales by St. David's Press, an imprint of

Ashley Drake Publishing Ltd
PO Box 733
Cardiff
CF14 7ZY

www.st-davids-press.wales

First Impression – 2022

ISBN
Paperback 978-1-904609-018
eBook 978-1-904609-025

British Library Cataloguing-in-Publication Data.
A CIP catalogue for this book is available from the British Library.

Typeset by Prepress Plus, India (www.prepressplus.in)
Cover designed by the Welsh Books Council, Aberystwyth

Contents

This book is dedicated to all the people who have been abused, taunted and laughed at, or simply made to feel inferior and self-conscious, because of their stammer. Whoever you are, and however bad you're feeling – remember, you're not on your own. My stammer led to a deep emotional pain and a psychological self-loathing that manifested itself in hate and aggression when I played rugby. I lashed out many times and did some terrible things which I now regret, but I found salvation through speech therapy which changed my life. I successfully channelled my aggression and frustration to smash the stammer – it doesn't control me anymore. Don't let it control you either.

Acknowledgements

There are lots of people who have preconceived ideas of me. Some of them positive, but probably a lot of them leaning towards the negative. I have done a lot of things that I'm proud of in my life and, to tell the truth, I believe I overachieved as a rugby player simply because I brought something to the table that not many 6-foot 5-inch guys did. I know I've also done a lot of things I'm not proud of - things I regret - but that was what got me to where I wanted to go. It made me not just another big guy with limited skills and big boots.

I've had a fantastic life from rugby and am so grateful to the people that helped me along the way: my dad, Richie Gregory, Ben Thomas, Dai Chard, Roger Thomas, Ron Waldron, Brian Thomas, Glen Ball, Tex, Dai Shaw, Berwyn, Les Miles, Brian Smith, Greg Mackey, 'Crusher' Cleal, Royce Symonds, Clive Griffiths, Mike Nicholas, Jim Mills, Paul Russell, Marcus Russell, Leigh Jones, Bob Jude. There are countless others who have had an impact on me. My old man, an encyclopaedia of phrases and quotes, often told me, 'Listen to everyone and pick their brains, then put all the good bits together and throw away the rest.'

I would also like to acknowledge the people closest to me. To my dad for guiding me in his own way. To my mam for loving me unconditionally. To Osian and Manon – I love you both so very much. To Izzy and Zara for being my energy and drive. To Pat and Malcolm for taking me in, and to Julia for putting me on the path to redemption.

The people listed above are the ones who spoke the most sense. For fear of sounding clichéd, when you play rugby you meet a lot of people and mix with an assortment of different characters. You are learning all the time. You learn in training from someone who has a totally professional attitude. You learn on the field when someone runs over you as if you weren't there. You learn subconsciously and you work things out. You do take all the good bits and you improve. There can be, though, a limit to your improvement, either you don't have the physical ability to perform certain skills or you could have a psychological resistance - the fear of failure - to stepping outside your comfort zone. Most of us are happy to stay with what we know: doing what we are good at and only bringing what we can easily bring to the party. The superstars are the ones who do the basics brilliantly, but their natural skills are enhanced by an ability to learn from others and improve every aspect of their game - that is what sets them apart. It is said there are water carriers and water drinkers. It's nice to be a drinker, but in my humble opinion, you can't drink if you haven't carried.

I did a lot of things in my life, the good, the bad and the downright ugly but that's the person I was. Looking back, many of the things I did were wrong, but they was a reaction to my circumstances – my daily, painful, personal battle to be heard.

To protect those I care about, I have occasionally hidden the identities of certain individuals when recalling some incidents. They may be great stories but the people involved don't always need to be mentioned.

This book reflects my opinion and no one else's. It's solely my perspective. One coach may love you, while another one hates you. That's their choice, their opinion. The most important truth, however, is your own. When you look in the mirror each morning, the person looking back at you is the one that matters. If you don't like what you see, it's up to you to change yourself. No one else can do it for you.

Enjoy!

Mark Jones
November 2022

Preface

Mark was the perfect No. 8.

In an era of amateur rugby, he was born to be a professional. He had all the attributes: big, strong and very quick he was almost impossible to stop, just ask the All Blacks who he faced a few times. Add to that an incredible physical presence and he was a man who could, and did, cause a lot of damage on a rugby field both at club and international level.

His particular fetish was for English forwards. Several have been recipients of his 'flamboyance' over the years.

At club level he loved scoring tries, so he would hang about in the outside half position waiting for a popped pass. If it was not forthcoming, he would take his frustration out on some poor prop's ribs which generally meant they went off injured never to return.

Thankfully there is another side to Mark which most people never see. He is witty, thoughtful, unselfish, very loyal and above all a great friend.

Glyn Llewellyn

Foreword

I have been privileged over the years to have played with, coached with, been coached by, toured with and drunk with so many great rugby people, but I can honestly say the player who made the biggest impression on me is Mark Jones – Scooby. From the first time I saw him playing for Tredegar – snarling face, long legs, huge stride and knees pumping to what seemed to be head height – his aggression and determination was enough to make the bravest opponent think twice about tackling him. I was playing for Brynmawr Youth, dreaming of playing for Wales (as were most of the boys from the Gwent Valleys), when I first saw Mark play. I then followed his career as he moved to Neath and looked forward to *Rugby Special* on a Sunday evening to watch the most formidable side in Wales at that time, with Mark dominating everyone he played against.

The first time I actually met Mark was in Blackwood RFC in 1988 when he presented me with the Clubman of the Year award for North Monmouthshire Youth (North Mon) – something that I am very proud of to this day. He shook (or should I say squeezed) my hand, looked me in the eye and uttered 'Sssstick at ... at it!' I never knew that this giant man had a stammer! It made me think that none of us are perfect, even this incredible athlete, standing 6ft 5 and full of muscle. A man who exuded confidence on the playing field, yet was so humble and almost shy off it. My respect levels for Mark went up even higher at that moment. Our hero, having recently starred in numerous games for Wales, putting himself totally outside his comfort zone, presenting awards to young lads in Blackwood on a Friday evening, giving something back to North Mon Youth. What a guy!

It wasn't too long before I graduated to senior rugby but by then Mark had 'gone north' to rugby league. I must admit to being quite relieved, particularly in those early years, not having to line up against Mark. Phew!

Many Welsh players successfully switched codes at that time and Mark was definitely one of them – he was a natural in the 13-a-side game. During my days at Sale Sharks I shared many a story with RL legends who had played with or against him, the great Paul Cullen for one. We instantly had something in common, Scooby stories! Old school rugby tales of thuggery and violence for the most part, but all the stories seemed to end in rapturous laughter – league was no different to union in that regard.

Mark was feared by many as a so-called 'enforcer'. Not many got the better of Mark, but if they did, he was the first to admit it, shake their hand and have a beer with them post-game.

In 1995 I was made captain of my beloved Ebbw Vale RFC. Malcolm Shepherd, a local businessman and club chairman, was pulling the strings following the great work of the Johnston brothers who got the club promoted back to the Premiership. Malcolm wanted to build a team of the best players from the area and targeted the likes of Byron Hayward, Dai Llewellyn, Jason Strange and Spike Jones who were playing for other first-class clubs at that time. We were becoming a decent side, a typical valley team I guess, tough and hard to play against, particularly at home. We were always on the look for players from Gwent and Breconshire. This was around the time that the game went professional. There was talk of players like Scott Gibbs, Scott Quinnell, Jonathan Davies and others returning from rugby league to play rugby union in Wales.

I will never forget one Wednesday night in September at Eugene Cross Park when we were playing Newbridge and Mark Jones was there, watching the game. I spoke with him briefly afterwards and he was still the very courteous, polite and humble man I remembered. He said he was interested in coming back to rugby union and had been talking with Newport. I went straight to see Malcolm Shepherd and the then president of Ebbw Vale, Paul Russell, to tell them the news about Mark. I said that if Mark Jones is going to sign for Newport, then I was going to sign for them as well. At that time in my career, I could honestly say he is the only man I wouldn't want to play against. 'He needs to be in our team!', I demanded.

Fair play to Paul and Malcolm, they set about their business and Mark soon became an Ebbw Vale player. The addition of Mark, along with Kuli Faletau and Suia Tomololo, took Ebbw Vale to new heights, reaching our first - and as yet only - Welsh Cup final and finishing in the Premiership's top four on a regular basis.

Mark brought mental toughness, resilience and professionalism to the team. The respect the team had for him was immeasurable. The fun we had, the memories (or should I say stories) I have, like the time we were travelling home from an away game in West Hartlepool, are legendary. We had stopped at a service station on the M5, tired, hungry and hung-over. The players were standing in the self-service food line when Mark saw a stray chip on the counter and decided to pick it up and eat it. When he got to the till the cashier demanded he paid for a full plate of chips. Mark refused, the cashier called security on the radio and within seconds a security guard bounded around the corner and headed towards the till, where Mark was singled out as the offender. This 5ft nothing, 20-year-old security guard, nervously walked towards Mark and as he got within 3ft of the big man, Mark growled at him, 'Come on. Earn your money, boy.'

The young guard, by now with shit literally running down the leg of his trousers, turned around and waddled away, followed by rapturous laughter from all the team. That was the last we heard of that! Another time we were playing Swansea at home and they scored early on. I felt we weren't at the races and I needed to get the boys fired up, so I organised the boys into a tight huddle and said, 'Scooby, Paul Moriarty is laughing at you.' Mark looked at me with a wry smile and muttered, 'Don't piss down my back and tell me it's raining, boy.' Once again, the team burst into rapturous laughter at my transparent, naïve and failed attempt at player motivation!

I have enough Mark Jones stories to last a lifetime, from witty to inspirational, and others that will bring a tear to your eye, and yes, of course, I can do a Mark Jones impression. It's only recently while reminiscing with Mark that I realise truly how difficult he found being in such a brutal piss-taking environment as Welsh rugby in the '80s & '90s, with a speech impediment. He tells me he has some regret about things he did or said back then, but for me, that was what made him the man he is. A legend amongst players and fans, and numerous stories are still spoken about on Saturday nights in rugby clubs around Wales to this day. I still find myself, 25 years on, using quotes in my coaching or everyday life that originated with Mark.

At times Mark could be a ruthless, brutal man, on occasion over the edge. If you were on the receiving end, you may think that Mark was a pig of a man, a dumb thug, but I can tell you otherwise.

That character was the on-field mask he wore, which hid a highly intelligent and caring man with a huge heart. A loyal man, my friend and someone I would choose to have beside me in times of trouble, every time.

Kingsley Jones

1

Personality Crisis (x3)

'On the field, Mark was a big, robust, ferocious player who never took a step backwards. But away from the spotlight, I found him to be a funny, social guy, who loved to sing a song now and again.'

Jonathan 'Jiffy' Davies

I sit alone on the front step of my house in Qatar where I now live. The sky is blue, the heat is relentless but as with most of my life, in my own mind, I can only feel the cold wind and see grey clouds floating above me. I'm trying to get my head around writing this book. I'm still not sure if it will be a good thing or not! It will mean me delving back into my life and dragging up all the pain and the hurt and the anger to finally tell the world about the real Mark Jones.

Communicating has never been easy for me, for all sorts of reasons. Having a stammer has firmly gripped every part of my life. It has owned me. It has been the most impactful thing of my entire life. It has influenced my every action, my every feeling. It's been a heavy weight around my neck from the moment I wake up every morning of every day until I fall asleep at night. There hasn't been a day that has passed where it hasn't affected the way I've behaved, the way I've felt, the way I've conducted myself. It has led to a rollercoaster ride through the dark emotions of self-loathing, hatred, anger, and endless insecurities. It has shaped everything I've ever done.

During my playing days, there were three Mark Joneses living in my body. Most people only saw one, the hard man on the rugby field. Some saw the second one, but no one saw the third one, and let me tell you now, there was definitely a third one. Not so much the father, the son and the holy ghost, more like The Terminator, The Party Animal and The Lost Soul. There was the 'On the Field Mark', the 'After the Game Mark' and then there was the 'At Home Mark'.

The 'After the Game Mark' and the 'On the Field Mark' were very closely linked, but the 'At Home Mark' was a very different creature altogether. A very detached species from the other two.

Millions of people who stammer will be leading an anxious, embarrassed, unfulfilled life. I am so lucky to have had rugby to provide the opportunity to achieve and to develop. I created two of the three personas to hide who I really was, and how I really felt. 'On The Field Mark' would put on the 'I'm 6 feet 5 and invincible' suit which would make him bullet proof. He could be a sociopath. That Mark had no empathy and no remorse for the things he did. In his eyes, when he crossed the whitewash and ran onto the rugby field, he was playing in a big boy's game with big boy's rules and he loved it. What went on, out there, stayed out there (unless I dragged up in front of the disciplinary committee). That suited 'On the Field Mark' down to the ground. The only person he had to avoid was the ref and winning was the only aim.

I am in no way condoning this mentality, looking to excuse my actions or looking for sympathy in any way, shape or form, but that is the person I was. I did not realise, until years later, that it was all driven by my stammer. I, just needed to rid myself of the pain and hatred that I felt building up inside me. When you have a stammer, every day is a struggle. Let me try and explain by describing a typical day in my life when I was growing up.

I would wake up each morning, bright eyed and bushy tailed, not realising or remembering that I had a stammer. I was alive and ready to step into a new day, ready to take on the world. I would start talking to myself about what was going on that day, where I was going, who I was going to meet and, very importantly, what I was going to say.

'Right Mark, we are going here today so we are going to do this and we are going to do that.'

I'd try to mentally put myself into different scenarios that I would and could face later in the day. I would then spend ages rehearsing each situation, like an actor learning his lines. I'd be totally relaxed in the safety of my bedroom, so whatever I said to myself out loud would be fluent and I'd think, 'Brilliant, I've cracked this. Today is going to be a good day. I'm going to be like any other guy in the street. I'm going to be normal for once.'

I'd convince myself that I was in control and I could beat this. I'd leave the house full of confidence and feeling I'd conquered my demon. Nothing was going to go wrong. 'I'll show them,' I kept telling myself.

Then came the first test – Rosie's shop, on the way to my comprehensive school. Ok, I know I could have not gone in to buy sweets, but that would be giving up before I even started, and I had it all rehearsed. I was ready. The shop was always quite full. Mainly schoolkids like me who needed a sugar rush to get them through another boring day of education.

As I waited in the queue, I began to feel anxious and started to sweat under my uniform. It was like I was waiting to go in to see the dentist to have all my teeth removed, not to buy a bag of bloody sweets. 'I'll show them,' I kept telling myself. 'I'm ready.'

Then it was my turn to order what I wanted. Everything seemed to go silent. In my mind everyone was standing there, staring at me. 'Come on Mark ... you're going to be ok. Come on, you've rehearsed it in your bedroom.'

'What do you want?' the shop keeper asked. 'I'll ... I'll.' I paused and took a deep breath. I wanted to say 'a quarter of sherbet bonbons' but could only manage 'I'll have a q....' I could only get as far as the q. The letter stuck in my throat. It felt like someone had rammed a basketball in my mouth, a cement mixer had started churning around and around in my guts, and 1,000 spotlights shone on my inadequacy as if I was a floodlit rugby field. I could hear the others sniggering away behind my back. Tittering above the silence. My body trembled, my face bright red. I felt anger and embarrassment at the same time.

For God's sake, I only wanted a packet of fucking sweets.

My mind frantically searched for another word to replace the word quarter. 'Half a pound,' I quickly blurted out, but I didn't want half a pound of sweets, or a pound, or a wellington boot full of sweets. I wanted a quarter, a quarter of sherbet bloody bonbons.

Life shouldn't have been that hard, but to me, it was, and it never got any easier.

So, within a blink of an eye, I went from feeling great, thinking I had cracked it, back to feeling a failure. The anger would engulf me, the frustration, the embarrassment, the self-loathing. That's what it does. It lulls you into feeling like you can get the better of it but then it totally destroys your confidence. It lures you in like the 'child catcher' in the film, *Chitty Chitty Bang Bang*: offering you amazing delights you've never experienced before but then, after you've been lured inside, the shutters bang shut and you're trapped in your worst recurring fears. It then laughs in your face, ridiculing you when you're at your weakest, lowest point - and that's all before you're out of your pyjamas in the morning. It's exhausting. It can really distort your outlook on the world and your place within it. This is your reality.

Every day, every minute, was like walking through a minefield waiting for your confidence to be blown to pieces. Every word, every difficult-to-pronounce letter, had the potential to undermine your self-esteem, every minute of every day.

The stammer even infected my sub-conscious, and on bad days I'd start stammering in my own head when just thinking about day-to-day things. Those were such low points. I just wanted to crawl behind the skirting boards with the woodlice and spiders.

It really affected the way I looked at the world. In reality only 10% of the people you meet will smirk or grin when you stammer and half of them do it because they don't expect it, and to be fair to them, they don't know what to do. It's awkward for everybody. That is the reality.

In my experience, it is only about 5 in every 100 who mock you, and enjoy doing it. They are the ones who think, 'Hahaha, look at that big, stuttering fool. What an idiot.' I knew that, but it was that 5% who fired me up. It was them who I focussed on. They gave me the spur. I drew on that fury and grew it into a big ball of rage. I used it to my advantage. I used it to fuel me, but I didn't realise until recently that the anger and frustration was also feeding the stammer, causing me to be even more tense. My continually racing mind caused the massive knot in my stomach. It didn't allow me to breath, didn't allow me to relax and so it caused the stammer to evolve and made it even worse - a proper 'Catch 22'. The feeling continually frustrated me. The feeling of wanting to put my head through a brick wall.

That's how I approached rugby. My *modus operandi* was to go out and cause as much damage to the opposition as I could. I had no desire to actually play rugby as rugby should be played. I didn't want to be like Sonny Bill Williams or Jonathan Davies, I just needed to beat the demons inside me, ease the pain in the pit of my stomach and defuse the anger that burned there. I needed it to flagellate myself. I needed to get rid of the hatred in me. I had no desire to offload the ball in the tackle, all I needed was the rush of smashing into an opponent.

It was the only way to rid myself of the feeling. To hit a ruck hard and to wipe someone out - give them some of the pain I felt inside. No one was targeted. Well, not for the first 20 minutes. It was the jersey I targeted, not the person. It could have been my best mate off the field but if he was wearing the opposition's jersey, and I had an opportunity to smash that jersey I would smash it. No regrets!

After the game I would sit alone in in the changing rooms, shaking. I wanted to make sure every bit of the hatred was exorcized out of me. Then, when I had cooled down, I would walk into the clubhouse with my head held high.

This was the second Mark Jones, the Mark Jones that I wanted you all to see. The 'After the Game Mark' was outgoing. He was loud, he was brash, and he was confident. If I had a good game there would be no stopping me. I was the 6-foot, 5 kid with the spikey, punk, hair-cut and the tight jeans. I was the guy at the centre of the room, drinking the beers with the boys, laughing out loud at the jokes and acting like I didn't have a care in the world.

It was, though, all just a mask, an act, because the personas of those two Marks only lasted a very short time. One, until the final whistle sounded and the other until the last orders bell rang. Then it was back to 'At Home Mark'. To the doubt and to the pain and the shame.

So, as I start to think back on my life so far and I feel the warm Qatar sun on my face, I think, 'OK, you lot ... this is the time to set the record straight and to finally tell the world about the real Mark Jones ... all three of them!'

So, strap yourself in - it's going to be a bumpy ride!

2

Stand Up! (Banged Up!)

'Mark was a legend, on and off the field. An Inspiration. Someone I looked up to. He took me under his wing and always 'looked after' me in games. One hell of a hard man....and I'm so glad we were in the same team.'

Lenny Woodard

'Let me out, you fucking pigs,' I heard someone shouting at the top of their voice from down the corridor.

Alone and fearful, I sat perched on the edge of the bed in the police cell. The taste of stale beer in my mouth and the stink of piss in my nostrils. My head was spinning, my heart banging in my chest. Questions raced through my 18-year-old mind at 100 miles per hour.

'When are they going to let me out? What if they don't? What if they send me to prison? What will my mam say? Will it affect my rugby career? What will my old man say? Shit ... shit ... shit.' I felt like crying. I felt so mad with myself.

The shutter in the metal door slid open. For a split second I thought the copper was going to say something like, 'Sorry Mr Jones, we've made a big mistake. You are free to go and don't forget to collect £200 pounds on the way out,' but this was Tredegar 'nick', not a Hollywood rom-com movie. No such bloody luck. All I could see was an eye at the slot and hear the copper's abusive words followed by his wicked laugh before it slammed shut again and he strolled off.

I lay down on the foul-smelling mattress, listening to the screams and shouts, bangs and slams, and lots and lots of swearing coming from the mostly drunken inmates in the other cells. I lay there scared witless, to be honest. Although I stood 6 foot 4 at that age, I was still a pup in the land of the big, vicious, street-wise and wild Welsh dogs.

How the hell had I got myself into this situation? How could I have been so stupid to get banged up? It had all started so well. It had been near the end of the rugby season - mid-April, 1983. Earlier that afternoon, I had played for Glanhowy Youth at home to a team from Nantyglo. We'd won and I'd had a good game. Now it was party time. We had gone back to the Royal Oak and got on it, big style. As the beer flowed, we played all the usual drinking games like buzz, round the brush, who stole the cookies and many more.

I loved the craic with the boys but the worse thing for me was that 90% of the drinking games we played involved speaking out loud. Either shouting out numbers, or words or phrases in a certain order. This I struggled with, more so when I was sober. As the game of buzz progressed and went round the circle from boy to boy, I could feel the glare of the spotlight getting closer and closer to me. My anxiety grew. I'd start to sweat. I wanted to make an excuse and go to the toilet. Anything to stop the spotlight lighting up my deficiencies, but I knew that would only prolong the agony.

My turn in the game of Buzz was only three boys away. Then two boys. Then one boy. Thankfully, Billa, messed up. The game stopped. He had to drink three fingers of his pint and, luckily, the direction of the game got reversed. I was off the hook ... for now. Round it went again. Back and forth it went, my nerves going this way and then that way like a tennis match being played on a minefield. It was nearly my turn.

Three boys – 'Please mess up.'

Two boys – 'Please, please mess up.'

One boy – 'Pretty please, with fricking bells on it, mess up!'

This time no one did. My face shone brightly in the limelight. Nowhere to run, nowhere to hide, I could feel every pair of eyes in the room glaring at me, praying that I would mess up.

'B... b... b... F... Fuck it,' I cried out and necked the half pint as the others howled with laughter. The maddening thing was, I knew what to say, I just couldn't say it.

That's how it was for the next hour or so. I got a bit better as the beer flowed but I ended up drinking way more than most because I couldn't speak when put on the spot and the pressure was on.

After all the free beer had been consumed, we headed off into town. A big gang of us walking down Scrwfa Road like the cast of *Reservoir Dogs* in our club shirts and ties. Up Church Street to the Con club. A few more pints there. Then to the next pub and onwards. All the nightlife was starting to gather around the circle where the iconic town clock was located and where all buses stopped. Every shape and size of creature you could imagine waddling around town in tight boob tops and high heels. The *Star Wars* bar in human form, but I loved it.

The weather was your typical nine degrees – a warm summer's day for Tredegar. My hometown is a place where even polar bears would trudge around in overcoats and gloves. It didn't affect us lot, though. We were way too hard to feel the cold. All of us pissed-up by 7pm - creating havoc, having fun. We rolled from pub to pub, queuing to get in to the next place on the crawl, finishing up in the Castle about 10pm. I know I was an absolute bloody nuisance by then. We all were, I guess. Just your typical 18-year-old lads, enjoying the craic, singing and shouting, laughing and joking. Causing trouble was the furthest thing on our minds.

The Castle was packed. Unlike today, 'Tred' was a hive of activity back in those days. There was lots of work around in the factories and down the mines which meant lots of money splashing about. Everyone was out enjoying themselves.

The barmaid rang the bell, it was 10.50 and 'last orders'. There was a massive rush to the bar to get two pints in each. I got mine in, safe and sound. I needing a wazz so I put my two full pints down on a table by the jukebox. When I came back, one of my pints had gone. I saw some guy standing nearby drinking a full pint. A smug look on his smug face. The reasonable part of my brain got by-passed. I made the decision right there and then that the pint he was holding must have been mine.

'Oh, you, cheeky git,' I muttered, 'that's my pint.' I reached out to grab it. He pulled it away. I stretched over and slapped it out of his hand onto the floor. He stared at me. The pub went silent. I wasn't in the mood for stand-offs so I slammed my head in him full force and he dropped like a stone. Then I, like an idiot, fell forward over him and landed on some of the broken glass. A large piece of glass embedded in my hand. I got to my feet. He got up as well, blood flowing down his face. His mates took him outside. I pulled out the glass from my hand and blood spurted everywhere. Someone threw me a bar towel which I used to wrap up my wounded hand. The sight of blood instantly sobered me up.

'You better go quick, Jonesy,' my mate said to me, 'the cops will be here now.'

I shook my head. I stood my ground. 'No, I haven't done anything wrong. I'm not going anywhere.' In my drunken mind, I was just serving retribution on a thief. So, I carried on drinking my other pint. My pulse still racing.

Within a few minutes, the police came through the door accompanied by the thief, now with the cut eye, and a few of his cronies. They all pointed at me.

'What happened?' the cop asked me. I was wound up tighter than a spring and of course, found it hard to get my words out. I struggled to tell them he had stolen my pint and deserved everything he got. 'We are arresting you on suspicion of assault and you need to accompany us to the station,' the cop announced.

My rugby mates tried to explain what had happened, but by then the policemen's minds were made up. I was guilty and they were nicking me.

When one of the coppers was cuffing me, he noticed the bad cut on my hand and decided to take me to the Accident and Emergency Department at the local hospital. I was now sat, handcuffed, in the back of the car. Gutted, I began to think about what I had done and where I was. My whole outlook began to change. I knew this was not just a little skirmish over a pint. I'd been arrested, and the victim wanted to press charges. It hit me that this wasn't a rugby field, where if I overstepped the mark, things were dealt with on the field and everything moved on. You'd get a punch in the face from someone or get a good stamping and you didn't do it again. That was how I'd been brought up. That's how I thought all through my rugby career.

I was bundled out of the car at the hospital and shoved through the door head first. Remember, this was 1983 – the Police were in charge and more than happy to remind you of the fact. This was before the days when the feelings of the prisoner were taken into account. I'd been a bad boy and deserved all I got. My head was taking the full brunt for my misdemeanors.

I then got presented to the nurse. A stern-faced matron who I wouldn't want to have met in a dark alleyway. I'm sure they had flown her in specially from Stalag 17 to work the Saturday night shift in 'Tred' surgery.

'Name?' she grunted. I paused. 'NAME?'

'Mmmmmm ... Mark....J....J....J....Jones.'

I sensed a grin lighting up the face of the policeman, now standing in the corner. He glared at me with a look which screamed out, 'You're not Mr Big Man now are you? You little stuttering boy.'

I struggled through the formalities of giving her my name and address and telephone number. With each word I tripped up on, I turned to see him smirking. Since I was 15 and leapt onto the punk rock bandwagon in my Doc Martins, I had become very anti-establishment. The police were the enemy. It was a proper council estate, working class attitude. So, seeing the arrogant look on his big, self-righteous face, only made me feel more and more resentment and anger towards them, towards him. Looking back now, my frustration was misplaced. I should have been angry with myself for being an idiot, not with the law man who probably only wanted to be sat in the warmth of his patrol car on a Saturday night, drinking hot coffee, not dealing with a teenage twat like me.

After the nurse had finished with me, I was stitched up by a doctor who I swear used a knitting needle to put the stitches in. I still have the scar today ... along with a few others I must add. With little or no sympathy for my wound, the cops piled me back into the squad car and transported 'their prisoner' to the 'nick'.

During the journey, I was trying to perfect my story in preparation for the police interview that would follow.

'OK, I'd bought two pints, then gone for a piss, came back, had seen that bloke – whatever his name was – drinking my pint. I asked him to please put it down and he'd told me where to go. I'd then reached to take it from his hand, the glass fell. I'd slipped and ended up falling on the glass on the floor. No, I didn't headbutt him. I must have accidently made contact with him when I was falling. At that moment, it sounded feasible. All sorted.

The cop car pulled up. I was dragged out and put through another round of torture as I again had to answer lots of basic questions: name, address, date of birth, parents. More stammering, more grins from the cops. More frustration, anger and humiliation for me and they knew it!

By now, I was totally upside down. I couldn't think straight; couldn't process anything in my brain. This was reality. I'd been arrested before, but then I was just thrown in the cell and left to sleep it off before being let go with a warning and a verbal clip around the ear, but this was more serious; this was the real deal.

I was that full of anxiety, I couldn't speak. They finger-printed me next. One cop roughly grabbed my hands. His finger purposely pushing into the cut on my palm

'Aaarrrrgghh,' I cried out as the tips of my inked-up fingers were rolled onto the little windows on the sheet of card.

When that was completed, next was the thing I dreaded the most - the interview. They sat me at a table in the interrogation room: a tape recorder on the desk, an officer opposite me, who was flanked by 'the grinner' who had arrested me. The other officer ran through the routine. 'Mark, this interview will be taped and whatever you say will be used in evidence. Understand?' I nodded. 'You, Mark Jones .... have been arrested for assault. You have the right to remain silent ....' His words span around my head. All I was thinking was I wish I could rewind the night back to the rugby club with the laughing and joking and horsing about with my mates.

'Mark, give me your version of events.' The pause seemed to have lasted ten minutes as I tried to steady myself. 'I ...I....I....I was in the C...C...Castle ...' I didn't care now whether the police were grinning or not. Actually, they weren't but, in my head, they still were and I hated them for it. As the time went on, I got more and more frustrated, more anxious but I finally spat out my side of the story.

'Well, he suffered a badly cut eye and needed stitches, so this must have been more than just an accident, Mark. We are charging you with common assault,' the policemen informed me. I was slammed in the cell with no shoes on my feet. So, there I found myself, locked up for a moment of madness over a pint I probably would have wasted anyway.

I stared up at the blank ceiling in the stinking excuse for a prison cell. I hated being locked up. I didn't want to spend my life being locked up on a Saturday night, paying fines and going to jail for some stupid nonsense. I thought about losing my job, becoming a piss head; living my life in 'Tred' with people whispering as they walked past me sitting in a doorway like a tramp, 'He was a good rugby player once and he could've gone far ...if ...if .... only....'

I didn't want that but I was on that slippery slope. 'I'm not,' I shouted out into the darkness, 'I want out ... I WANT TO PLAY FOR WALES.' I wanted to walk down the street and for people to say, 'That's Mark Jones ... the rugby player'. I didn't want to be known as the stuttering 'Lanky Jonsey from Cefn' who's been in and out of prison for being a first-class prick.

That night I had reached my own personal crossroads. I sold my soul and vowed to not get locked up ever again. I had already won a Wales Youth cap by then, but I wanted the real thing. It was a way out of the misery and the pain. Where I was brought up, only the odd boxer and snooker player got to see the real world. Everyone else was stuck in the same old rut.

After a few hours of self-inflicted brain torture, I managed to control the panic taking over my body. I must have fallen asleep because I got rudely nudged awake by a size 12, shiny, black boot. 'Mark, are you alright?' I was too dazed to reply. 'Are you alright?' the copper asked again. I nodded my head. He walked away. This went on every half an hour or so. 'Mark, are you alright? Do you need a piss? Are you sure?' Then they would walk away leaving me wide awake again. Mental torture.

I went down to a dark, old crossroads during one of those brief interludes of sleep that was respite from the stinking hole that was the cell. There was someone sat on my shoulder that night. An invisible presence who bombarded me with more questions than answers. 'That's a lot to ask Mark, you playing for Wales? Having people to respect you? Look at you, you are sitting in a prison cell, alone, scared, talking to yourself. You want a lot of things but how can that happen? What are you prepared to do to get all that? How will you pay? You will have to feel pain; you will need to suffer. You will need to fight every inch of the way, boy. Are you ready for that?' After hours and hours of mental torment, I thought, 'sod this'. I sat on the piss-stained mattress and swore I wouldn't get locked up again.

It was a massive relief to be let go at 6.30 am. I was charged with Actual Bodily Harm (ABH) and walked home through the cold, damp Tredegar streets. When I ambled through the front door, my father was waiting up for me in the front room.

I expected him to give me a wallop, but he didn't. My old man was a kind fella. He never put a finger on me. He often said because his old man had beaten him with a belt when growing up, he would never touch us, me and Sandra (my older sister of five years), and he never did. I think he came close with Sandra a few times during her teens. She was wild. but although he was pushed at times, he always kept his word.

Instead, he sat me down on the settee. 'What are you doing, son? You are ruining your life. You will be going to go to jail if you carry on like this. You are going to lose your job. You will end up with nothing.'

I felt so ashamed to be sitting in front of him having this conversation. 'Dad, I swear this will be the last time I will ever get arrested. I'm not being locked up again.' I told him that one day I was going to play for Wales. This was the one thing I thought would make him proud of me, and I meant every word of it.

'I bet you will son,' he replied, 'but it isn't going to come easy. You will have to fight for it, every step of the way, especially with your... your.' He couldn't bear to admit that I had an affliction. He stopped mid-stream. 'I know I will, Dad. I know I will.'

He smiled at me. 'I remember the day you were born.' I rolled my eyes, here we go again, I thought. 'You were born 10 lb 6 oz and with two black eyes and a broken nose.' It's something he had told me a million times in the past. I sat and listened again to the story. His face lit up with delight. Maybe he was right. Maybe, when I had fought my way, kicking and screaming, into the world on 22 June 1965 at St James' Hospital in Tredegar - in the beating heart of the South Wales valleys - to Elizabeth and Benjamin Jones, I was just getting prepared for what was to come.

The whole episode about getting arrested and spending the night in the cell had made me sit and think and try to fully understand how I had got into this situation and more importantly what I needed to do to move forward with my head held high. I wanted to make my parents proud of me; I wanted to make myself proud of me.

I can honestly say I came from a good, decent, hard-working family. My father was a collier and worked for 40 years in the mines. He had left school when he was 14, during the war, unable to read or write, to work down the pits. Originally his family were farmers who came from the Ledbury area to find employment in the iron works. He never missed a day's work – a fact that made him very proud – often doing double shifts. However, money was always tight in our house. We had no extras, just food and basic clothes. We never could afford the little luxuries in life. Yet what we did have was pride. It was bred into me and my sister. We never had a car and never had a foreign holiday. The furthest we ever got to was Barry Island during 'Miners' Fortnight'.

Until I was four, our family lived in three rooms on the ground floor of a rented house. My parents had one bedroom, me and my sister shared the other and we had one living room which also included the kitchen. It was only a few years later, when we moved, that I had my own room! I slept in the tiny box room (7 foot by 8) until I was 25, by which time I'd played for Wales 15 times! In our first house, we only had an outside lavatory. A small, redbrick outhouse which bred the biggest garden spiders in the world ... ever! I saw some raspers down there, hiding in the corners, ready to pounce. At night, terrified, I'd be in and out of that place like a flash of lightning.

My dad was the vice-chairman of Tredegar Ironsides RFC and that gave him a huge buzz. He was a full-on rugby man though he never played. I still reckon if you had cut him in half, he would have bled the colours of the club. He would sit in the clubhouse like thousands of Welshmen from all over the country and analyse every game, every player. He would watch the Ironsides every week. He would watch Wales on the telly, shouting at the ref, cheering and chastising with his one, red and white, biased eye blazing with passion.

He also loved his garden. He could grow anything; tomatoes, lettuce, peas, beans, cabbage, cauliflower, beetroot, the lot. He spent hours and hours, planting, weeding, pruning, digging and whatever gardeners did with their spare time.

'He loves that garden more than he loves me,' my mother often joked. Well, I think she was joking. My mother, Elizabeth, was only 5'4' tall. A very frail little lady who was very shy but very strong and was fiercely protective of her 'little boy'.

They never really talked about how and when they met. Probably in some dance in the social club I'm guessing.

My mam was severely afflicted with rheumatoid arthritis which, from the age of 45, made her a captive in her own home. She had a wheelchair but wouldn't be seen dead in it: 'The shame,' she often said. All through my childhood I can recall my mam going into hospital for numerous therapies and operations. It wasn't an easy time for any of us, especially for her. She must have felt like a pin cushion with the number of injections she had to endure each week. She had injections in her knuckles, knees and elbows and relied on ibuprofen tablets to dull the pain. Her battle against the arthritis and its crippling pain continued well into my rugby career and after my father had died,

By the end, the disease had forced her to have numerous joints, ankles, knees, elbows and wrists fused in order to take away pain but also to remove any movement in those joints.

My old man often said that Mam's illness came after I was born. As a kid, hearing that and having the immature mind of a 10-year-old, I sometimes thought that it was me that caused all the suffering to Mam. It was a spiteful thing for him to say. As I've got older, I've read numerous papers and it's been hinted at that the trauma of childbirth could be a catalyst for the onset of the disease, but the gene for the disease had to have been passed down from Mam's parents. Over time, I've come to an informed conclusion that genetics was the main reason for her illness, not my arrival.

Although, she was small in stature, quiet in personality and ill most of the time, Mam was still the boss in our house. She was very strong willed and could be stubborn. Although she ended up not being able to walk, she was not a walk-over by any means

On one occasion I recall that we were moving out of Scrwfa House when I was about four. Me, Sandra and Mam went to my nan's house in Abertysswg for the day, leaving my father and his mates to move our stuff to the new council house in Cefn Golau. I loved going to my nan's in Arthur Street. My cousin lived four doors up from her. I'd either go the field behind the houses and feed the sheep, cows and horses with bread crusts and peelings, or play garages with my toy cars using my nan's walking sticks as the garage.

When we went home and got off the bus at our new house, all the lights were on, the front door was wide open and most of our furniture was sitting in the garden – sideboard, sofa, chairs. My mam led the way, tottering in through the door.

'Benny ... Benny.' she called. I could hear voices in the back room but the door was closed. Mam grabbed the handle and pushed it open. I squeezed up behind her peering round her leg. There in the back room were about seven guys all sat round in a circle on barrels of Watney's Red Barrel, laughing and joking and, of course, drinking. There was instant silence when Mam walked in. 'Oh Elizabeth,' my father piped up, 'we hadn't expected you back so early.'

'I can see that Benny,' she replied. My father tried to water down the situation. 'Here's my boy, come here ... here he is.'

'Benny,' Mam's voice voice was calm, 'can I see you for a minute?'

'Yes, love.' He winked at his mates as if to say, don't worry lads, I've got this under control. They walked to the front door from where I heard muffled voices while sipping a cup of beer that dad's mate, Billy Gregory had given me. In an instant, my father came back saying, 'Ah, c'mon boys let's finish this job and clear up, is it?'

Within two minutes the furniture was in and all the men had gone, taking their Watney's Red Barrel with them. That was the last party that house saw until my sister and her mates trashed the place and killed my gold fish on her 18th Birthday.

My mam didn't like crowds but, like most women of that era, she loved bingo. Sadly, as her health deteriorated year-on-year, she went from going to bingo two days a week, and to the club on a Saturday, to not leaving our living room. My father became her carer as well as working shifts down the pit. He even stopped watching his beloved Tredegar Ironsides because he couldn't leave Mam. He needed to be on hand, just in case.

Watching the Ironsides was his main pleasure, his only real release. He had a set pattern of going up the club then popping back to check up on Mam. He would go to the Recreation Ground (The Rec) at 2.30pm, watch the game and be back by 5pm to check she was ok. He would often go back down for a few if she was alright and settled down. We lived about 300 yards from the club but it was a vertical climb back. By the time he was 50, my father had pneumoconiosis and the walk home from the club would take him an hour. So, he often told mam, 'I'd better stay and have three more pints and run up the hill.'

They say you can't remember things from when you were a nipper. I don't know what age they say you start cementing memories but I can remember quite a bit. I don't know if these things have been told to me later in life but some of them were pretty traumatic and they have stuck with me. Two in particular.

When I was three years old, Dad was working nights and I was out with some of the boys, playing on the street. We didn't have much money, just enough to survive hand to mouth. Nevertheless, I was always trying to be liked, as kids do, and said to my gang in the street, 'Who wants an orange? I've got some in the house.'

Their eyes lit up and their tongues hung out. I snook into the house like a commando crawling through the jungle. Once inside, I put three oranges down the front of my jumper and crept out the back door. As I was going across the yard. I heard a rat-tat-tat on the window behind me. I swung round and my old man was stood in all his glory, white vest and Y-front pants in the window - he had just woken up after a nightshift. If you have never worked a night shift, they are bastards, let me tell you. They make you as miserable and cranky as hell. My old man was no different. In fact, he was a black belt in being cranky at times. He glared at me as I held the bottom of my jumper tightly making a bag so that the big, juicy oranges wouldn't fall out. Then the dreaded finger beckoned me inside. I was terrified.

'You're a thief ... a thief,' he said as he began his interrogation. I was too scared to even explain why I had taken the fruit. What a bollocking I got. After that there was no pinching for me. He didn't need to hit me. Just a short sharp blast of shouting and swearing was the cure for that little boy. I never, stole anything else again in my life (Well, that's a little white lie. All will be revealed later during a mega session in France!).

Like all good mothers, my mam stuck up for me on that occasion but, of course, I ended up upsetting her as well a while later. I remember getting sent to the shop for a loaf of bread – uncut – for our tea. On the long walk home, all of about 10 yards, I felt hungry so I sat by the river and ate the middle out of the loaf. I went home and presented it to my mam, thinking maybe she wouldn't notice. This time she gave me the mother of all bollockings while my old man sat on the settee laughing his head off: 'He's a growing boy, Liz,' he teased.

In the summer, I used to play down the river with the other boys. We'd go looking for fish and frogs and other creatures. Back in the '60s there was a load of barabits and bullheads, (millers' thumbs), massive frogs hopping about and plenty of other types of wildlife. The banks of the river were steep and covered in stinging nettles and those plants that you could make pea shooters out of (the weapons of choice for a working class four-year-old at that time).

I remember one day we were playing in the lane by the river bank and, for no reason other than I was taller than him, Terry Jones pushed me straight in the stingys and down the banking. I was stung from head to toe. On my arse, my bollocks, in my eyes, my mouth. the lot. I remember racing home screaming like I was on fire. In agony and in panic, I ran straight into my house. My mother, and my aunty who was visiting from Birmingham, stripped me off and plunged me into the tin bath full of cold water. I don't know what was worse, the stingys or the cold water. This was 'Tred', where back then there was no central heating and there was always ice on the water outside in the bucket until the end of April. It was freezing. After being immersed in this ice-bath for what seemed like an eternity, the pain eased. I was covered in nettle rash and had to be doused in calamine lotion for a few days afterwards, but at least I'd stopped screaming.

It wasn't until the age of around six I became aware that in certain situations I became tongue-tied and struggled to get my words out. I was different to my mates. School highlighted it and the more I tried to be the same as everyone else the worse it got. Over the next few years, this became a real issue in everyday life and after getting advice, my parents sent me to have speech therapy. My parents did the right thing but they didn't know the psychological issues I was facing daily. I was introverted and very shy.

I don't remember ever being asked how I felt about it, or how I dealt with it. The subject simply wasn't talked about. Never once did my parents sit me down and try to explain. They didn't really know how to deal with it to be fair to them. Maybe they saw it as a weakness in themselves. It must have been tough for them as well. In my mind, it felt as though every kid in short trousers in our street could read the book, *War and Peace* fluently, aloud, standing on their heads while I, on the other hand, was struggling to recite the first page of *Dick and Dora*.

The speech therapy sessions I recall going to were pretty basic. It normally meant me reading aloud and being talked at. There was no emphasis, I recall, on things like breathing techniques or working with my parents to create an environment where I felt more relaxed and confident about talking and developing my, and their, communication skills. Maybe there was, but nothing at home felt different. Today it's all about parents speaking slowly and trying to calm their child – encouraging them and listening to them. Modern techniques emphasise the nurturing of children's speaking skills and bringing children into everyday conversations – making them feel comfortable even if they are struggling.

We weren't affluent enough to have private health care so that was all I got. Would it have made a difference if I'd had more in-depth one-to-one coaching? Who knows? The more I've read up on the subject, however, the more I believe it may have helped me. I read that treatment for stammering is often successful in pre-school age children if they get the right type of help. About 5% of children will go through a stammering phase when they develop language. Most of them will recover fluent speech without any intervention necessary. However, one in five of that cohort (1% of all children) will be at risk of persistent stammering so early intervention, as soon as possible after onset, has the best chance of success.

I was in that 1% who never shake it off. As you can imagine, even though I was a tall and imposing specimen, I was mocked, teased, and taunted as I grew up. I was never in the in-crowd, always felt an outsider and was never in the cool cliques even from that young age.

Growing up in Tredegar in the '70s and '80s was, I assume, no different to growing up on any other council estate in Wales or across Britain. There were loads of bored school-age kids looking for things to entertain themselves with. We all played out on the open space and in the playground in the middle of the estate. We would play football, cricket, British Bulldog, mob, and knock-knock ginger. I was always outside. They were great times. We would go out (or be ejected from the house) to play when the sun came up until it was dark, or when we were hungry. There were no computer games or mobiles. We didn't have a phone in the house until 1980. I never thought I would be saying things like this. When my old man would talk about his youth I would think, 'shut up you lamp, that was then' but now here I am, exactly like him!

Cefn Golau was real cowboy country. There was a load of teens who loved riding the ponies that grazed on the mountains surrounding the estate. More than once, I was woken by a stampede of ponies with the young scallies jumping on their backs and riding them up the hill, all pretending they were riding *Champion the Wonder Horse*, or there were cows and sheep being herded through the estate. It was common to wake up in the morning, open your curtains to be stared at by sheep that had wandered into the garden.

Like most towns in Wales at that time, we had our share of interesting characters. Henry Carpenter lived in a house at the end of my road. He had made the common land at the back of his house into a small-holding where he kept chickens and sheep but his main thing was mountain ponies. There was always one in the corral along with a couple of mad border collies. He was definitely living the cowboy life. I remember him riding his trusty steed round the estate, thinking he was the *Lone Ranger*. He wore a long off-white coat, stained with all sorts of stuff, that draped down over his legs to his gum boots that he'd pimped by painting sheriff's stars on the side and cutting sergeant stripes into them.

Henry liked to show his prowess on horseback and often rode his nag through the town, doing a lap around the town clock and rearing up his horse in front of everyone. He was known to lasso the cigarette machine that was screwed to the wall outside the Queen's ballroom in the town, attach the rope to his saddle, whip his horse and ride off shouting, 'Giddy up! Ya ya'. There were rumours he was a sheep rustler and that he would gut the poor animals in the bath of his council house and decorate the taps with the heads of the beasts.

Another top character was the local strongman, 'Georgie Muscles', or 'Strang the Strong' as he was often called. His real name was George Davis, who was quite famous in the mid-1970s. He would travel the world giving strength shows, ripping telephone directories in half, bending frying pans, and having paving slabs smashed on his chest by a sledge hammer.

Each year there was a summer carnival that took place on one of the bank holidays. On one of these occasions, George set up a performance area on the field with an odd-looking frame taking centre stage. No one knew what was going on. After doing his usual tricks, we heard his voice over the PA system: 'Ladies and Gentlemen, I will now attempt to perform a feat unseen before. I will lift a horse off the floor above my head.'

The atmosphere was tense to say the least. The horse appeared and was clearly agitated by all the drunken fellas shouting their encouragement. It stamped its feet, eyes ablaze, and it was somehow manoeuvred into the frame. Then Georgie positioned himself and took a few deep breaths. To this day I cannot find a picture or remember how he did it but he actually did the stunt. He actually picked the horse off the floor and above his head. The man was a legend in the town.

In a place like that, as you can imagine, there were no social graces – no refinements. We were all in the same boat and all got on with it. We weren't nasty kids, but sometimes we did things that got us into trouble. I would be egged-on by the older kids to knock people's doors and run away. This was fun until the day I got caught by some bloke and clipped around the earlobe. I never did it again.

In the winter, the snow would often fall deep in Cefn. We had some great adventures when it did snow - it felt like a different world. I knocked around with some older kids and one snowy day, I called for one of them, Hedgy. He was in his garden with some other lads rolling a big snowball. It was massive, at least waist height to the boys. They must have spent hours rolling this thing. His garden was up some steps and he had a coal shed recessed into the wall. You could walk from the garden up onto the coal shed roof. The boys had pushed this colossal snowball on to the coal shed roof. This was another instance of me doing something to be accepted by the older kids. Hedgy started winding me up, 'You play rugby, Lanky. You're hard, I've seen you. You are the master. Let's see how hard you are.'

They knew what they were doing. I puffed out my chest to show how brave I was. How dull more like!!

'Stand by there.' He said, pointing to a spot by the coal shed. 'Now shut your eyes.' I did what I was told and waited like an idiot. I could hear the giggling but it didn't twig with me. I heard him run up the steps and wanted to open my eyes but he was older than me and I didn't want to disobey him. I desperately wanted to be one of the gang. I faintly heard, 'quick, push' then heard a loud 'thoooop'.

The next thing I remember was 'BOOOOOSSHHH'. It felt as if I had been hit by a dumper truck. I crumpled to the ground and then everything went black. I didn't remember a thing and then started to hear faint voices in the distance: 'Lanky, Lanky are you ok? ... wake up ... wake up.'

I came-to with the boys frantically shovelling snow off my head with their hands like something out of the film *Ice Station Zebra*. The bastards had pushed that huge snowball onto my head for the craic and I'd been stupid enough to stand there with my eyes closed!

It wasn't the last time in my life I acted like a twat.

3

I'm an Upstart(er)

'I have nothing but the utmost respect for what Scooby did on and off the field. Fair play to him, even though he had his battles throughout his life, he was a fantastic player for whoever he turned out for and a great human being.'

Kevin Ellis

Back in the 1970s, Welsh rugby was riding high on the wave of success because of that great team, one of the best Welsh teams of all time. The likes of Phil Bennett, Gareth Edwards, Mervyn Davies, JPR and JJ Williams, Gerald Davies and, of course, the infamous Pontypool front row, plus many more. Every little kid wanted to be like these guys.

During that period of national euphoria, mini-rugby in Wales was born, led by Ray Williams and his famous coaching leaflets. These leaflets were sent out to clubs explaining the fundamentals of coaching rugby union to all levels which, in turn, gave birth to an abridged version of rugby that kids could play. At its core, it promoted the three basic skill elements of catch and pass, run, and tackle, which, if you look at it in the cold light of day, is all rugby is. The All Blacks have been doing it for years and years. The mini-rugby game consisted of nine players - four forwards and five backs - with rolling subs, no scrums and no lineouts. Mini-rugby was springing up throughout Wales.

Teams were being organised by parents of lads from eight years and over, and it gave the children a focus, to get them off the streets and stop playing stupid games like 'knock-knock ginger'! It not only gave them more confidence, it also nurtured the kid's dreams of one day playing for their country. It also gave them life skills: how to react appropriately to success and failure and how to be part of a team.

It wasn't all about the individual anymore. Team sport is all about working together, about covering your mate's arse if he messed up. At the time, we didn't have a clue about all that stuff. All we wanted to do was run about with a ball and be like the blokes in the red jerseys who we watched on the TV. It also brought communities together and it gave a lot of us kids a purpose in our lives.

The Tredegar Ironsides' mini-rugby team had been formed at the very beginning of this project by Richie Gregory, a scrum-half and salt-of-the-earth bloke. I started playing for them at the age of eight. As you can imagine, my father was chuffed to bits. Mini-rugby was a new thing back in 1973 and we had regular games against all the teams in our valley. All mining villages and all within about nine miles of where I lived. This was the same all over Wales.

Within a couple of years, the mini-rugby set-up had grown and grown to such a point that regional tournaments were established. We did quite well in these competitions and the club also struck up a friendship with a club in Coventry, 'Barker's Butts', and we went to play in a festival organised by them. This became a regular, annual occurrence and we would play them home and away. It was a massive thing and we even had singing practice for weeks before the festival so we could learn *Hen Wlad fy Nhadau, Calon Lan* and *Sospan Fach* to sing to our opponents in the clubhouse after the matches. I loved it. The feeling was out of this world.

Even though, at eight, I stood head and shoulders above all the kids in the team, I was a bit of a coward, and not at all brave. Some would say probably the least brave one in the team.

We started training every Wednesday at the end of summer and, unlike some of the other kids, I didn't have a pair of proper rugby boots so I trained in my black daps, the ones you had to have for PE in school, or my trainers from Woolworths. With my father being a collier, and with Mam not working because of her rheumatoid arthritis, we didn't have any disposable cash so things were tight. I didn't have a penny to throw at a mad dog.

There was no Adidas or Puma or other fancy labels in my house. Not just because we were poor, but another reason being I was continually growing. I was eight years old with size eight feet! If my parents had invested in a pair of branded boots or trainers, I would have grown out of them in a month. After a few weeks training in my daps, which did the job because the ground was hard, things changed in September when down came the rain. I was constantly asking my old man for a pair of boots. The same answer came, 'Mark, we can't afford it. Sorry, you need to make do with what you got.' Or, 'You may not stick at it. I'm not wasting money on brand new boots for you to leave them sitting under the stairs.'

When the season started, I kept on and on at my dad. Then I heard, 'I'll see what I can do,' although he didn't look up from watching the telly. Even so, that meant a lot, because I knew then he was doing all he could. It must have broken his heart not to be able to just go out and get a pair of rugby boots for his son, like many other fathers could. I bet he would have robbed a bank just to get money to kit me out in the best gear.

A week before the tournament, he came home from the club with a plastic bag under his arm and a smile on his face. As he threw the bag to me, he said, 'Have a look at them.'

I managed to catch the bag and tore at the plastic. Out fell a pair of Adidas Flankers. They had a scratch on the toe but looked brand new. Square toe, ankle protection and three white stripes. 'Thanks Dad, thanks Dad,' I said, thinking it was Christmas and my birthday rolled into one. 'Well, try them on,' he said, his face beaming, 'let's see if they fit?'

They were size 7s and I was already a size 8 by then but I didn't care one bit. I didn't care if they made my toes fall off, they were Adidas Flankers! I jammed my feet into them like the ugly sister trying on the silver slipper. They were a bit snug, to say the least, but I didn't want him to know that. 'They fit fine, Dad.' The joy was evident on both our faces.

'Be careful mind,' he said, 'I've borrowed them from John Thomas down the club. He's hurt his knee and won't be playing again for a while, so you make sure you thank him when you see him.'

'Thanks Dad, I will.' I was super chuffed. I'm sure I slept with the boots next to me for a few nights. I was like a man, sorry, boy possessed running out on the field after that.

However, after wearing those borrowed boots for a couple of weeks I had feet like a griffin. Post-match my toes would be curled under and almost facing my ankles. I could hardly walk. I either needed to cut my big toes off, or get a bigger pair. Again, I was too scared to tell my old man that they hurt so much and my toes were curling under. I feared that he would call me ungrateful, but he must have realised because, a few days later, he came home again with another bag under his arm, and we went through the same ritual. I tore at the bag and a pair of Bukta rugby boots fell out. They had seen a few scrums these ones. They were very scuffed and split a little on one side but with a bit of polish they'd come up like a pair of Dr. Martens.

'Now, they're size 9's' he said. 'I had them off Benny Thomas. He doesn't need them so thank him in training on Wednesday and, by the way, stop growing!'

Those boots lasted me the rest of that season and were one of the reasons I stuck at rugby and progressed. By the start of the following season, he must have seen something in me, because he really splashed out and got me a brand-new pair of Gola Forwards – size 10, 'So, you can grow into them,' he said - from the Littlewoods catalogue. They probably cost dad £2.15 per week for about 100 years!

I had to wear two pairs of socks to start with just to stop my feet from flapping around in them. So, thanks again, John and Benny for the boots. How can I ever repay you? Fair play to my old man, deep down he had a heart of gold. I remember a few years later, I must have been about 12. It was coming up to Christmas and he asked me what I wanted. 'I ... I... I want a new bike, Dad,' I replied full of the excitement of youth.

The bike I already had was a reconditioned one. It had been done up nice, mind, painted red with a bell and a padded seat, but it had no gears so pedalling up the hills near my house was a bit tough. I'd had it since I was nine but I was 12 now and still growing. It was a bit small and my knees kept smashing into the handle bars and my chin. I must have looked like a circus clown cycling around the big top.

He looked at me, looked over to my old bike, then muttered, 'OK, son.' Thinking that now was my chance to strike while the iron's hot, I quickly added, 'I've got my eye on one in a shop in town. It's brilliant, Dad.'

'How much?' he enquired. Now for the tough part. I took a deep breath. 'It ... It's £75,' I revealed, and before he could say anything, added, 'It's got 10 speeds, a derailleur and everything.' Nowadays £75 is a lot of money for a Christmas present, so back in 1977, it really was a massive amount. Something approaching two weeks of my father's wages.

For a while he said nothing. He just sat there. Then he looked at me and, in his best John Wayne voice, he came out with a pearler. 'BOOYYYY, you can keep your eye on it ... you'll NEEEVER get your arse on it!' I didn't know if I should laugh or cry.

Come Christmas morning, the bike was wrapped up in the front room. I have no idea how they paid for it, although we had books of Green Shield stamps piled high on the cupboard, right up to the ceiling, but they'd got me the bike I really wanted. Love you Dad and Mam.

My second-hand rugby boots were doing the business and we played our first game, away to Pontllanfraith RFC. We travelled down the Sirhowy Valley, all of nine miles although it seemed like 90 at the time. I felt really nervous. I was scared, had developed a 'Bard Stomach' just before kick off and had to be coaxed and nursed to even get changed. In my mind, they were all going to be enormous. I was finally persuaded to play after it was pointed out that the opposition weren't that big. That made me feel better and a little braver. I ended up scoring two tries, running through the opposition at ease, and we won 8-0. However, the phantom 'Bard Stomach' came on a few more times in the next three years or so - I wasn't the bravest kid on the block

By the time I'd progressed to the Under 11s, we had assembled quite a decent team that was being coached by Algy Thomas (a former Wales flanker). He was a top fella and lots of fun who never put any pressure on us. His aim was for us kids to just enjoy it. His son, Richard (also a flanker) was in the team. We also had Ian Williams, the son of another Wales cap and British Lion, Denzil Williams. We didn't realise it at the time but that's some pedigree. The rest of the team were, 'Tank' (prop), Harriman (hooker, who went on to play for Wales U14 but died tragically young), Me, 'Billa' (scrum-half), Leon (outside half), 'Nelly' (centre), 'Doris' (wing), Laughton (wing/full back), Ledington (wing), and Gerwyn (wing). Some real talented lads in there and a gang that even back then would look after each other. We were having a good season, winning games and tournaments regularly. Our small living room was awash with trophies, all displayed with pride on the mantlepiece, around the Rayburn fire and on the unit in the alcove.

There was a big tournament coming up in Pontyclun - I didn't have a clue where that was – in the the Welsh National tournament and the winners would play in the final as a curtain-raiser to the Welsh Cup Final in May 1976. 'C'mon boys let's have it,' our coach said. 'I feel we have a good chance of winning it.'

We picked up the training, working on our tap penalties and other set moves for weeks. I don't recall ever working on defence, but that's how it was in the '70s, no one practiced tackling. We all wanted to be Phil Bennett.

On the day of the tournament, we got to the club and jumped on the bus, all very nervous. After each tournament we always had a box of Fleur De Lys or Peter's Pies and a carton of squash and a bag of crisps. I could see them all packed up for us on the front seat. A celebratory feast or just a snack if we lost.

We arrived at Pontyclun for 9 am, ready for the first game at 10. Richie registered our team and led us to our patch, where we kept our bags and equipment. The fields were massive, all divided up into enclosures with ropes around each pitch. You could fit two pitches on one rugby field, playing side to side. As I'm writing this, all the memories are flooding back to me: the sounds, the smells, the nerves, the emotions. I was looking around at the size of the other kids in the other teams - some of them seemed massive so I got a bit panicky. I didn't fancy going up against them. I knew I couldn't play the 'bard stomach' card again so I gave myself a good talking to in the toilets of the changing room: 'C'mon Mark, you're bigger than them... you can do it,' I tried to convince myself.

It worked. I pulled myself together, piece by piece, and I'm so glad I did. We played all day and won the competition which meant we were through to the final to be played at Cardiff Arms Park in May against a team from Barry.

I had been to Barry Island before, but never to Cardiff. On the annual club trip to the seaside with my parents we'd travel on a bus, like an old charabanc, and once there, I was given 50p to go play on the fair after a day messing about on the beach. Or, if I was really lucky, also have a go on the trampolines. My dad, with the rest of the men, would go for a pint or six and my mam and the other women, would sit on the benches on the promenade holding the bags.

On this occasion, our little team were heading to Cardiff Arms Park to play before the main event, the 1977 Schweppes Cup final between Llanelli and Swansea. I had only seen Cardiff Arms Park, with the overhanging lights and the dog track round the outside, on the telly when Wales were playing at home. The dog track was where Gareth Edwards had famously rolled, head over heels, into the corner while scoring a wonderful try against Scotland, and then appeared on our screens with a face of muck while the rest of Wales went absolutely berserk.

There was also the clock. The famous clock that hung on the stand, right in the middle of the beer advert that hadn't changed for years, which read 'Welsh Brewers, NEVER FORGET YOUR WELSH'. The stand had also changed, but that clock was always in the same spot. Ten or more years later, when I was in the Welsh squad, Clive Rowlands, who was chairman – and president and a load of other things – came out with an iconic pre-match speech for one of our important games. It was well known, that Clive loved to get in amongst the lads. He was a true motivator, a proper Welsh warrior. His words came from the heart, a heart which was as big as a coal tram.

'Right boys. Sit down, get your heads on, focus and listen to me.' Clive was on top form. The room was buzzing. Vaseline was being smeared on faces and rugby balls being smashed onto chests, to the sounds of loud grunts and random screams. There was noise everywhere and I could hear my teammates shouting 'C'mon boys', 'ave 'em', 'kill 'em' and plenty more choice phrases. To an outsider it must have sounded like the annual conference of the Welsh Tourette's Society. I couldn't resist, I couldn't wait to get into them – SMASH! I put my head through the wall!

Clive was now standing in the middle of the room, speaking to us with a dragon's fire in his eyes: 'Picture this – last ten minutes, you've run your guts out, you've tackled everything, you've been kicked, punched, raked, and your jersey dripping with sweat and blood. We are losing by three points and there's a scrum five metres out from our own line. We don't just need to keep them out, we need to get the ball back. We need to get up their end to score to win the game. You're absolutely fucked. You look up behind you to THE CLOCK to check what time is left and then you see it, those words, those four words that will inspire you and take you to the gates of hell and back.' He left a short pause before bellowing out, 'NEVER FORGET YOUR WELSHHHHHH....AARRRRGGHH,' he roared. We followed his lead like a bunch of wild banshees. What an inspiration Clive was. Absolutely superb.

OK, sorry for bouncing around, but I'm 10 again and we are heading to the capital city followed by the entire village, all dressed up in their Sunday best to support their lads. They trailed us in buses and cars and trains and aeroplanes. Ok, ok I exaggerated the last bit, but it felt that way.

The entire day was a blur. The trip down, the nerves before the game, going into the dressing rooms, seeing who we were playing against. They looked older than 11. Bloody hell, one of them looked about 46! I sat myself down, 'C'mon Mark ... guts, guts.'

We walked out of the tunnel across the red track and onto the pitch. I knew my parents would be up in the stands, shouting their hearts out. Bloody hell! I didn't realise the dog track was red - we still had a black and white telly in those days so to me, most of Wales was drab and colourless.

Wow! The grass was so green and lush. How soft was it? Like walking on air. I even thought that I wouldn't mind falling down on that. Then I looked up and I saw the clock. I looked passed it and gulped at the size of the stands. I couldn't believe how high they were. They seemed to go on forever. For a kid of 10 to have the opportunity to do that was amazing, not that we fully realised it back then. Its only when you're an old bastard like me now, and you start looking back on things that happened in your life, at important turning points, that you realise the significance of things. That was where it all started for me. I ran out of the changing rooms and onto that field a few times in the future. It had altered a bit but the one thing that remained constant was the clock and Clive's words of war. It kept on ticking. Knocking off the minutes, knocking off the hours, knocking off the years, until I came to what was my last ever time to run out on that hallowed turf over 30 years later, on the same Welsh Cup final day in May, playing for Neath v Caerphilly. A game in which I bowed out in a blaze of glory ... NOT!

Back to age 10. We all got set up for the team photo. We did all the passing, the ball warm-up and then, thud, the kick off. I'm not going to fib and describe anything about the game except the odd flash of a green jersey (us) running amongst blue and black (them), or a permed hairdo which flashes from the depths of my memory because I don't remember a thing of the game, except that we lost. Maybe if we had been successful, I would have remembered every last detail, but it was not to be.

There were thousands there to watch the main event, the Schweppes Welsh Cup final, plus most of Tredegar had made the trip to watch us. I recall the disappointment of losing as we collected our runners up medals. We were ushered off the field, back to the changing rooms under the stand. We got out of our kit and were led into the kid's enclosure with our Fleur de Lys pie, crisps and carton of squash. We were upset but we had played on Cardiff Arms Park, the sporting cathedral and the mecca for all Welsh kids.

The players from Llanelli and Swansea then came out and got on with the business. We were allowed to stay to watch the match. All I can remember is the booming voices of the thousands of drunken Taffs singing *Calon Lan* and the roar of the crowd when the two main teams raced out and when someone scored. The game was won by Llanelli 16-4, then we were escorted back to the bus through the sea of red and lilywhite jerseys. I was terrified that we were going to get washed away in the tsunami of bodies as they all rushed to get out onto Westgate Street and back inside the boozers.

Our bus crawled out of the car park, past the Angel Hotel and back up the A465. Win or lose, our club was bouncing that night but us kids were all knackered and went home, while the dads, and the wives, got on the lash and talked about how proud they were of their little boys and how there were much bigger and better things to come.

That was it, my first experience of running out at Cardiff Arms Park – but luckily for me, it wasn't my last.

4

Teenage Kick(ing)s

'Mark was a rugby athlete with few peers. He was incredibly dynamic and powerful, allied to being fearless and ruthless. What he achieved in both codes representing Wales and GB is a fantastic feat. I truly believe that without his stammer and the demons it created, and with the right management, he had the ability and athleticism to be the best No. 8 we have seen in a Welsh shirt. He was that good.'

Gareth Llewellyn

Being young and naïve, I didn't think my speech was a massive issue because I thought the taunting and comments were normal. Sometimes, of course, I didn't like it and would fly into a rage and my tormentors, but that's the way it was. I had a temper but it would take a major incident for it to show itself. Once, when I was around nine years of age, I can remember throwing the fire poker through the door in our lounge after losing it when my sister had been winding me up for hours. When I did lose control, it was as if my eyes had rolled back into my head and two demonic red shutters had dropped down in their place. For the next 10 seconds my mind would go blank as I turned into Tredegar's versions of the *Incredible Hulk* – albeit a very skinny and pasty version of the green man-monster.

When I reached the top end of primary school the penny dropped. I didn't need to be a rocket scientist to realise that there was going to be a big - no, a HUGE - difference between being teased and picked-on in primary school because of my stammer, and the physical and mental bulling I'd face in secondary school, which can be evil, unforgiving places if someone is different. I witnessed kids getting bullied beyond belief and breaking beyond repair and, right from the outset, I knew this was going to become problematic for me as well. All the kids in the town and surrounding areas went to the same school, the very creatively named Tredegar Comprehensive. The founder of the National Health Service, Aneurin Bevan, was born in - and was MP for - Tredegar, and surely the school should have been named after him. Such logic was, and still mainly is, beyond the grasp of local government.

My sentence at Tredegar Comp started in 1977, where I found myself 'doing time' with over 1,300 other inmates - spotty-faced pupils with all sorts of backgrounds, from council estate kids to doctors' sons and architects' daughters, and many from mining families. The cross section of characters from across the stereotypical valleys working-class town resulted in many clashes, from disagreements and feuds to outright bullying and full-on, all-in, fighting. Every breaktime there would be scraps in the yard with the pupils encircling the fighters, screaming 'Fight, fight, fight.' I'm sure some of the teachers would join in now and again.

The pressure on me just to get through each day was immense. It felt that not only was I ridiculed by the schoolkids, but the teachers could be very unsympathetic too. Hearing 'C'mon, boy, spit it out!' wasn't good for your confidence or street cred. I hated it, and hated them for treating me with such distain. It was just the way things were in those days. Again, unlike today, I just had to grin and bear it. I lost it at times. Some of the abuse and mickey-taking, really got to me and tipped me over the edge.

With all this madness swirling around me, I found myself sinking down inside my own private shell. I became more of a loner than I already was and felt pushed out and alienated from the world. To say I was constantly bullied would be an exaggeration, but I was targeted by some of the bigger boys due to my height, and being teased about my stammer gave me major insecurities, both physically and mentally. Then two events happened that caused everything to change.

The first major incident which triggered the chain reaction came when I was 14. In a nutshell I took a right good old kicking.

Tredegar in 1979 was smack bang in the clutches of the so-called 'winter of discontent' and, being a collier's son, I experienced its worst effects. The town was cold and wet, and most people were skint. The sense of hopelessness led to a dark foreboding across the people of the south Wales valleys who wrapped themselves up tight inside a blanket of personal and community depression. I did what all teens in industrial towns did back then, I hung around the streets and the town centre, getting moved on by the cops. Back then there were still cops on the beat in Tredegar. We had a big police station and you would often see them, walking in pairs, like guards patrolling the perimeter of a prison, HMP Tredegar. To me and many others that's how it felt.

I didn't hang around in a gang - I was too paranoid that they'd be laughing behind my back - so I generally just wandered around talking to a few people here and there, going to the leisure centre to play pool or just sitting in the few cafés dotted about the town. That was what our life revolved around – there wasn't anything else. I can't really remember what I really did in those lost years other than walk about aimlessly, talking about music and trying my best to talk to girls. Lots of the kids I knew were sniffing glue. That definitely wasn't for me. I saw the state some of them were getting into - proper brain-dead zombies.

I just kept my head down and tried to stay out of trouble. Others were breaking into places, smashing windows and pinching stuff. My father had drilled the anti-theft message it into me and had scared me to death with the incident with the oranges, so I didn't go down that route. There were loads of teen gangs around but I would try my best to avoid them. Whenever I saw them, I would head off in the opposite direction.

A lot of these boys were the so-called trouble makers. You knew they would give you hassle if your paths crossed, so I learnt early enough to stay out of their way. A few of them had been kicked-out of local schools and sent to the Tŷ Mawr 'approved' school in Abergavenny. Some had even been sentenced to a period at the young offenders custody centre, or borstal in old money, in Portland, Dorset. It was basically a kid's prison which was known for housing all the hardened teenage criminals. All sorts of stories surrounded these places. When the TV drama and film *Scum* was released in the late 1970s, it graphically showed what those places were like. That definitely wasn't a place for me! I wouldn't have lasted a night there. It was truly horrific and some of the scenes in that movie still haunt me today.

I kept an extra wide berth from anyone I thought had been to borstal. One kid, who I didn't know but knew of him, was rumoured to have recently been released from Portland and was a tough nut – definitely not to be messed with. He had a crazy grin and an evil laugh. His mouth would turn up into a smile but his eyes were manic and burnt deep inside anyone he glared at. Seemingly always on edge, and very unpredictable, he was always causing trouble and you never knew how far he'd go if he took a dislike to you.

I remember one cold night – I know it must have been very cold because I was wearing my blue snorkel parka – I'd been to the leisure centre for a wander. Then I'd bought chips and headed to the station to catch the bus home. When you are young and want to keep yourself to yourself, you try to blend into the background. Everyone does it. You pull your hood up, shove your hands in your pockets, look at the floor and hope no one sees you. It's as if you think you become invisible, but you don't! Well, on that day I didn't anyway.

I was stood by one of the concrete benches on the station concourse, waiting for the bus to pull in, when there was movement and noise to my left. I looked up, and at the top of the steps to the ugly, brutalist structure of the shopping centre, I could see a gang standing on a balcony. That was bad news but what I did next was a basic schoolboy error. I turned my back on the group hoping they wouldn't see me. No chance.

I heard a shout, 'Hey Lanky, what you doing?' I turned my head around to face them. 'Nothing,' I replied. 'Just going home,' then turned back to look out for the bus. Although I did my best to sound unconcerned and calm, my inner fear was clearly audible by the way I trembled when I spoke. There were more muffled voices in the background. I then heard someone say, 'Don't. Leave him be. He's alright.'

It was freezing cold, and the water vapour billowed out of my mouth more heavily as my breathing quickened. My snorkel hood was fully zipped up and I stuffed my hands deeper into my pockets. I wanted to disappear. I hunched up my shoulders, trying to make myself look smaller, and hoped they'd just leave me alone for long enough that I could reach the sanctuary of the Hill's bus that was due any minute.

I stood there, afraid to move. 'Where's that bloody bus?' I said to myself as I took a sneaky look over my shoulder. Through the fur-lined rim of my hood, I could see him coming down the steps. He stood on the concourse with his hands in his pockets trying to look nonchalant as he moved towards me. I stood facing the wall, now shaking with fear, wishing I could be on that bus and on my way home. I sneaked a quick glance to my right. I couldn't see him. Panic set in. Where was he?

At that very moment, I felt the bottom of my legs being grabbed from behind and it seemed as if I was being lifted in to the air. He'd got hold of my ankles and was ferociously pulling my feet up to waist height. I toppled over like a felled tree, my legs now horizontal to the ground while still frantically trying to get my hands out of my pockets. I must have looked a sight – all 6 foot 3 inches and 11 stone of me. Gravity had kicked in and I plummeted down towards the concrete bench where I'd been sitting a few minutes earlier. All this happened in a split second but it played out in slow motion. As I fell, I could see the edge of the seat coming closer and closer. This was going to hurt.

WHACK! POW! BANG!

Like the sounds from a Batman movie, I felt the impact and quickly tasted blood. A loud bell rang in my head and then the lights went out. What happened next was just a blur. I remember being helped inside the bus station waiting room, then sensing that the police had arrived, before realizing that the sting of the alcohol wipes and the sensation of the stitching needle piercing my skin meant I must have been in hospital. I also recall the pain. More than one. Sharp pains all over my body. My head ached and my mouth was a mess - split open where my teeth had been pushed through my lip. I couldn't eat for a few days. I kept snorting out clots of blood from my nose and a big scab formed on the side of my face where the skin had been scraped off. A few days later I remember waking up after a deep sleep that had been aided by the best pain killers I've ever taken. The pillow had stuck to my face and was stained with the plasma that had seeped out of my wounds.

The police got involved from the off and I had to make a statement. My old man, wanting to avoid any repercussions for his son, was not comfortable with pressing charges. Then the police explained that I couldn't press charges, because they were going to do it, which eased my father's concerns. I didn't know if it was the thought of me getting targeted for retaliation by the lad if I'd pressed charges, or whether my father wanted me to live by the law of the jungle meaning that I needed to deal with this myself, but it was a harsh introduction to the nitty gritty of life. The law took its course and news that the thug had been prosecuted eventually filtered back to me.

I'm not saying that experience turned me into a better person. A person full of empathy for others, fully considerate of people's feelings and a champion of the oppressed. I wasn't going to pull on a red cape and prowl the streets protecting the weak, but it made me acknowledge that my shying away from confrontation had left me defenceless. What had running away from aggression achieved? Absolutely nothing except the constant feeling of fear in my guts when I saw the big boys. The shame of being thought of as a big wuss, and someone who just lay there and took a good kicking played on me.

I made a huge decision. Never again. That was it. I'd always been told to stand up to bullies but had never had the guts to. Now things had changed. I'd taken a kicking because I'd run away, a kicking for trying to blend into the background. It dawned on me that if I'd stood up for myself it couldn't have been any worse than what happened, and at least I would have been able to get a couple of shots in. It was as if my injuries, both physical and mental, had desensitised me.

Of course, this didn't happen instantly, but my attitude definitely changed. I wouldn't avoid the places where the others were. I now went into and left Tredegar's Circle café through the back room, where a known gang of lads always hung out. Mind you, I was still on my own but I started to put myself out there. I started to mix a bit more and not run away. I had to front up even though it didn't come easy to me.

Being the aggressor wasn't, at that time, in my DNA. One Sunday morning, when I was 14 and still a scrawny, brittle totem pole of nothingness, the Tredegar Ironsides under-15s had a fixture against Llandaff North in Cardiff. Under-15, my arse! Their players had beards and looked like they were on day release from Alcatraz.

Right on cue, the 'bard stomach' came back! Where was my parka? I wanted to be invisible again! 'Look at the size on him,' one of our team said, pointing at one of their players who looked like a cross between Goliath and Grizzly Adams. 'who's going to jump against him?'

I quickly looked around at our team. 'Him,' I said pointing at a lad 4 inches shorter than me. 'He's... he's... he's taller than me.' What a shithouse thing to say and I knew it as soon as I had said it. There was a silence and then Richie, our coach, said, 'Mark, its best if you do. You can jump higher and you're bigger.'

I was taller but as thin as they came. They didn't call me Rizla for nothing. Anyway, my old man glared at me and dragged me aside. 'Don't you ever embarrass me like that again. Act like a man.' I felt so ashamed. Everyone could hear what he had said to me. He hadn't held back.

My conversion from retreating from confrontation ended that day. I would never again shy away from a battle. My personal Rubicon had been crossed and at that moment I vowed to always stand up for myself and my teammates. I ran out on to that field and piled straight into Llandaff North's man-child. I got hurt but I didn't care. My fight or flight mechanism had been firmly switched into fight mode. I had always run away from the big boys but those days had gone. 'Fuck it', I thought. 'That's not happening again.' I did not want to be laughed at. I did not want to be ridiculed and known as stuttering, Lanky Jonesy for the rest of my life.

My transformation did wonders for my confidence but it did have a down side. From that moment on, I have to admit, I began to turn into a right idiot. At school I became the prick of the class. I got louder, and very disruptive. Most of my bad behaviour stemmed, I think, just to hide my own inadequacies. To cover up the cracks. With each day, week, month that passed, I seemed to be getting worse and worse. Transforming into a right knobhead.

I decided the best form of defence was full-out attack. Almost overnight, I turned from being the bullied into the bully. I'm not proud of it, but it helped me to get through my purgatory and was convinced it deflected the spotlight away from me. I didn't think about people's feelings. I didn't care. I couldn't stand being mimicked and ridiculed anymore. I realized I could finally do something about it. I also noticed that being aggressive was a release for me. It made me feel like someone. It would block out my inner, stuttering, turmoil and I was, for the first time in my life, putting down a marker of my choosing. If someone took the piss, I would do something about it.

Probably the worst thing I did was when I was having a particularly bad day in the fifth form. During the morning break I had kicked a lad up the arse with my Dr. Martens for taking the mickey, but it was me who had instigated it by calling him Shorty. That's what seemed to happen a lot. If I had said nothing there would not have been an issue, but I was stupid and my behaviour was spiralling out of control.

The world hated Jonesy and I hated the world. After lunch, which for me was a daily diet of a cob and crisps from the local bakery, I'd sit alone on a bench in Bedwellty Park. I had an English lesson after lunch which I hated with a passion, mainly because the teacher sometimes made us read passages from books to the rest of the class. Like anyone with a stammer, being forced to read aloud was probably my biggest fear at school so I decided to deflect my anxiety and act the fool. That afternoon, I sauntered into the lesson trying to disguise my angst. I plonked myself down at the back and began an endless stream of banter and interruption. We were being taught comprehension. The male teacher, who always went for a pint at lunch time, must have been hoping for an easy lesson, but with me in the room, that wasn't going to happen. After a few, 'Jones, will you shut up' he changed tack. With a grin on his face, he said, 'Jones, read the next paragraph.'

There was silence. The whole class wanted to hear this. After my non-stop disruptions, everyone wanted to see me floundering. It was pay-back time. The basketball-shaped block in my mouth, the concrete mixer in my stomach, and the brightness of 1,000 spotlights scorched my brain. Then my skin felt as if I had stepped in to a shower. I started sweating as if a monsoon had erupted inside my school jumper.

'W... w... when the lady in t.... t.... the pink g... g.... gown'

From behind his desk and through his smirk, I heard, 'W... W... What was that, s... s... sorry?'

That probably wasn't how the teacher said it, but to me – with all that was going on in my head – that was exactly what he said.

BOOOOOOM!!

I blew every fuse in my body. I threw the hard backed text book followed by my desk at him and screamed out, 'Don't ever take the piss out of me.'

There was a look of shock and more than a little amusement on the faces of my fellow fifth formers. I barged out of the room followed by the teacher, who called out, 'Mark, Mark ... stop.' All I could say was, 'Y... Y... you took the piss. You took the p... piss.'

The teacher denied it and the Head was summoned. Eventually things cooled down and I went to the next class to face row after row of teenage derision. There were probably a few in my class who thought, 'serves you right, Mark, for being such an arse.'

I, though, didn't care what anyone thought of me. I was angry with the world and most people in it. I was going nowhere but desperately needed someone or something to believe in. Then it happened. A momentous thing (or 4 momentous youths, to be more precise) which changed my outlook on life, as well as changing my appearance and my attitude. Music didn't just float into my life, it marched into my very existence, through every pore in my skin.

I had a few friends who I knocked about with, and one of them had an older brother who had bought *Never Mind the Bollocks* by the infamous Sex Pistols. Punk didn't really arrive into Tredegar until about 1979 – about three years after it hit the King's Road and Carnaby Street in London, and even two years after it had landed in Merthyr! Even though they had split up by then, the Pistols were still public enemy #1, #2 and #3. I couldn't wait to listen to it. One lunch time, on the way home from school, we sneaked into my mate's house to hear what all the fuss was about.

The needle of the record player was placed on the edge of the vinyl and, seconds later, the noise of jackboots stomping and the opening bars of *Holidays in the Sun* filled the small room with such anger and an energy I had never heard before. My mate didn't like it but it blew me away. It was a WOW! moment. The power, the lyrics, the attitude, the swearing. It was what every 14 or 15-year-old schoolkid should have in their lives; some rebellion, something to call their own, something that sticks two fingers up at the rest of the world.

My parents would have killed me if they knew I had listened to it but I was hooked from that moment on. Punk rock just added more fuel to my ever-spreading fire of confidence. I started to dress in tight ripped jeans, Dr. Martens boots, and sleeveless T-shirts and began acting the part. Yes, I was imitating the bands I saw on TV, but it was deeper than that. It was an escape. I was fleeing away from being me. Running away from the stuttering, Lanky Jonesy. Teenage rebellion felt different and I wanted to be different. The anger and aggression about my speech now mixed with my high-octane teenage hormones, to which I added the alcohol and great music. The result ... Boooooooom!

I had to make all my own gear because we couldn't afford bondage trousers and other punk accessories. There was no money for me to go shopping to Paradise Garage in Cardiff or the King's Road in London's West End. My mam, riddled with rheumatoid arthritis, couldn't sew, so I had to do it. I was really taking the punk ethos to a new level. My father went mad because I wore ripped jeans, the shame!

The introduction of punk put my life into a new context – the bump in the bus station, my father's embarrassment at his shit-house of a son, and years and years of pent-up anger – and changed me into a new person. Punk reflected my aggression, my teenage angst, and my rebellious, anti-establishment sentiments. The old Troggs song *We Gotta Get Out of This Place* played on repeat in my head. It wasn't being in Tred that I wanted to escape from, though. It was me. It was the person I was in Tred that I couldn't handle.

I'm no different to millions of others who have wanted to do something with their lives. I wanted to be something, but for me it was deeper than that. I needed to reinvent myself. Mark the Punk. It helped feed my hungry emotions. It made me realise that there were others like me out there. We didn't like ourselves and didn't like what we were. Punk gave me a connection to that world. I used the music as a catalyst. I would sit in my bedroom, alone, listening to The Damned, UK Subs, Sex Pistols, and the Angelic Upstarts. Every night from ten until midnight I would listen to the John Peel show on Radio One.

Because I was a total knob at school I never stood a chance of attracting any girls my own age. I was a bit of a late developer, to be honest. I started to notice them, but I was always useless at small talk as I couldn't find or say the right things. So, from 15 to 16 I had a few girlfriends but they were all younger than me. They hadn't seen me misbehaving in lessons so were oblivious to Mark, the class arse.

During the school holidays, I would spend hours and hours coarse fishing. A million miles away from the anarchy of the madness in my head. I guess it was another way for me to escape my surroundings. To sit on the banks of the local pond for hours, just me, the rod and the maggots. I loved it because I didn't need to speak to anyone or have any interaction at all. It was the same for the next four or five years. Every summer, I was there by the water, rain or shine. Punk and fishing were my escapes from the turmoil and frustration of being me.

Because of my size (six foot four, 12 stone – and still growing) I was encouraged, or let's say, pushed, to play second row. It was the logical position for me but I hated playing lock. My old man told me to tell them I was a number 8 and I didn't want to play second row. He had very savvy advice for his young rugby-mad son: 'You will never show up in that position,' he warned me, 'you need to be seen. Wear a head band so people can see you like Mervyn Davies and take kicks at goal like John Taylor.'

'Dad,' I quickly replied. 'The only thing I've ever kicked on the field are a few heads.' I wasn't joking. He meant well and just wanted me to stand out from the crowd. I knew what he was saying, but this was Wales, and in Wales at that time big boys played second row, fat kids played prop and the good-looking ones played in the backs and the nerdy types went to chess club.

Me and a few others from the school had a district trial for North Monmouthshire (North Mon) under-16s. As expected, I was shoved into the second row for the first half. We were losing and I hadn't really touched the ball other than catching a few line-outs. My dad was right. I was unseen, almost invisible. At half-time, I wanted to tell the teacher in charge to move me to number 8 but kept chickening out because I didn't want him to hear my stammer and I kept getting the cement mixer in the guts every time I thought about speaking to him. I knew I had to summon the courage and raise my concerns, so I finally approached the teacher – my guts churning.

'I... I... can p... play number eight sir.' He looked up at me, thought for a minute then said 'Ok, Jones, if things don't get any better, I'll switch you after 10 minutes.' True to his word, ten minutes into the second half, there was a stoppage and changes were made. 'OK, Jones,' he shouted at me, 'you go to number eight, and you, Williams, go to flanker on the other side.'

The game restarted. Within a few minutes, there was a scrum in the middle of the field, a fair distance out from the try line. The ball came to my feet at the back so I picked it up and ran. I could blag it that I fended off five players and ran in a try under the posts and no one could argue that I didn't, but I won't. I did run for a fair bit though, and through a few defenders before getting tackled. I felt alive. I felt pumped, and it wasn't the only time in the rest of the game that I made good yardage. So, by the end, the word was out that Lanky Jones could play number eight and was actually quite good. My second row days hadn't quite gone for good but were, thankfully, numbered.

The trial was a success and I made the North Mon district under-16s team, which really boosted my confidence. Soon after, I was also named in the Gwent Schools under-16s team to play away against Pembrokeshire schools. This was my second rugby adventure after the game at the Arms Park when I was younger. We went up on a minibus, which must have got lost as the drive took over four hours, before being farmed out to stay with the families of our hosts. I didn't a say a lot that night.

I can't remember where we played, but that's neither here nor there. I was someone. I had played for Gwent. There was only one other lad from Tredegar Comprehensive, Ian Harriman, who had played at a higher level, Wales under-14s, so this meant a lot.

I was also enjoying playing football, as a goalkeeper, for the school. Not quite Mark 'The Cat' Jones, but I didn't mind diving around a bit and getting dirty. I knew falling over didn't hurt so I would try to make spectacular saves like Ray Clemence of Liverpool and Paul Cooper of Ipswich. I actually met Paul years later, when I used to have a pint in Stockton Heath, in Warrington, where I played rugby league many years later. I saw him across the bar and said, 'I recognize that fella' to one of the boys when we were having a beer. 'That's Paul,' he replied. Ping! the light came on. 'Paul Cooper, wow! I used to watch him on *Match of the Day* as a kid and used to try and pretend to be him.' I was awestruck, and because I'd had a few pints, I bounded over to tell him. What a lovely bloke he was too.

Tredegar Ironsides was my club from when I joined, aged eight, to when I was 16, playing through all the age group from juniors to youth. It was only when I was 16, though, that I started training regularly. We would run up to the tump of stones on the mountain, touch them, then run back. It was the Ordinance Survey's highest point on the mountain above Tredegar, but it was just the tump of stones to us. That run became a ritual.

In the late 1970s most of the men in the Gwent valleys worked in the giant steelworks in Ebbw Vale and Llanwern or as miners in the many pits operating in the area, or in the companies supplying heavy industry. Although jobs were relatively plentiful, the value of wages was reduced by high inflation and many families struggled to make ends meet.

My old man had worked all his life down the pit but could still only afford to rent a council house. At least I had a house with a garden, there were a lot worse off than us. Wages lagged behind prices and the unions were constantly going toe-to-toe with the bosses of the nationalised industries like British Coal and British Steel. This was the era of the strike. Working people were fighting for a living wage and sheer survival was the name of the game. Unlike the well-fed posh boys playing rugby at private schools, the sports-mad boys growing up in the valleys of south Wales existed from meal to meal with the cheapest brands and a very basic diet. Our mothers always gave us the best they could afford, but filling our stomachs took precedence over nutrition, and I would eat a loaf of white bread a day. My genetics gave me a head start, standing at 6 foot 3 when I was still only 15, but I was painfully thin and my diet wasn't the best. Three years older than me, my sister Sandra told me that her friend, who was also 18, saw me dashing up the stairs in my Y-fronts and said I was the thinnest person she had ever seen. As an athlete I was definitely still 'work-in-progress'.

Friday was big shop day in our house. I can recall waiting at the front door for Mam to get off the bus, which out of courtesy would stop by our gate. I would rush out and grab the bags off the steps of the bus while she hobbled into the house. Then came unpacking time. Tins in the cupboard and detergents under the sink. Our bread, eggs and milk were delivered, so were already in the kitchen, and my dad grew all the vegetables himself. All that was left were the treats – sweets and meat. We didn't get many sweets and when I say meat, I don't mean T-bone steak or lamb chops. Remember, this was 1970s working-class Wales. The meat was either in a tin, corned beef, Pek (chopped ham and pork), or slices of haslet – to this day, I still don't know what it was! We had tins of sardines, sometimes mackerel if we were lucky, and always had a Sunday dinner – chicken or beef. Lamb was an extravagance. It was very expensive. We even had rabbit a few times. I would eat half a loaf of bread with every meal. Well, that's not entirely true but you can get the idea. I was growing fast and needed to eat something.

A Saturday lunch was always a Vesta beef curry, while sat at the table watching Grandstand or World of Sport. It was lovely at the time, but I had one a few years back to relive my youth. It was horrible and the beef pieces just tasted of old bits of cardboard, but that was the one meal we had as a family when I would sit with Mam, Dad and Sandra, and talk about stuff. Then Dad would go to watch the Ironsides, or, if Wales were playing, sit in his chair to watch the match. Even though my belly was full I had no chance of growing muscle because my protein intake was just too low. My understanding of nutrition didn't kick in until my late teens.

Representing Gwent Schools at 16 was a major turning point in my life and resulted in Tredegar Comprehensive giving me the Billy Morgan rugby bursary during its annual awards evening, but me being me I didn't turn up for the presentation. As a punk I was just rebelling against authority but the second, and most important, reason was because I thought I might have to make some kind of acceptance speech. There wasn't a chance in hell I would have done that. Graham Price, the legendary Welsh prop, was there to present the award and my old man played hell with me when he found out I hadn't gone. Price was one of his all-time rugby heroes. To be honest, I deeply regret not going. It was a stupid thing to do. It was an incredible honour but I simply didn't realise it at the time. What a complete idiot.

In the summer of 1981, I'd just finished my 'O' levels and turned 16. I didn't do too badly in my exams and left school with five O' Levels. I even went back and re-sit maths and history – not too shabby for a thicko from Tred!

The economic impact of Thatcherism meant we, like many other working-class families, couldn't afford to have a family holiday that year so I went to Brecon, to stay with my aunty, my dad's sister, for a few weeks. Her daughter, my cousin, was married to a squaddie, as were a lot of the girls in the town. He was a Geordie and was the first to introduce me to weight training. When he said he'd show me his magazines I wasn't expecting his body building mags! 'How could these guys be so big?' I thought, as I saw the big arms, enormous thighs and amazing physique of Sergio Olivier, Mike Mentzer, Lou Ferrigno and Arnie Schwarzenegger. I wanted to look like that, but how?

I was then lucky to get an apprenticeship as a fitter turner in the steel works. I also went to the NCB (the National Coal Board) and passed all the tests to become an apprentice fitter with them too. I actually had a choice and the money was a lot more working for the NCB but my old man told me not to go down the pit. So, I didn't, and opted for the British Steel plant in Ebbw Vale instead.

Life was improving. I had a job, was continuing my education at Ebbw Vale College – every Monday, on day release – and I even started going out with a few girlfriends (but not at the same time). I began to spread my wings a little and meet new people and go to new places.

Now I was earning and had a bit of cash, I could finally eat like an athlete. I'd never had steak until I was 17, but I was now able to buy it myself. My diet changed from jam sandwiches, to scrambled eggs; from tinned Pek to fresh steak. My physique changed accordingly. I trained in the spare room for two years and the change was noticeable.

Youth rugby became an outlet for my aggression. I can imagine Tred was like numerous other industrial towns, with wild young men all trying to find their way in life, to find their place in the pecking order, vying to be the alpha male. Rugby was where you could bash anyone who got in your way and have a gut full of beer after the game. Tredegar offered a fight if you wanted it and, if you were lucky, a snog and a grope on the walk home. All this was put into words by Elton John and Bernie Taupin in their anthemic *Saturday Night's Alright (For Fighting)*, with the classic line: 'I'm a juvenile product of the working class, whose best friend floats in the bottom of a glass.' That was me, and thousands of others.

Youth rugby was full of testosterone-filled yobs, with some games starting and ending in massive fights. I'm not sure what it's like nowadays, but it could be 75 minutes of scrapping and 5 minutes of actual rugby. Being destructive on the field appeared normal to me.

The boys I hung round with often took the mick out of my stammer, as teens do. I didn't find it funny, though, and just wanted to smack everyone, but that wasn't possible so I had to find another way to vent my frustrations. Rugby seemed to offer that opportunity. It felt like I could do anything on the field and not be held responsible. What happened when you were on the field, stayed on the field. It became my little world, my place, where I wasn't laughed at. I could kick, punch, stamp and release all the anger and not be held accountable, well, up to a point.

It was around that time when I was taken under the wing of club secretary, David 'Dai' Chard, who must have seen something in me because he took me everywhere. My old man couldn't drive so David stepped in. He was a godsend, not just for me but for the whole team and youth rugby in the town. He took me to all the Wales Youth training sessions and all the games, the lot. I have massive respect for the man. I haven't seen him since the late 1980s but I need to thank him from the bottom of my heart for what he did for me. I would have still been stuttering, 'Lanky Jonesy' if he hadn't invested as much time and effort in me as he did, which helped me get my first big break.

Up to that point, it was my sister, Sandra, who was the real sports star of the family. She represented the county at school athletics and was the all-round athlete in the family. My old man often said, 'If she was a boy, she'd have played for Wales.' That was like showing a red rag to a bull

Sandra was one of 'the in crowd' in school. She had a good social scene and was a popular girl. I think I embarrassed her to tell the truth. This lanky, misfit punk rocker who she had to call her brother.

Unlike me, I think she enjoyed school and college. It seemed like she had a great time. I was the awkward one growing up. We got on okay but the age and gender difference didn't pull us tight. It was only after our father, and then our mam, passed away that we became really close and still are. We both realised that it was only us two left and we needed to both make a bit more of an effort. Sandra had the brains, went to college and worked hard for her degree. She became a successful nurse practitioner. Now retired, Sandra often visits us in Qatar.

As well as David Chard, Tredegar also had a coach called 'Popular', because he lived in a house called The Poplars. He looked like Roy Wood from the glam-rock band, Wizard. He definitely connected with the boys and that gave us a bit of an edge because we wanted to play for him. He was a top man. Roger Thomas was also one of the main guys behind Glanhowy Youth in Tredegar. What's more, Roger also happened to be the secretary of Wales Youth. He was also a top guy and between them both, they opened the door for me to a new world.

I was really loving rugby – the stereotypical 'eating, sleeping and breathing rugby' obsessive – and each bit of success which led to another step up the ladder fed the ravenous emotional appetite I had for the game. The support from the coaches bolstered my confidence and made me feel appreciated, but it also heightened my desire to perform well and I found myself getting more and more wound up before games. I may have only been 13 stone but I was aggressive and loved driving into rucks and mauls. I couldn't use my shoulders for the hit because I didn't have any, so I just ran into them head first, like a crazy giraffe!

Thanks to Dai and Roger, I was selected for Wales Youth and for the two years I was involved in the team I regularly moved positions between lock and number eight. Even my old man didn't moan about me being in the second row when it meant me winning a Welsh cap. He was over the moon. So was Mam. This was a Welsh cap, and hopefully the start of a great adventure for me.

I was also training regularly with the Ironsides senior squad every Wednesday, which was invaluable. As a kid you learn so much from the old, wise heads – all the little tricks, the do's and the don'ts. Training with guys who were heavier, stronger and more street-wise forced me to grow up very quickly. I was an apprentice at British Steel in Ebbw Vale and serving my rugby apprenticeship with Tredegar

Ironsides. It gave me a massive edge when I went back to playing against opponents my own age.

One particular lineout practice session with the Ironsides when I was 17 sticks in the memory. It was a long, hard session focused on catching and driving. There were some wizened old bastards there. One of the props, Ian Price, had been around the block a few times and knew all the tricks.

At each lineout, as I began to jump, Ian would step on to my boots, nudge me, or pull my shirt, to disrupt my jumping action. He was really pissing me off, and enjoying every second. I couldn't let this go on and hatched a cunning plan. At the next lineout, the hooker cocked his arm and threw. I dummied to jump but moved forward quickly to get away from him, then planted my feet to jump. I thought I'd out-foxed him but, as my arms came forward to give me the momentum I needed, I could see his hand swing across and hit mine down. Once again, he'd done enough to stop me jumping and I fell sideways, only getting about two inches off the turf.

He wasn't the only one grinning. Lots of them were. That was it. I swung a fist at him out of pure frustration, with a childlike 'Piss off ' for added effect, but with no real intention of connecting. I was just lashing out.

Luckily for me, he ducked and my fist flew over his head.

'Woah, butt, what was that about?' he asked.

'Take it easy Jonesy,' the coach piped up, 'its only training.'

'He... he... he was f... f... fu... messing me about.'

I could hear the muffled chuckles from the rest of the players. We quickly moved on to some touch rugby and that was the end of it.

Later that night, my father came home from the club and sat me down. 'I heard you tried to knock Ian's head off in training?' I told him what happened. 'Ian was pushing you to see how far you'd go,' my old man told me. 'He wanted to teach you the dark arts, the tricks of the trade. You surprised him. He didn't expect you to swing for him.' I stared down at the floor, waiting for a bollocking that never came. Instead, he finished off with one of his famous quotes about life throwing adversity at you and how you must always try to overcome it – how it's easy to give in, and not to forget that only dogs lie down. Then he started laughing and winked at me, saying, 'Good boy, now go and put the kettle on.'

For me, that was the green light to carry on. Showing aggression was the only way to deal with things on the field and if I was being messed about – and the ref wasn't going to sort it – I had to. Rugby is a tough old game without allowing someone to take liberties. That's where it started for me.

My first Wales Youth cap was against England at Kingsholm, the home of Gloucester. I was 17. There were a few up-and-coming stars in the squad, like Paul Moriarty, Lyn Jones, Jonathan Griffiths, Roger Bidgood and Mark Perego. We lost, I think. It was a really wet day and the field was like a bog, giving their big forwards an advantage. They were huge. They looked more like grown men than youth players. Ron had got us fit with 'last man standing' runs, but we couldn't match them or I felt I couldn't. Facing me in the second row that day was Nigel Redman who went on to play for Bath and England. He was bald even way back then. I just ran around tackling and getting dirty in the mud.

The next game was against France at Stradey Park. They had a load of stars in their ranks who went on to be full internationals. This was a much better game. Again, I'm not sure if we won, but if we didn't win, we came bloody close. I recall Lyn was in a heck of a battle with their seven – two top players. He was a real link man with the backs and gave the team continuity. Conditions were dry and we spread the ball far more than we did against England. I really enjoyed that game.

The following season, Ian 'Turkey' Williams and I were both lucky enough to be selected for Wales Youth to play France in Toulouse, I think. Now in my second year with the Wales Youth squad, I had a bit of a swagger and thought I was 'Jack the Biscuit', the chocolate variation. This led to me getting above myself and being a bit of a dickhead. I think Ron Waldron, the coach, had a bit of a soft spot for me as I got away with a lot of shenanigans off the field that would have seen others kicked to the kerb. This sort of thing also happened when I played under Ron for Neath. He really did look after me. As a young buck, finding your feet, you need someone to keep you on a lead. Like most teenagers I thought my old man couldn't teach me anything, which again was nonsense, though I was neither humble or mature enough to realise it. I needed a father-figure, a guiding light, a strong influence and Ron became that person. I'm eternally grateful to him and his family for what he did for me (I'm actually writing this with a tear in my eye).

When I moved back to Neath years later, after my exploits in rugby league, I lived round the corner from Ron. I'd see him regularly and we'd chat about old tales and the stupid stuff I got away with. I had grown up a bit by then so wasn't as petrified to speak to him as I had been as a lanky, wet behind the ears, 18-year-old pup. What a top guy he still is, full of wisdom and guidance to this day.

The Wales Youth squad landed in southern France on the Thursday before the game, like excited eight-year-old schoolkids on a trip to Bristol Zoo. We started preparing with a bit of a run out on the local field and then got back to the hotel. After changing, a team meeting was called where we were told, in no uncertain terms, to keep off the beer. Ron gave us the old spiel that we were representing Wales, this was a big honour for us and our families, and to not do anything to let people down: 'You can all have a good drink after the game, but not before.' Good rousing stuff.

There was a bit of time before dinner, so me, Turkey (Ian) and Ginge (Carl Jenkins from Abertilery) decided to go for a stroll to stretch our legs and work up an appetite. This was only the second time I'd been abroad, first being a school rugby tour to Germany organised by Alun Pask, head of middle school at Tredegar Comprehensive and another British Lion, so I was excited and buzzing to be in a new country. We walked up the street talking about the game, passing shops and cafés from where the aroma of strong coffee, strong fags and strong lager wafted into our nostrils. Each street released the same smells; the same atmosphere; the same sounds. We were valley boys on tour. What could go wrong?

'Shall we have a quick one?' I asked them.

'But what about Ron?' Ginge replied.

'Only a quick one. He won't find out.'

We couldn't resist and ducked into a café on a side street. For a boy from Tredegar, it was amazing. The French guy behind the counter had a ciggie wedged in the side of his mouth and one eye shut as the smoke drifted up, blinding him. A proper, greased, wrap-over hair style and a once-white cotton vest, strained over his beer gut, stained with blotches of lager and coffee. He glared at us, shrugged and grunted 'Uggh', which we assumed was French for, 'What the hell do you Welsh morons want?'

Now I had been around Ron long enough to know that what he said he meant, but like any teen with the punk rock spirit of Sid Vicious running through their veins, I liked to stretch the elastic. So, being what I thought was street smart I pointed to the lager pump, raising one finger and then picked up a discarded espresso cup on the bar and also raised one finger. I liked France. You didn't need to speak, just point. Sorted. Maybe I should have moved out there. The other two just asked for a beer. The ice-cold lagers quickly appeared followed by a single, strong coffee for me. I suspected Ron would probably be taking in the sights before dinner, like us, but also on the lookout for Wales Youth players up to no good, like us. So, as soon as the lager was on the bar I skulled mine down in one go and put the glass on an adjoining table. I then sat down with the tiny cup of espresso rocket fuel in front of me.

'Bloody thirsty Jonesy,' said Ginge.

'Bloody right' I replied.

'What have you got that coffee for?' I was asked.

Before I could say a word, our world stopped. A big figure appeared at the door. Turkey stood frozen in time, with a glass of lager in his hands, in the motion of raising it to his lips, reminiscent of his father, Denzil Williams. Ginge was caught red-handed too. As the familiar flaming beard and piercing eyes of Ron Waldron, with his big fierce butty, Pat Walsh, blocked the door of the café, I looked up at them.

'What are you doing Jones?' Ron yelled.

'Nothing Ron, just having a coffee.'

He looked at me as if to say, 'You lying bastard.' I picked up my coffee cup and smiled. He glared at the other two with disdain, in a way only Ron could. He delivered a one liner that summed up everything the situation had presented to him: 'and Williams, I knew you'd be here. Like father like son eh! Follow me!' He then proceeded to frog-march us back to the hotel. Sometimes, not often, I was a lot smarter than I looked. Well, I thought I was, but in the game against the French, I smacked a couple into their second-row who had come off-side and flattened our scrum-half. Sadly, I caught him on top of his head and broke my left hand. I played on but the damage to my hand ruled me out of the England game at home a week later.

Three from our district team were capped that season, and being a Wales Youth international brought with it a bit of fame, invited to presentation dinners at local clubs and to other events in the valley. The district team played South Africa schools at a game in Monmouth that attracted a group of anti-apartheid protestors. At that time I didn't know what all the fuss was about. South African politics seemed a world away from my life in Tred. We won the game, although it was a bruiser, and as a result two more of our district team won Welsh caps. North Gwent rugby was flourishing and many onlookers were saying we all had first-class rugby careers ahead of us. I was still the punk; still anti-establishment; still a clown. I was still a little lost. I tried to forge this new identity for myself, the rugby star, but when I went home, I still couldn't answer the phone or go to the shop for my mam. It was so frustrating.

Winning a Wales Youth cap was huge for me. It gave me some credibility and boosted my confidence. For once, things were moving in the right direction. The dark days of hiding in derelict houses with the punks and glue sniffers were gone. In the Gwent valleys, we played lots of local – but not so friendly – derbies with the likes of Blackwood, Blaina, Brynmawr and RTB Ebbw Vale. Many battles were fought on those fields but, strangely enough, I did make some friends for life. Pitched battles on the turf until the final whistle and then a few beers in the bar with the boy who you had fought with for 80 minutes.

In my last year of youth rugby, we reached, for the very first time, the quarter-final of the Welsh Cup. We'd beaten Lampeter in the previous round – no one knew where the hell it was; we'd never been that far west – and were now drawn to play Carmarthen Quins. It meant another trip to west Wales and the same questions were asked by the boys from the Gwent valleys. Where is it? How far is Carmarthen? Is it near Barry Island?

We got there on a Harry Hill's bus and were all well up for it. Bosh, Billa, Leon, Turkey and me thought we could do a job on them. How wrong could we have been? They had a winger and a scrum-half who were something else. They outplayed us from the opening whistle. We tried to bully them but that didn't work either. It turned out that the scrum-half was Jonathan Griffiths, who went on to play many times for Wales, while the winger was none other than the brilliant Ieuan Evans, who later starred for Llanelli, Wales and the Lions. Well, that's what I was told. If that is wrong, I stand to be corrected, but if it wasn't them, those players were superb. On the way back to Gwent we got absolutely hammered on cider, and drowned our sorrows even more in the Royal Oak when we finally got back to our little bit of God's country.

Going on the lash and creating havoc in Tred after a game became a normal part of life. One evening I was at my awful best – loud, rude and blotto, and ventured into The Cambrian (The 'Cam'), a great pub on the corner of the circle, opposite the town clock, run by Val and Neil. Val gave the impression she was of royal blood and regarded herself as the Queen of The 'Cam' while Neil was an educated, civilised landlord who had brought the atmosphere of a country pub to the centre of Tred. The colliers and factory workers loved it and you had to queue 20-deep to get in every weekend. On this particular night I'd got in and the place was packed. All the seats were taken and you couldn't turn without knocking a pint over.

Being 18 and tanked-up in that environment was a recipe for disaster. The loved-up couples, and highly protective Welsh males, didn't take kindly to my unruly behaviour. Tensions rose, then rose again as I took little notice of their growing impatience.

'Look out, you. Watch my pint. Oi! Behave will you!' some guy yelled at me.

His words poured petrol on my inebriated fire. How dare he? I had played for Wales Youth.

'Piss off, the lot of you,' I snarled back. Then, finding a bit of space, perhaps just two-foot square, I turned my back, unbuttoned my jeans, pulled 'em down to my knees and bent over showing my arse to the lot of them. Laughing like a fool, I straightened up, pulled up my jeans and was buttoning back up when ... Slam! I felt a huge clout just before the lights went out.

I came to, face down on the floor with my tongue tasting the beer-stained carpet. Getting to my knees, I began to come to my senses, then finished buttoning my jeans before being thrown out of the back door. I didn't have a clue who'd bashed me, apparently with a bar stool. It served me right, though. I even had to appear in front of Val and Neil to apologise for my behaviour, and receive a two-week ban from The Cambrian. I was gutted. So, you could see I was a little out of control.

This wasn't the person I wanted to be, so I sorted my head out and set my goal of playing for Wales.

5

(Playing With) The Rude Boys

'Mark was a great mentor, an immense player and still is a good friend. The few of us that got close to him knew about his demons and how they brought out his biggest asset on the field; his physicality. Off the field, we could also see how he battled those demons and thought more of him because of it. This is because, in reality, we all have them in one shape or another. He is a big man in every sense of the word and someone I will always have a lot of respect and time for.'

Chay Billen

The door to the promised land was now ajar and I was going to make sure I kicked it open and walked right through it. I began to take my rugby seriously and I had a goal, to one day run out in the red shirt of Wales. During pre-season, Billy Bennett, the physio for Abertillery RFC and a mate of my old man's who drank in the Ironsides, took me under his wing. He had me training there through the summer of 1984.

If anyone doesn't know Abertillery, it's a town nestled in a very narrow valley with a river running along the bottom and the rugby ground located on the river bank. The mountains tower above the ground and cast a permanent shadow over the pitch. It was once voted the most picturesque rugby ground in Wales but I've also heard it said that it goes dark in Abertillery two hours before anywhere else in Wales!

It was a grey and damp town surrounded by coal tips, which we used while training. One of the drills was to run up the shale tip and back down in a zig zag. It was horrendous. My legs turned to jelly and my heart pounded so violently I thought it would jump out of my chest. I managed the first uphill section without any issues, but when I turned to run back down my legs buckled uncontrollably, as if

I was pissed. It was a crazy sensation but I just had to keep going and finish the session. The next few days were torture, mind, and I could hardly move my legs. They ached and throbbed every time I moved and I couldn't walk down the stairs without holding on to the hand rail. After those sessions in Abertillery with Benny, running up the mountain to the tump of stones was like a stroll in the park on a quiet Sunday afternoon.

Rugby in the Gwent valleys in the 1980s was thriving at all levels particularly at the top table. This was the Merit Table era where teams like Tredegar, Abertillery, Newbridge and Ebbw Vale were all big and successful clubs. The forwards were always huge, hard guys like Brandon Cripps, Sid Wharton, 'Bunter', 'Phyllis' Thomas and Clive Burgess plus a few dozen more. The game was still amateur so all these guys had manual jobs and most just turned out on a Saturday for a bash about and a gut full of beer after the match. As a skinny 18-year-old I quickly experienced the full-on brutality of valleys rugby. I got slapped round the ear or smashed in the face if I stepped over the line, or for even just being in the wrong place at the wrong time. There was no sentiment, no empathy because I was a youngster and a newbie. 'Let him learn, just like we all had to,' was the unspoken understanding of those granite-faced beasts of men during those long and hard 80 minutes of battle.

I'd come out of youth rugby thinking I was definitely on my way up. Even Ron Waldron, my coach at Wales Youth and the coach with Neath RFC, had pulled me aside at one Wales training session and whispered in my ear, 'Jones, I'll be keeping an eye out for you next season. Got a feeling you're going to make your mark.'

I didn't know if that was a good thing or a bad thing. I didn't know if he said it to scare me and keep me in line, or was it to give me a boost to make me play better. I think it did both!

I learnt my rugby at Tredegar Ironsides but they were just one of three clubs in the town – the Ironsides, Tredegar RFC and Trefil RFC – and there was no love lost between the three. Tredegar RFC was the premier club and played in the Merit Table, but loyalty to the Ironsides ran deep in me. I wanted to play for them, not Tredegar. My old man got wind of this and pulled me up one day. He told me to have a serious think about what my aims and goals were. 'You can go higher than the Ironsides, so use your head.'

It was evident what he meant. Ironsides were his team, his love and joy, but Tredegar were a better and bigger team. They had some cracking players and if I made my mark there it would definitely be a good stepping stone to bigger things. Taking my father's wise words on board, I joined Tredegar RFC along with five or six other lads from the Glanhowy Youth team including, Billa, Leon and Turkey.

I had played with all these lads through all levels from the age of eight with the Ironsides. Turkey was a good player, but due to his dad's stardom I would often wind him up. He took the banter but I could see it didn't go down too well and he got his revenge by smashing me a few times in training and trial games. Billa, our scrum-half, was the son of the Ironsides coach Richie Gregory, and Leon was the outside half, always the first guy picked. A natural footballer, as cool as a cucumber in a fridge.

Of the six former youth players who stepped up for trials with Tredegar's 1st XV that year, two of us had been capped by Wales Youth and the other four had won district caps. It looked like there would be a decent team running out in Tredegar colours for many years to come. Competition for places was tough, though, as there were some good players already established at the club, such as Ian 'Pepper' Lewis, John Dixon, Wally Jervis, Nicky Hunt, Martin Burridge, 'Phyllis' Thomas, John Doc, 'Dwty' Moore, and Chris Jarman. So, when I was picked for the team, I made sure I played as well as I could.

It was scary, as a 19-year-old, being pitted against grown men who were work-hardened and not afraid to dish it out. The game then was all about intimidation. If you could stop your opposite number playing, there was no need to worry about his rugby skills. If he feared you would smack him at any time, he would be too afraid to play.

Most of the bigger, skilful guys I came across often turned out to be utter shithouses. They would be fantastic in the unopposed team training sessions on a Thursday night – running, jumping, catching and passing – yet, when they ran out on the field on a cold, rainy Saturday, faced with a gnarly old bastard like John Perkins (Pontypool), Adrian Owen and the O'Callaghan brothers (Aberavon), or Gareth Howls and Clive Burgess (Ebbw Vale) it was a different matter. Those hard men would actually grip you in a line out and hiss in your ear, 'You jump today son and I'll fucking have you.' The shithouses would stand there, shaking in their boots and looking down at the grass. They may as well have gone and had a cup of tea with their mothers in the stand. A verbal threat from the hardmen would render them useless for the rest of the game.

I found myself on the receiving end of that type of intimidation but my internal response was immediate and blunt. 'Why don't you fuck off?' I thought to myself. 'I'll jump, you old has-been. I'll jump right on your fucking head.' Being young and a little naive, I always jumped. No one was going to frighten me. Saying that, I got done on a few occasions and was helped off the field with a head full of stars and seeing double but, as my confidence and my reputation grew, I made sure that the next time I faced them, they didn't have their own way. I wasn't going to let them have me again. It would be me issuing the threats. Me telling others not to jump.

Playing for Tredegar against Ebbw Vale was one of those games played right on the edge. I wanted to prove myself to guys like 'Phyllis' and John Dixon so I was a bit over zealous at the start, kicking and stamping on everything and anyone that moved. I was really enjoying myself. I got to one line out and the legend that is Clive Burgess, the famous Ebbw flanker, said very quietly to me, 'Calm down, Mark, you're a bit excited.' Clive may have looked and played like he had been carved out of stone from the local quarry – craggy and indestructible – but no one was going to boss me around anymore. I tossed a nonchalant glance at him as if to say, 'Fuck off old man ... it's my time now.'

The ball came into the line-out. We won it and it was moved sharply to the midfield. Our crash-ball centre got tackled and I raced across to join the ruck, entering it as I had done earlier, feet first, as if I was taking part in the long jump.

BANG

A bell started ringing in my head. Then nothingness. No sound, no vision. Next thing I could hear was a voice, far off in the distance. 'Mark, Mark. You okay?' The voice got louder and louder. 'Sniff this, Mark.' I remember breathing in the smelling salts and the haze started to lift as I came out of my enforced slumber. The noise of the crowd filled my head and the daylight scorched my slowing opening eyes. As I got to my feet I saw a river of blood pouring past my eyes from a deep gash to my head, and realized that Albert, the physio, was leading me off the field back to the changing room.

'We'll get that stitched,' Albert muttered, 'the doc will be here in a bit. You won't be going back on.'

'Oh,' I slurred, 'What happened?'

'Don't worry,' he said, 'you just caught one. A good one.' As he mopped the blood away with the magic sponge!

Now here's an enigma. The magic sponge! That sponge was used for everything – cut heads, bloody noses, grazed knees, busted nut, smashed teeth, the lot. It just went straight back in the bag of water, had a quick rinse and was ready for the next injury. The infections that thing must have spread. I bet there's been many an STI caught from the magic sponge!!

Years later, I regularly went for a Sunday pint to the Rhyd-y-Blew in Ebbw Vale. This was Clive Burgess' regular haunt too. Someone asked me if I'd ever played against Clive, who was standing with the group.

'Yes,' I replied, 'Once for Tredegar, when I started out.'

'I remember that,' Clive uttered, a smirk curling up his top lip. 'You were the one stamping and shoving your weight about.' As I started to puff-out my chest with pride, Clive delivered his knock-out punch. 'You weren't on long though, were you?'

Whooooosh it all came flooding back. 'You?' I looked at him. 'You did me that day, didn't you? I always wanted to know what happened but no one would say.'

His smirk turned into a big wide grin. He clutched his fist which was the size of a Cornish pasty. 'Yeah,' he laughed, 'it was different back then.' Everyone else joined in laughing. He finished up his beer and then brought a round for me and the rest of the boys. He was a truly humble bloke and a true legend.

As a rugby-mad teenage boy, it wasn't the exploits of the silky-skilled players that interested me. It was the stories of the hard men, like Brian Thomas playing in his bare feet, Paul Ringer's charge at the English outside-half at Twickenham, or the skulduggery of Clive 'the claw' Burgess. Then there were the really hard bastards who had 'gone north': like Mike Nicholas, Glyn Shaw diving off the bar into a box of crisps, Jim Mills stamping on the head of a Kiwi after he'd scored under the posts, and Paul Woods, another Tred boy who held the unofficial rugby league record for breaking jaws. These stories would make my eyes light up and got my blood racing. To meet all these guys as I grew up was a real honour and for one of them (Clive) to feel the need to actually give me a clip was the biggest compliment ever.

When I played for Tredegar it wasn't just on the field where boots and fists were flying. The miners' strike was raging and we had a lot of players who were colliers, and a lot of our parents and other people involved with the club were also working in the pits. Some of our players – like 'Phyllis', John Doc and 'Dwty' Moore – were regulars on the picket line and on many Saturdays they would be picketing in the morning, then giving their all on the field in the afternoon. Emotions were running high, against the scabs and the cops, and with the threat of losing their job adding to the tense atmosphere in mining communities. The film Billy Elliot summed up the whole aura that was present at the time.

Back then each team had its enforcer; its 'daddy'. The guy who dealt with any nonsense on the field, and often off it. He was also the guy who took care of the youngsters – who righted the wrongs and, in those days, there were a lot of wrongs taking place. 'Phyllis' was Tredegar's daddy. A six-foot two-inch, hard-working, hard drinking, and one hell of a hard bastard miner. Yet one of the nicest blokes you would ever want to meet. He was a legend both on and off the field. We'd heard tales that on Sundays, his wife would bring his roast dinner to the pub for him! All the young valleys boys aspired to be like Phyllis. He didn't take any nonsense.

One weekend that winter we played away to Waunarlwydd in the Welsh Cup. All the talk on the bus was about the strike – about the cops, the pickets, the scabs, and how most families in the valleys were struggling to survive. Everywhere you went, similar angry conversations were being had about the strike. It was a civil war, a class war, and the scars and the wounds it caused are still deep and painful today. There was talk on the bus that there were a few policemen in the Waunarlywdd team. That was all the pep-talk we needed.

The pre-match atmosphere in the changing rooms was unlike anything I had witnessed before or since. I could see the hatred in the eyes of some of our players. As you can imagine, the game was played in a very bad spirit from the first whistle to the last. Off-the-ball incidents and skirmishes were kicking off all over the field. I don't remember the score. I'm not sure if we won or lost. The bad blood had poisoned the game. I was more interested in how many faces I had punched than how many points we had scored.

After we got showered and changed, the team went in the clubhouse for some food and a beer. In retrospect it was probably the wrong thing to do. Both teams were in the same room and the queue at the bar was four or five deep. You could cut the atmosphere with a machete. I was sat down, having a chat with Steve Fealey, our new scrum-half who'd joined us from Dowlais, when suddenly the volume and tone of the bar noise changed. I looked up and several of the Waunarlwydd players were stood by the bar in their police uniforms ready to go to work. The rumours were correct. As you can imagine, the sight of the 'enemy' wasn't appreciated by the miners in our team. Whisperings and rumblings circled around the room like vultures circling around a dying man in the desert. Daggers were drawn in the eyes of our players and knuckles were clenched under the tables. An eerie silence engulfed the clubhouse.

Shoulders were bumped. Beer was spilt. Things were said. The words were inaudible but the tone and emotion was obvious. You could taste the tension. Something was about to go off, big time. It didn't take long.

Within seconds, tempers flared and the room erupted. Glasses were smashed, chairs flung across the floor and tables over-turned amid the chaos. Those who didn't fancy a fight fled from the bar, leaving the true pugilists to go at each other, showing no mercy. Me and Steve scarpered through the door, out into the car park and the pouring rain. Steve grabbed my arm, shouted 'Look by here' and gestured towards the window of the function room which was right next to the door. I rubbed away the rain, cupped my hands to the glass and peered through like a starving kid by a cake shop window.

It was like a scene from a wild west film. 'Phyllis' and 'Sparky' were stood back-to-back in the middle of the room, throwing punches and kicks at whoever came near them. The off-duty yet uniformed policemen were sporadically attacking Tredegar's terrible twins, then retreating when they took a short-left jab to the nose or a boot to the nuts.

Things quickly subsided when people realised they weren't going to get the better of 'Butch Phyllis' and 'Sundance Sparky'. Pepper, our captain, quickly rounded everyone up and we got onto the bus, leaving broken glass, smashed furniture and random teeth on the blood-splattered, beer-soaked carpet. Once back in the safety of Tredegar RFC, everyone got pissed, had a sing song and then staggered home with a bizarre tale to tell for the next few years.

That season, I was also picked to play for Crawshay's against Bridgend. A fantastic set up, and a halfway point between club and full representative honours, Crawshay's meant good rugby, good drinking and good fun. When the letter arrived, inviting me to play, it looked so official and important. It made me feel a million dollars.

Dai Morgan, the Neath number 8 was named to start and I was on the bench. I had seen him play in the Welsh Cup final the previous year when Llanelli had defeated the Welsh All Blacks. He was so explosive and a real handful. I wasn't yet 20 and it would have been a lie to say I wasn't frightened. I was playing against men who had big reputations and I was scared – about not playing well but also about the physical side. In those situations, my dad would always say, 'They have two arms and two legs just like you, boy. They can't kill you.' He also reassured me by saying, 'if it does kick off there is always that little man with the whistle who will stop it.'

Dai Chard gave me a lift to the game and as I walked into the dressing rooms Neville Walsh greeted me at the door. 'Mark, thanks for coming. All the boys are in there,' pointing towards the changing rooms. I wasn't going to speak, no chance, I didn't want to be considered an idiot. My guts were churning. I was shaking and sweating. There was a load of 'Alright, Mark,' as I pushed through these men to find myself a spot and put my bag down. I turned round to face the wall and timidly took my shirt off.

I bent over to take my jeans off and turned at the same time. 'Clunk.' My head hit something hard and I straightened up. 'What the hell was that?' I thought. It was a colossus known as Russell Cornelius. I muttered an apology. He grunted. He never said much. I carried on changing. After a while Neville came over. 'Mark, Dai's not here yet, it looks like you're starting. You ok with that?'

'Y...y...yes,' I spluttered, my head spinning like a top.

I put on the Crawshay's jersey and the team ran out to the pitch for a warm-up. I was nervous but buzzing. I caught a practice throw at a lineout. 'Yes,' I thought. This is going well.' I was as enthusiastic as a kid playing in a sandpit. Lineout calls learnt; scrum moves learnt; I was ready.

With about 10 minutes to go to kick off, we were back in the changing rooms making our final preparations when Dai turned up in jeans, a check shirt – unbuttoned to reveal his hairy chest – with his face half covered by thick black stubble and a cigarette smouldering beneath a huge jet-black moustache. He looked like a reincarnation of Charles Bronson.

'Alright boys,' he grinned, as he walked in carrying his boots in a plastic carrier bag. He took his shirt off with a swagger, his cigarette still hanging from his mouth. No wonder he had the confidence to turn up late. It looked like he was carved from granite. I had only seen things like that in cartoons.

Neville came over to me, looking sheepish. 'Sorry Mark.' He took the shirt off me and gave it to Dai. No worries. I couldn't compete with that at 19. I was in total awe of the beast of a man.

Dai played 30 minutes then came off and I played for the rest of the game. To play with men like that, and against the late great Gareth Williams, was definitely one of the highlights of my career. I learned so much from those guys. I also took a huge hint from Dai: 'Get on the weights, Mark.'

Well, I was on the weights, but in my bedroom. I'd gone as far as I could with my array of plastic weights, a bench, a curl bar and bits and pieces. I needed a proper gym. Seeing Dai and Russell Cornelius gave me the guts to join the local gym: Body Masters. Previously, I didn't have the confidence to go to a gym because I thought I was too thin and scrawny, but when I got in there it took me to another level. I spoke to Mike, the local body builder, about training routines and diet – about the benefits of amino acids, protein powders, eggs and milk.

Within six months I must have upped my calorific intake three-fold. I was eating six raw eggs a day, six pints of milk, a whole chicken, 12 Weetabix, two jacket potatoes, an 8oz rump steak, salad, assorted vegetables, and pot of ice cream. I must have gone from a daily intake of 2,000 calories to 5,000 calories. There were also the supplements: amino acids, ultimate orange, ephedrine powders, and potions that were laced with all sorts of stuff which would be banned now. Drug testing was not taken seriously. It was in its infancy so who knew what people were taking. I certainly didn't. Things that weren't banned then would be banned now and I was not on my own. Players were beginning to weight train, and attend gyms. You needed to be bulkier, more muscular and physically stronger if you wanted to dominate on the field. I got bigger and stronger very, very quickly. A mixture of diet, training and supplements – boosted by my raging late-teenage hormones – were putting right the wrongs of years of poor dietary decisions. I went into that gym a boy, but came out a man.

Over the next couple of years, I got drug tested a few times and the results were always negative. Maybe if the parameters were the same as they are now, myself and a lot of players would have been disqualified from playing, who knows? A lot of things were different 35 years ago and I reckon players would have been banned from playing for doing a lot more than taking a supplement. I got in the Welsh squad at 20 and in one session we were asked, 'Who is training with weights?' Only three of us raised our hands. What shocked me more was one of the back row stars saying, 'I don't do weights because it's boring.'

In that moment I knew I was ahead of the game and focused on getting bigger and stronger. I didn't have the exceptional skill of others so I needed to make the most of what I had.

After my first appearance for Crawshay's, against Bridgend, I was invited on their tour to Narbonne, in southern France. The squad was full of great players such as Mike Richards, Wayne Hall and Ray Giles.

One aspect of playing for Crawshay's I wasn't prepared for was their legendary initiation ritual. It's a secret never divulged by any of those honoured to have played for the team – including me. I have no real recollections of the matches we played, but I do vividly remember two incidents.

The first was when I latched on to Mike Richards. He was the Neath hooker at the time and had taken me under his wing as soon as I walked into the changing room for training. It wasn't long before he christened me Scooby Doo. I can only guess at the reasons, but there was more than one similarity in looks and personality between me and the cartoon dog. We arrived in France and as always on a Crawshay's rugby tour, the bags were dumped in the room and the boys were quickly out on a 'bonding' session – lots of beer, snacks and chat. These sessions were essential for the guys to get to know each other. I was rooming with Mike. I was young and naïve and he took it on himself to take care of me!

I made the most of all the freebies on offer. Wherever we went we were treated like V.I.P.s and I had no need put my hand in my pocket. Narbonne was lovely and the tone of the trip was all about having a bit of fun and playing exciting, entertaining rugby. This suited me and the boys. As was tradition, everyone had to give a song. I was told this and had been rehearsing. Wayne Hall started with Delilah. He was absolutely fantastic. What a voice! Even though I was nervous, I jumped in next. No, that's a lie, I was thrown in next. I felt like Eminem in his song, Loose Yourself, but I'd been practising and hit 'em with the 1961 classic, *Big Bad John*.

'Every mornin' at the mine you could see him arrive
He stood six-foot-six and weighed two-forty-five
Kinda broad at the shoulder and narrow at the hip
And everybody knew ya didn't give no lip to big John
(Big John, big John)
Big bad John (big John)'

I'd practiced for weeks in mam's box room and I got through without a glitch. Thank God. 'Yesssssss,' I was one of the boys.

We had a great session, laughing until we cried. One of the places we visited was this very posh establishment, some kind of stately home, decked out with all sorts of weird stuff. Dark mahogany panelling with paintings of rutting stags and stuffed partridges in glass cases. It was bizarre. A million miles away from the orange painted walls in the social club in Tredegar, but pretty soon we relaxed and got the beer down us. Then I saw it. Wow. A giant eagle carved out of black marble. It was exquisite.

'Look at that Mike,' I said.

Now Mike was one hell of a wicked bastard. 'You like that do you Scoob?'

'Aye. It's...it's...it's brilliant,' I replied.

'Why don't you have it? They wouldn't ever miss it.' He planted the seed in my drunken mind.

Bollocks, of course they'd miss it but it was all for the craic. I was brought up in a culture that allowed the rugby boys to get away with blue murder most of the time. If a car was turned over in the street in Tredegar, people would say. 'Ahh it's only the rugby boys ... they were just having a laugh.' If a gang of skinheads had done it, it would be, 'bastards, they should be strung up.'

I have been involved with many a street sign going missing and traffic cones being rearranged down the years, so 'removing' an eagle in a posh pad in France would be small potatoes. Everything would be excused. So, we had a few more beers and kept close to the eagle. By the time it was time to go we had formulated a plan. I took off my burgundy Crawshay's jumper with the green and white leek on the left breast and casually walked over to the bird. Just before we were leaving, I threw it over the bird. It hid it perfectly. A few minutes later I grabbed the jumper with the bird underneath and made a brisk exit through the door.

'We got it Mike, we've got it,' I said excitedly.

'Shhh shhhh,' you fucking idiot ... keep walking.'

We struggled to carry it up the street to the hotel. Christ, it was heavy. Halfway home, Hally passed us

'What you got there, boys?' he asked.

'Nowt.' We carried on walking.

We finally got it back to the bedroom, laughing like two school kids who had just pinched crisps from the corner shop. Our stolen prize was placed in its position of honour on the wash stand in our hotel room. It looked fantastic, very majestic. I stood back to admire it. God, that bird was beautiful. I woke the next morning with a thick head and a mouth like a dustbin. I rubbed my eyes and saw the bird looking at me.

The memories of the night before flooded back, but deep down I was proud of my achievement. With a smile on my face, I headed down for breakfast. As I was about to gorge on scrambled eggs and streaky bacon French style, Hally pushed past my chair and out of the side of his mouth I heard, 'Where eagles dare, Scoobie, boy.' He smirked and walked off.

'Shit, he knows,' I thought.

We jumped on the bus. Had a light training session. A few passing drills and some lineouts. All the time I was whispering to Mike. 'We were seen, Mike. Hally knows .... Shit, shit.'

'Calm down, Scoob. It will be all right.'

We returned to the hotel and within no time a team meeting was called. The boss man, Neville Walsh, addressed us. You could cut the atmosphere with a kitchen knife. In his best solicitors' tones, he said, 'Boys, a very expensive and rare item has gone missing from the establishment we were in last night.' I didn't know where to look. I started sweating like I had malaria on a slow boat down the Nile. 'They want it back,' he added.

I looked straight at Mike, trying to remain cool and composed but I was sure that everyone in the room knew it was me and were slyly glancing over in our direction.

'I need it returned to reception in 30 minutes. Thank you.' Neville left the room.

I grabbed Mike and rushed upstairs. Hally was grinning like a Cheshire cat who had all the cream.

'Shit Mike ... it was only a joke. We're going to get sent home in disgrace.'

'Calm down Scoob. Just wrap it up, take it to reception and leave it there without anyone seeing you.'

The jumper came out again and was used to conceal the prize for a second time. I almost dropped it going down the stairs. There was no one at reception, I placed it under the counter and fled.

'Phew ... I've got away with this,' I thought.

On my way back to my room, I was confronted with Hally's grinning chops. 'Where eagles dare, Scooby, boy,' he whispered and shook his finger at me. 'Where eagles dare.'

Nothing came of it but that vision of him still haunts me to this day.

After the first game of the tour the boys were back out on the beer and we had the initiation ritual. It left me a bit sore. Sudocrem was good for that sort of thing, but it's a bugger to get out of grey stay-pressed trousers. What happened? My lips are sealed. It's a Crawshay's secret.

We then went on to a club which the French guys couldn't wait to show us. I'd had a few by then and as I walked in, I saw what I thought was a mirage. The place must have been about 70% women. They were all 6ft with long hair, very slim and dressed to kill.

'What the hell?' I said, 'this is more like it. Why didn't we come here earlier?'

There was champagne everywhere and we were all chatting, laughing, and loving it. I was right in the middle of festivities and one gorgeous blond had latched right on to me. I thought I was David Hasselhoff. I was up on my feet dancing. I was chatting, the stammer lost in the enjoyment. I was having the time of my life then I felt a tug on my arm. It was Mike.

'Heeeeyyy, Mike, this is a superb place.'

'Come here a minute, Scoob.' He motioned for me to follow him.

'No butt, I'm in here.'

'Come here, quick.'

Like a kid whose mother had told him to come in for tea, I reluctantly walked behind him to the bar, shouting back to the girl that I would be straight back with her. She smiled and blew me a kiss.

A few of the older players, Neville Walsh and the management team were lined up by the bar, talking and drinking by themselves. What a bunch of old, boring bastards I thought to myself.

'C'mon Mike, what you doing mun?'

I heard it again. 'Calm down, Scoob.'

'But look, Mike, what a place.'

'No Scoob, you look.' The other players were belly laughing by this point. I wasn't sure why. Probably taking the piss out of me yet again. I was getting mad.

'What do you mean?' I hissed at him.

'Scoob.' Mike looked me straight in the eyes. 'See that lady sitting on the table over there?' He pointed to a stunner with long, black hair in a tight red dress. I nodded. 'Well, how big are her hands?' I checked her out. They did look pretty big to be honest. Like shovels. 'And look at that one's face, on the next table. Notice anything?' he continued.

I must admit her chin was a bit darker than her forehead but I thought it was the lighting. The penny still hadn't dropped. The others guys were more or less rolling on the floor laughing at this point. 'And that one's swallowed a cooking apple and it stuck in her throat,' he added.

Wallop. It hit. It was like a scene from The Kinks' song *Lola*.

'Fuck me, they're all blokes, Mike.'

'Yes, Scoob,' he laughed, 'that's what I've been trying to tell you. You were the little boy and Lola was gonna make you a man.'

That was it. It was time to leave ....Taxi!!

So, my first year out of youth, I played for Tredegar but was intermittently training with Neath. Back then there was a WRU ruling that a player's first season out of youth had to be spent with his mother club. I reckon the reasoning was to repay the club for the investment in the player, which was a commendable approach.

That April, on a Sunday about half three in the afternoon, I had just come back from having a few jars in Dowlais with the boys, and had devoured my chicken dinner. Dad was back from the club, sat in his chair, and I was on the sofa, relaxing. My rugby career was starting to take off: Wales Youth caps, Tredegar RFC 1st XV and now Crawshay's. Everything was heading in a positive direction. I was settled and happy. Suddenly, there was a knock on the door.

'Who's that? It can't be the cops,' I thought. I'd been a good boy that week. Maybe it was the French police come to arrest me for the Great Eagle Robbery!!!

'See who that is Elizabeth,' my old man said drowsily to my mam.

Mam toddled off to the door. She later told me that it had 'gone dark' with a huge frame standing there, blocking out the sunlight. There, standing in all his leather biker gear was Brian Thomas the

Ayatollah of Welsh rugby; he had ridden his Harley Davidson from Neath. My mother nearly collapsed in the hallway.

'Hi Mrs Jones, I would like to have a chat with Mark please,' Brian said.

My old man was out of his chair quicker than a labourer off a hot toilet seat. He ran into the passage and stood there transfixed. 'Brian F......g Thomas, in my house !!' he kept muttering. Brian just smiled.

After things had settled and mam had made tea, we sat round the table and Brian talked me through the plans they had for me at Neath and how things would work next season. Train two days a week, games on Saturday and Wednesday, with transport provided for each trip.

'What do you think?' he asked.

I was lost for words. I was the proudest 19-year-old in the valleys. It was a dream come true. I was going to play for Neath!

A new and incredible chapter in my life was about to begin

6

Neat(h)! Neat(h)! Neat(h)!

'I first met Mark playing in the youth set-up. I could see straight away he had a raw talent that could be developed. He blended into the Neath way perfectly because he had the right attitude, he was vigorous, committed and always willing to learn. A very special player indeed.'

Ron Waldon

I'm putting this out there, and I would argue until the end of time, that for anyone who played for Neath between 1985 and 1990 it was simply beyond remarkable. The situations and the experiences I personally went through with Neath set me up and put me in a place that nothing else could come near.

At my first training session, which was three days after my 20th birthday, I didn't get off to the best of starts. I'd been out on the weekend with my mates from Dowlais. As usual, after a mad night on the town, we ended up in Fealey's parents' house. There were about 15 of us, all crashed out, listening to music, drinking and trying not to be the first to fall asleep. It was one of those gatherings which was deadly if you dozed off first. That night, because I'd had more to drink than normal, I crashed out. When I woke in the morning all I could hear was giggles coming from the boys laying around in the front room.

'Oh no,' I guessed what had happened. I raced into the bathroom and swore out loud. 'Bastards.' They had shaved the right side of my head completely bald.

'Thanks boys,' I stormed back into the front room. 'I've got training with Neath on Monday.'

'You look great ... a real trend setter,' one of them shouted out from behind the settee where they were all hiding.

'The bastards.'

When I got home, my mother was beside herself. 'Mark, what's happened?'

'I fell asleep, that's all, mam.' She looked confused.

A while later, I thought 'balls to this', so I shaved the other side too and turned up on that Monday night at the Gnoll with a Mohican haircut. There was a deadly silence when I walked into the changing room. I must have looked a sight. A lanky Tredegar upstart with a ridiculous haircut and kitted out in punk gear. The guys told me later they thought, 'who the hell is this idiot?' Mike Richards, who had already adopted me and christened me Scooby Doo on the Crawshay's tour, introduced me to the boys and the name has stuck with me ever since.

The first thing I noticed when I turned up to training was we didn't see or touch a ball for the first hour. It was just run, run and run. The whole ethos; the whole Neath style was based around out-running and being fitter than the opposition. The aim was to put constant, unremitting pressure on them and not allow them to relax for a second. Its more or less what Barcelona football team did in their prime.

That full-on style wasn't for everyone, mind. A number of good players were asked to come along and train with us, with a view to joining us at the Gnoll, but after seeing what we did in training it was usually the last we saw of them. Maybe they didn't want to put in the hard yards or maybe they thought they didn't need to. It was their choice.

Being the coach of the Wales Youth team, Ron Waldron was exposed to a lot of young players with ability and promise, and looked for certain qualities in a player. The right mentality seemed to be right at the top of his wish list. It wasn't the most skilled lads who got approached. Neath had a certain style and players needed to fit that style to be considered. Ron took a punt on me. I wasn't the best lineout forward, I wasn't the quickest off the back of the scrum, and I wasn't the best passer, but he must have noticed something else I offered as a player.

Ron's ethos and methods while coaching Wales Youth didn't sit right with the players of other clubs, and that's why none of them played for Neath. The methods had made Neath unbeatable for a number of years, because every player bought in to the club's ethos.

My playing style and attitude must have been what he was looking for, and I fitted in from day one. Brian Thomas, Ron Waldron and

Glen Ball believed in me. They believed in us all. That belief enabled us to climb – or run through – the mountains that stood in our way and made Neath RFC not only the premier club in Wales but perhaps the most successful and feared team in Europe.

The Neath ethos was also obvious off the field. Unlike other clubs there wasn't a club blazer and tie in sight. They were not big on formality and pomp. Just turn up, get on with it and get the job done. It was as simple as that. Brian and Ron were in charge and they created a different, highly effective organisational culture. Our team spirit was unbreakable and we didn't need a blazer and tie to win games.

Brian Thomas' tactical nous and man management was way ahead of its time. He was the first person to suggest I may need speech therapy but, stupidly, I didn't think there was anything wrong with me. I was in denial, or simply embarrassed, and didn't take up his kind offer. Even though he was a giant of a man who demanded abrasive rugby, he definitely had the human touch. I was made to feel part of the family. He had an open house policy and there were no barriers. If you needed a little help in life Brian would give you the guidance you needed. He is another who I am deeply indebted to.

He was the brains behind Neath. He had a plan, a master plan and sought out players who were a little unconventional. He then moulded his band of brothers into a lethal yet loyal force. We would die for each other and go down fighting, for Neath.

The players who pulled on that feared black jersey with the Maltese cross on their chest were all first class, many of them world class. With the likes of Jonathan Davies (the Messi of Welsh rugby), Allan Bateman, Brian Williams, Kevin Phillips, Jeremy Pugh, Phil Pugh, Barry Clegg, Stuart Evans, Dai Joseph, John Davies, Dai Morgan, Rowland Phillips, Lyn Jones, Gareth Llewellyn and Glyn Llewellyn, Neath were a formidable unit. The Welsh All Blacks were not only good enough to challenge the best club sides in Europe, they could stand toe-to-toe with the world's strongest teams such as New Zealand, Australia and South Africa.

All our players were top drawer. All had certain attributes that set them apart and made them worthy of pulling on the Neath jersey. Jiffy was mercurial while Jeremy was a ball of ginger anger. He could have a rumble in an empty house, and regularly smashed holes in the opposition's defences. Allan Bateman was so silky, so quick, so skilled and totally unflappable. The most unassuming guy ever. While many of us were swallowing amino acids and creatine before a game, Allan would dine on ham, egg and chips – and still out-played us all. Dai Joseph was the minder. He wore the tux on the field. If he said you weren't coming in, you weren't coming in. He was a one-man '*A Team*'.

We also had Gareth and Glyn Llewellyn, the Welsh Kray Twins. Gareth was scouted by Ron first. He came at 19. He was raw but you could see the talent. There was no lifting in the lineout then. Second rows had to jump. I reckon that was one of the reasons I was allowed to play back row – jumping wasn't a strength of mine. There were players like Wales' Rob Norster and Ireland's Donal Lenihan who were both exceptional jumpers and Gareth was right up there with the best. He was the last of the great leapers and played through both eras, achieving huge honours in both. He didn't mind a scrap either. I remember him playing for Wales under-21s at the Gnoll. The Neath team had trained that morning so we all watched the match afterwards. I was stood with Glyn at pitch-side, adjacent to Clive and Margaret Rowlands who had turned up as dignitaries to watch the match. There were nice smiles all round.

'Hi Mark,' Clive said.

'Hi Clive and Mrs Rowlands,' I politely replied.

Around 10 minutes into the game there was a lineout a few metres from us. The ball was thrown in. There was movement from the players but the ball sailed over the top of both team's jumpers. Something had happened. It all kicked off when Gareth steamed into their second row. It was utter pandemonium. It would be an understatement to say that I got a bit excited. 'Go on Gar... get in there.' I was fighting for him on the touch line. The referee finally gained control and when the situation calmed down I glanced across to my left, to see Clive and Margaret frowning at me in disbelief. In no uncertain terms, Clive told me that was no way to behave and that I should conduct myself in a proper manner.

Feeling like a chastised child, I dropped my head, said 'Sorry' then sloped off, dragging my finger along the wall, feeling about 9 years old. I saw them both regularly in the years after that. The incident was never mentioned. I hope they forgot!

Gareth's brother, Glyn, quickly became my best mate. Glyn loved doing the unseen, unglamourous stuff that every good team depends on, and he was bloody good at it. We had three cracking years playing for Neath and spent so much time in each other's company that we often joked his parents had adopted another son. When I came back to Wales from playing rugby league, Glyn joined Ebbw Vale for a couple of seasons and the fun all started again. Seriously, Glyn was a top player and is a top man.

Neath made me feel special and appreciated. They also took care of me on and off the field. As a young player I was still finding my feet, but at Neath I developed a strut!

Neath weren't a fashionable club, but we worked hard and did the job. We had a fitness coach, Alan Roper, who was a marathon runner and we also had the head of South Wales CID John Williams, who was another fitness fanatic.

Each training session was preceded by a 3k run, which was eight laps of the field and had to be completed before 6.55 pm. A few of the guys found this tough but everyone had to do it, even Jeremy Pugh who constantly complained of jogger's nipple. 'My nipples are like iced-gems,' he often cried out to all our amusement.

Neath's mantra was 'fitness is king'. We would 'hit and hit and hit' in the first half hour to wear them down, then spread it wide and clock-up the points. I was told to charge through the number 10 channel and I scored a shedload of tries – 26 in one season, a record which still stands to this day. That beat the 25 tries scored in a single season by the legend Dai Morris. I'm made up with that.

During the light nights in July, August and September, we would run up to the fourth pond in the Gnoll park. It was roughly a four-mile circuit. Some of the boys would go missing and hide in the trees on the way up to have a fag and join in on the way back but the management cottoned on when Phil Pugh and Dai Morgan came in before everyone else on a couple of occasions. After that, Roper and John would follow us, running up and down the line like two sheep dogs picking up any stragglers and roasting any slackers. When we got back to the club, we'd have a quick stretch before starting the training session.

Neath were big exponents of continuity – keeping the ball alive or using quick rucks if you were tackled. Hours and hours were spent on simple routines like 'drop, pop and roll' drills. The emphasis was on getting up and back in the game, and giving constant support to the ball carrier. The importance placed on interplay amongst the forwards was huge. We employed short little passes, with big men coming through at pace – hit, spin, offload and always fight to stay on your feet. Hitting the deck was the last option but if you had to go to ground, the imperative was to stop the game being slowed down and to make the ball available as quickly as possible. We wanted to play our game and not allow teams like Pontypool and Pontypridd, who liked the slower driving game, to play to their strengths.

The forwards were coached to keep it tight and support each other. We were brutal and anyone who stood in our way was swallowed by our black tsunami, chewed into pieces then spat out the back. It wasn't a place for the faint-hearted, but there were a few gutsy flankers and tough second rows around at the time who took us on.

A young Richard Webster had just come on the scene, playing for Swansea, and was making a name for himself. He would kill the ball in games and often get a bit of a shoeing, but he seemed to love it. We played Swansea at St. Helen's one cold December afternoon, facing the Moriarty brothers and Maurice Colclough up front, with Rob Jones, Malcolm Dacey, Mark Titley and the other backs looking to spread the ball from side to side. I always hated playing at St. Helen's because the field was huge and the Jacks could play, particularly at home. Webster had been a gutsy nuisance, putting his body on the line, forcing us to play with slow ball. In those days only the ref had eyes on foul play. The linesmen were normally one-eyed, biased club officials so you can imagine the dubious calls and the extra metres that were made on kicks to touch.

The laws were different back then so, to avoid being done for stamping, a few of the forwards would link up and join the ruck together. If they moved forward as one, it was seen as rucking. I know that's totally alien to what you see now but there was no wrestling on the floor, no bridging over the ball and very few pile ups that nowadays can lead to serious back and neck injuries. No one would lay over the ball. Well, some would and they were dealt with. It was something you looked for. Giving someone a good shoeing was part of the game.

During the game a lineout was awarded on the far side. We pinched it and Huw Richards burst through the Swansea defence. Webbie chased back and managed to bring Huw down but was now on our side of the breakdown as we charged in. With a Swansea Jack lying in front of us, no one in the Neath team needed a second invitation and we put the poor bugger through the shredder. As we hit the ruck, Webbie was kicked, raked and stamped on. It was bad, and the ref knew it. The whistle blew: 'peep, peep, peeeeeeeep,' and the Neath rucking machine ground to a halt.

The injuries were shocking. He was peeled off the turf like a large slice of fresh Gower gammon. Webbie's shirt had been ripped off his back, with streams of blood soaking into the frayed edges of cotton where studs had torn open the fabric. I could see the long deep welts on his back and his head had been cut open by several size 12 boots. He was a hard man but the tears of pain and frustration ran down his cheeks as he was shouldered off the field and into the arms of the waiting medics.

We assumed his game was over but a few minutes later a bright white figure appeared on the touchline. Patched up and wearing a clean new jersey, Webbie came back on. Not only that, he played exactly the same way for the rest of the game. It was a clear statement that he wasn't going to be intimidated by the Neath threshing machine. Fair play to him. What a player he was, and what a character. Respect where respect is due. Nevertheless, we won and Huw Richards scored a hat trick!

The lack of reaction from the Swansea players was, for us, shocking. In all the teams I had played for over the years, the 'one in, all in' ethos was uniform. Some teams just wanted to play rugby, believed that retaliation solved nothing and trusted the ref to sort things out. A great idea, if everyone had the same thought, but not everyone did.

I was schooled that if anyone hit or kicked one of yours, you were obliged to take things into your own hands and deal retribution to the perpetrator. That was the unwritten, (dark) golden rule of rugby at the time. That is how I and many others played the game, and I did so right up until I retired. You felt obliged to and you expected the same from your teammates. However, at St. Helen's that day, no one retaliated. No one piled in to defend him. No one fronted up to us.

That match at St. Helen's was a wake-up call for me. A realisation that not everyone, not every team, would sacrifice themselves for a teammate. Not everyone would be drawn into a scrap. To me this was a weakness in a team and it was something to exploit. If we (Neath) knew a team were not inclined to retaliate it gave us a mental edge. We knew we could impose ourselves physically on them. We could beat them, and beat them up. It wasn't all violence and intimidation, though. We recognised that we needed to be strong in both aspects to solve the rugby jigsaw. We needed the 'one in, all in' mentality yet also needed to be able to play a decent game of rugby. It was all about having the right balance to be successful. Too much of either and you would come unstuck in big games, as Pontypool often did when the cameras were at their games and they couldn't use their usual tactics of beating players up from the first whistle to the last and get away with it.

Neath always had big battles with Pooler. They had all the stars upfront, Pricey, Steve 'Junna' Jones, Staff, Boris, Perky, Eddie Butler, Mark Brown, Chris 'Madman' Huish and Jeff Squire, as well as their ninth forward, Dai Bish, at scrum-half. It was the who's who of Welsh and world rugby. That pack could match any international side in the world. It was an international pack in itself. It's easy to see just how they went so well for so long. A few of them were ageing when I got to play against them but quality is quality at any age. To me, the best of them all was Jeff Squire. Pricey is a legend and has had all the accolades but Squire is often forgotten. He was big, tough, skillful and a real top bloke. He was 'man of the tour' for the Lions on one of the trips. Well, he was in my eyes. So, to get to play against him was an honour for me.

Neath played Pooler away and took their ground record. Phil Pugh went into a maul, came out the other side with the ball and ran 40 yards to score with his blonde hair flowing behind him in the breeze. The place was packed with fans, right up the bank as far as the eye could see and the stand was overflowing. What a sight for a 20-year-old. All I could hear was 'Pooler, Pooler' and I could see their fans salivating as they shouted. At a line out in front of the stand, the ball was thrown to the back where myself and Mark Brown got tangled in the jump. Shirts were grabbed and we stood there for a second in a mini-Mexican standoff. I thought, 'What do I do? He's Pooler, I'm Neath. Hit him before he hits me?' So, I did. He hit me back and I hit him again and he hit me back. We carried on this blow for blow exchange until we flew over the advertising boards and into the crowd still clutching each other's collars and still punching. The crowd loved it.

'Pooler, Pooler,' rang around the ground.

'Neath, Neath,' came the response from our set of fans.

We stopped punching and climbed back onto the field and carried on as if nothing had happened.

One of the great Pooler characters was Dai Bishop. A quality player and probably the best scrum-half in Wales for many years, Dai was as tough as old boots and a player you'd rather have on your side than facing you. I was lucky to play alongside him for Wales RL and remember Bish calling 'Hammer time!' when he thought we were flagging and needed to lift our game. He demanded total commitment from his teammates and wouldn't accept anything less. Wales squads were always interesting when Mr Bishop was around.

I've always loved the atmosphere among the squads I've been involved with. There's always a load of banter flying around. One minute, you're the butt of all jokes, the next you're the one leading the charge. It's all part of the squad mindset, but sometimes it can go too far. My trigger was cruel banter about my stammer. I could normally control myself in those tense situations and most days I'd have the boys giggling and laughing if I was talking and had a speech blockage. I made light of it and shrugged it off by saying things like 'give me a minute' or 'hold on'.

The great thing was that, for 99% of the time, no one gave a toss that I stammered, and in that situation I didn't either. I sometimes found it difficult to call moves but if I could see something was on, a gap to run through, I'd have to set myself up to call it. I'd breathe, think, then speak, although sometimes the opportunity had gone by then. I learnt that I couldn't be spontaneous or do anything off-the-cuff. Everything had to be rehearsed. I would keep things short, to just one word: 'yes', or 'mine'. In Neath, Lyn Jones, our flanker, introduced a move off the back of a scrum which was a simple run around off the number eight (me) with the blind-side flanker receiving the pass and hitting the scrum-half who was running the loop. He wanted to call it 'Tin of Beans' (God knows why!). We tried it once. I decided to call it: 'T... T... T....' It was too late. Opportunity lost.

It was even more difficult when I played rugby league for Hull many years later. We had all sorts of different calls. The only one I could manage was 'one up'. It saved confusion and my embarrassment.

At Neath, there were a few times off the field and in the clubhouse that I got ridiculed. This wasn't ok. It was out of order. Often, I felt a blind rage taking over me. It was times like that I knew things could have got out of hand. After a game when I hadn't played that well, I went to a pub in the town for a quiet pint. I needed a bit of space to myself. As I walked in, I clocked two guys sat on stools by the bar, positioned in a way so they could see the whole pub and both doors. They could 'survey their manor'. They looked like the local, fat, roid-head, gangster types, with their typical Duran Duran haircut and lots of cheap, gold chains poking out of their half unbuttoned shirts.

There weren't many in the pub as I strolled up to the bar. I stood, trying to order a drink. The barmaid in front of me, patiently waiting. The basketball returned to my mouth. I couldn't get my words out. From behind me, I heard a comment followed by a few sniggers. I tried to ignore him, but I thought 'You, cheeky twat, having the nerve to laugh at me, looking like that.'

I didn't turn around and just pointed to the beer pump and signalled to the barmaid. One of the blokes walked up beside me. He stood about two metres away from me. I could tell he thought he was a bit of a comedian. He started shooting his mouth off.

'Fucking rugby players, they can't even order a pint.' His mate laughed. 'Do you want me to order it for you boy?' The mood in the bar changed. One or two of the other punters, took their pints and escaped into the lounge.

I can remember looking over my left shoulder, lining him up. Within seconds the red shutters came down again and all I remember was seeing the guy on the floor and being ushered out of the side door of the pub by the bouncer before the police got there. To be fair, that wasn't the norm with the fans. Almost all of them were brilliant.

Neath went on to dominate Welsh rugby at the end of the 1980s. For two years or so we swept all before us, winning regularly by 50 points. Life was made easy for me by the players around me. The pack was full of wonderful hard men who could play a bit as well. In my eyes they did all the work, the hard shift which left me the time and space to run like a man possessed at little backs who didn't like tackling at the best of times. It felt fantastic.

We were as mad off the field as they were on it. After one game at Newbridge, the committee had kept the players hanging around on the bus as they gorged themselves on the free whiskey in the club's board room. We sat around, impatiently, as the committee staggered back on the bus, 30 minutes late, with wide grins on their smug faces. Someone said that we needed to teach them a lesson. The unlucky committeeman on that trip was the club secretary Dai Shaw. To great delight from the players, he was stripped of his clothes as we came down the Glynneath bank and his garments were disposed of through the sky light of the bus by Paul Jackson. But that wasn't enough. As we drove through the village of Glynneath, a decision was made.

'Let's throw him off at Resolven!' someone yelled out.

'Yessss,' came back the cry from the rest of us.

So, it happened. The driver was told to stop and Dai and his shoes were thrown out into the hedge. To be fair to us, we had some consideration by giving him his shoes. Some didn't want to even do that. As we sped off, all that was visible, sticking out of the weeds on the side of the road was Dai Shaw's fat, white arse. 'That will teach him to keep us waiting.'

Reports came in by our Monday training session that the talk of Resolven was of some perverted, peeping Tom who had been seen naked but for his shoes jumping over garden walls and pinching clothes off lines on Saturday night.

You would have thought the committee had learnt their lesson, but alas, maybe they were thicker than they looked. There was another incident when we played away in Gloucester. Again, the committee were dawdling, getting hammered on whiskey chasers in the clubhouse. The free beer for the players had finished so we were ready to leave.

'Right, that's it,' was the call, 'we're off. Bollocks to 'em. They've been told.' So, with a few crates of beer for the trip, and the driver press-ganged into doing what we said, off we drove back to Neath minus our committee. It was one of the funniest two-hour journeys ever with us playing a game of one smart fellow, which was always suggested by Phil Pugh. I'm sure he always suggested it to expose my weakness and give everyone a good laugh when I was fined, again and again, for slipping up on the phrase 'four smart fellows and they felt smart'. I always seemed to drinking five times as much as everyone else. That may have been funny for them but it wasn't for me.

I soon got over it, though, and we arrived back in Neath absolutely hammered. Well, I was anyway! We all spent the early part of the night in the club waiting for the committee to get back. They had to get taxis back to Neath and pay for it out of their own pockets. They weren't happy. The cheers from us when they walked into the club could be heard all the way back to Gloucester. From what I can remember, the players were never ever kept waiting again ... funny that. Nothing was said. We were winning everything so we had a licence to do whatever we wanted.

At each home game we would attract crowds of five to eight thousand, crammed into the Gnoll. It wasn't a huge stadium, like the Arms Park in Cardiff or Stradey Park in Llanelli but they certainly knew how to pack them in and create an atmosphere. The spectators would stand close to the touchline, with just a 3ft high advertising hoarding separating the crowd from the players. At a lineout you could smell their breath as they screamed 'NEATH, NEATH, NEATH'. It was superb. If you couldn't be inspired by that, there was no hope for you.

Neath were not only the best side in Wales but we were crowned the best team in the Britain after playing the English champions Bath, twice, for the title two years on the bounce.

In the 1980s, there was no Heineken Cup and no Aviva Premiership. Welsh teams played Welsh teams in the Merit Table and Welsh Cup competitions. There were also some friendlies (in the loosest sense of the word) against English clubs when there was a spare weekend but there were no cross-border competitions.

Bath were regarded, by the London-based media as the best team in Britain. The London press was much like they are today – lauding English rugby and decrying Welsh or Scottish talent as second class. It was 1985, I had just turned 20, and was fully signed-up to the Neath revolt. A rugby revolution was in the air. We had three or four internationals in the team and the rest were strays, adopted and taken in by Ron and Brian. The Bath team was awash with 12 internationals such David Sole, 'Coochie' Chilcot, Stuart Barnes and Richard Hill. Their team sheet was a who's who of world class players.

Paul Thorburn and Elgan Rees were two of our three, the other was Barry Clegg who won his single cap against France in 1979 while playing for Swansea. He had been around for an eternity and was the old buzzard of the team. Our captain was hooker Mike 'Silent Death' Richards, who had sat on the bench for Wales many times and was another who had a wealth of experience. He was lethal. Once, he had just thrown the ball into the lineout, and the ref and the opposing hooker were watching the ball as it flew over their heads towards the back. As he ran past his opposite number he sharply and firmly flicked his elbow. Blink, and you would have missed it. Everyone got to the maul in mid-field, except their hooker, who was sat on the five-metre line with a busted jaw. A proper tough old bastard was Mike.

Barry and Mike led our pack of mongrels – Lyn Jones, Jeremy Pugh, Brian Williams, Phil Pugh, Huw Richards and myself – all non-internationals and quite new on the scene. We were very rough round the edges, but all of us went on to represent Wales. We were given no chance of beating the champions of England. Bath and their fans must have expected an exhibition game. As we got to the Rec, their home ground, we could see all the rich mob in the car park.

Rolls Royces and Land Rovers all parked up, driven by the Barbour jacketed brigade in their tweed hats. The ground was rammed, with the smell of hotdogs, cigars and beers wafting around. I was a raw, punk rock upstart from Tred. The culture was completely alien to me. There were lawyers, doctors and accountants everywhere, all having a jolly afternoon with their wives: 'Let's play rugger, yah.'

Looking like the gang of rogues in *Oliver Twist*, we clambered off the bus and strode into the dressing rooms. They were a bit larger than the ones at the Gnoll, under the stand in what can only be described as a dungeon, with what appeared to be the same fixtures and fittings from when they were built at the end of the 1930s. The showers at the Gnoll were supplied by a water tank that always ran dry. The wise old heads would go off injured with 10 minutes to go just to get a warm shower. When the team were all in the changing room, I can only describe the conditions as being similar to the inside of a Russian submarine in the Baltic Sea. You would be sat down tying your boot laces and a big hairy arse would be shoved in your face. The smell of deep heat and liniment was overpowering, as were the manure infested clothes worn by the farmers who'd come straight from milking the cows. There was also the spectacle of a 20 stone prop sitting on the bog, with the door wide open, shouting for toilet paper. What a charming place. It's strange how those conditions can bring you all closer together!!

In comparison, the changing rooms in Bath were palatial. There was room to move about and to stretch. Plus, they hadn't hosed them down with cold water like we used to do when teams came to visit us. The wooden duck boards didn't have splinters and were in good repair and we even had a separate physio room. Wow! All this went to fuel the resentment we all felt towards the wealth and privilege we saw on display. It was topped off with the fact they considered themselves to be a superior team, as did the press. They were also English. That was more than enough to really incur the wrath of the boys.

They should have realised this wasn't going to be a nice relaxing day for them, English champions or not. It was late November, cold, damp, misty, and the Neath boys were in town.

We raced out of the sheds like the hounds of hell, snarling and yelling. They didn't stand a chance. As the rain fell and faces got criss-crossed with streams of blood and sweat, the primal grunts of

'Neath, Neath, Neath' slowly drowned out the polite calls of 'Bath, Bath, Bath'. It sounded absolutely beautiful and drove us on.

The home supporters were soon silenced. It was tough but, on that day, no one was going to beat us. We won 13-7 and I was so pleased to have been part of it. We were loving it and none of us wanted to hear the final whistle. This was a major victory in the rise of the black storm from Neath and laid a foundation for the team to move on and dominate rugby for a number of years. The following season, at our home patch, we stuffed them again just to prove that our first meeting wasn't just a lucky punch. Neath really were the best team in the land and I was honoured to play my part.

We had some right legends in that team, none more so than our prop, Brian Williams. A lot has been written and said about the formidable farmer from deepest west Wales but it still doesn't reveal a fraction of the awe and respect he had in rugby circles. He was a super hero – cast in iron – with a will to match. Whenever he entered a maul, they don't happen much these days but back then they were a common occurrence, it was guaranteed if he could get a finger on the ball, and was coming out with it. He was Popeye without the pipe. His forearms looked as if they had been transplanted from one of the Titans. He had a six-inch upper cut that could take your head off, and it left more than one limp body in the middle of a maul. Stuart Roy, the Cardiff second-row, reportedly said Brian had the 'punch from hell'. There were tales of him running after sheep in his wellies, as his pre-season training. I once watched him pop his dislocated shoulder back into the socket as he was running from a scrum to a maul. He was a machine.

Once, after playing a match in the Basque region of France, the team visited a farm that bred cattle for the bull fights. We were all on the lash, 30 of us sat in a circle in the farmyard with two, galvanized steel baths in the middle. We were given a Basque feast of ham, cheese, baguettes and salami, then drinking games started. That was okay, but they were followed by a kangaroo court, which is daunting if you happened to be one of the people brought up to face the judge. No one was allowed to leave the circle, so all liquid waste had to go in the two separate baths: one for pee, the other for vomit. There was a lot of liquid in both.

I was being targeted, yet again, and there were belly laughs all round. I kept it together reasonably well, though, and the attention turned to others in the circle. A few of the boys were mathematically challenged so they took a bit of a hit.

The festivities had hit a bit of a lull when the guy that owned the farm summoned us to the training ring. The farm hands were in the ring with a young calf. It looked like they were teasing it and getting it to charge at them. It was set up like a proper bull ring with two wooden hides on opposite sides to escape behind if the calf got too close. We were loving this. The beer was flowing and some of the lads were beginning to think they were matadors. We all wanted a go. The farm hands obliged but removed the young calf and introduced its sibling. This was a mean looking creature, and much bigger, with brass balls screwed on the end of its horns!

The Neath team had a bit of an off-field rivalry between the colliers and the farmers and it had been raging on this particular trip. The collier faction went first as Phil 'the murderer' Jones entered the bullring. As macho as they come, he was tossed a red rag and left to his own devices. I'm sure I could see a grin appearing on the face of the beast as it struck the dusty ground with its hoof. With a quick snort it shot towards Phil who, to jeers from the rest of us, ran and dived behind the boards to safety. The spirit of Rorke's Drift had vanished behind the safety of the hide.

Next up was Kembers, all six foot eight inches of him, with his long flowing blonde locks. He was right up for the challenge – so was the steer who was keeping the farm hand occupied across the ring when Andrew stepped over the barrier, carrying his scarlet table cloth. There were a few shouts of encouragement from the Basques and the animal turned its head towards Kembers. 'Yeesss, another idiot,' it snorted as its eyes stared menacingly, weighing up its new challenger: 'This one's a big lump. Let's see how fast he can move.'

Imagine the scene; a face-off between a two-metre beer-filled giant and a one-metre ball of pure muscle. It happened just like it would have in the movies, with snorts and pawing of the ground and even a little bellow. The cow charged straight at Kembers. As we watched and cheered, we saw Andrew wave his tea cloth to the left of him, then to the right of him like a proper bull-fighter. We all thought he knew what he's doing. 'This is what you're supposed to do,' he yelled.

The animal had covered half the width of the ring by now and you could see the intent in its eyes, it read, 'this blonde twat is having it.'

My Mam and Dad, Elizabeth and Benjamin (Benny). They didn't have much but whatever they had was shared with me and my sister, Sandra. It was a loving and close family and I'll be forever grateful for what they did for us, and what they sacrificed for me. A miner, who served for years as vice-chairman of Tredegar Ironsides RFC, Dad loved rugby and encouraged me to fulfil my potential. Mam suffered terribly with rheumatoid arthritis but remained cheerful and was so kind and supportive. I miss them both. We had a lovely holiday in Blackpool in 1976, when I was 11, and these photos bring back so many happy memories.

Rugby is what I'm known for, but I was also a keen footballer as a boy and played for Earl Street Primary School in Tredegar. As a tall lad, I always seemed to be picked as a goalkeeper! The teachers, Mr Price (top left), Mr Maynard the head teacher (top middle and bottom right), and Mr Davies (top right and bottom left) were always very supportive.

I loved football, but quickly realised I was good at rugby, and started playing with Tredegar Ironsides' mini-rugby team. Here's the first known photo of me scoring a try, aged nine! We were also quite successful and, aged around eight, I enjoyed my early experience (bottom photo, second from left) of winning a trophy – a mini-rugby U11s tournament in Pontllanfraith.

By now a pupil at Tredegar Comprehensive, I was progressing through age group rugby at the Ironsides, here with the U12 mini-rugby team, and several cups!

The first sign that I had a bright future in rugby was in 1983 when I was selected for our district team, North Monmouthshire (North Mon) while playing for Glanhowy Youth. It was one of many proud moments in my rugby career, and one I shared with my good mates (L-R) Neil 'Billa' Gregory, Andrew Baldwin, and Ian 'Turkey' Williams.

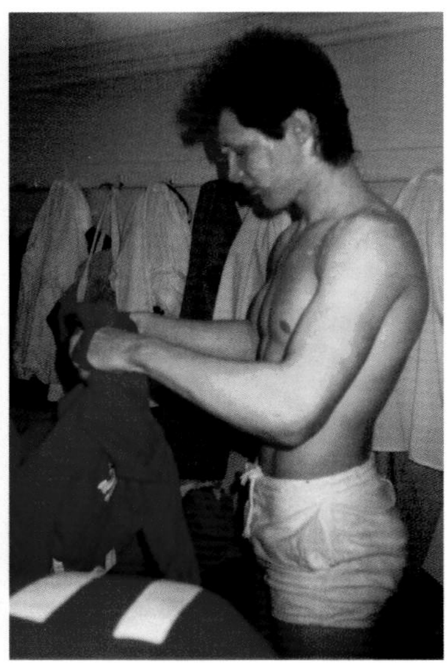

From North Mon, the next step was Wales Youth, coached by Ron Waldron.

Ironsides chairman, Tommy Gregory (black jumper), presented me with an award in recognition of my achievement, watched by my proud dad.

My first match for Wales Youth was away to England at Kingsholm, Gloucester – we lost. A few future Wales internationals lined up alongside me that day: Mike Rayer, Roger Bidgood, Mark Perego, Lyn Jones and Paul Moriarty.

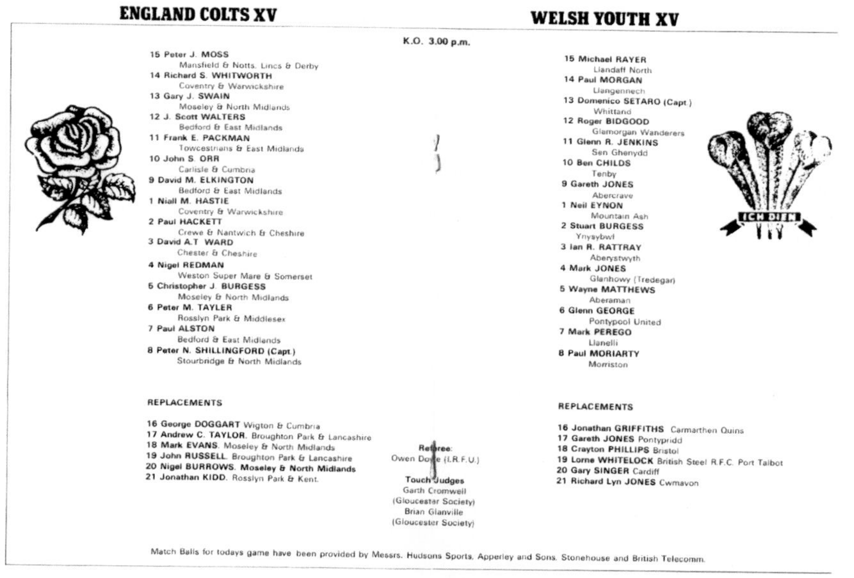

ENGLAND COLTS XV

K.O. 3.00 p.m.

15 Peter J. MOSS
Mansfield & Notts. Lincs & Derby
14 Richard S. WHITWORTH
Coventry & Warwickshire
13 Gary J. SWAIN
Moseley & North Midlands
12 J. Scott WALTERS
Bedford & East Midlands
11 Frank E. PACKMAN
Towcestrians & East Midlands
10 John S. ORR
Carlisle & Cumbria
9 David M. ELKINGTON
Bedford & East Midlands
1 Niall M. HASTIE
Coventry & Warwickshire
2 Paul HACKETT
Crewe & Nantwich & Cheshire
3 David A.T WARD
Chester & Cheshire
4 Nigel REDMAN
Weston Super Mare & Somerset
5 Christopher J. BURGESS
Moseley & North Midlands
6 Peter M. TAYLER
Rosslyn Park & Middlesex
7 Paul ALSTON
Bedford & East Midlands
8 Peter N. SHILLINGFORD (Capt.)
Stourbridge & North Midlands

REPLACEMENTS

16 George DOGGART Wigton & Cumbria
17 Andrew C. TAYLOR. Broughton Park & Lancashire
18 Mark EVANS. Moseley & North Midlands
19 John RUSSELL. Broughton Park & Lancashire
20 Nigel BURROWS. Moseley & North Midlands
21 Jonathan KIDD. Rosslyn Park & Kent.

WELSH YOUTH XV

15 Michael RAYER
Llandaff North
14 Paul MORGAN
Llangennech
13 Domenico SETARO (Capt.)
Whittand
12 Roger BIDGOOD
Glamorgan Wanderers
11 Glenn R. JENKINS
Sen Ghenydd
10 Ben CHILDS
Tenby
9 Gareth JONES
Abercrave
1 Neil EYNON
Mountain Ash
2 Stuart BURGESS
Ynysybwl
3 Ian R. RATTRAY
Aberystwyth
4 Mark JONES
Glanhowy (Tredegar)
5 Wayne MATTHEWS
Aberaman
6 Glenn GEORGE
Pontypool United
7 Mark PEREGO
Llanelli
8 Paul MORIARTY
Morriston

ICH DIEN

REPLACEMENTS

16 Jonathan GRIFFITHS Carmarthen Quins
17 Gareth JONES Pontypridd
18 Crayton PHILLIPS Bristol
19 Lorne WHITELOCK British Steel R.F.C. Port Talbot
20 Gary SINGER Cardiff
21 Richard Lyn JONES Cwmavon

Referee:
Owen Doyle (I.R.F.U.)

Touch Judges
Garth Cromwell
(Gloucester Society)
Brian Glanville
(Gloucester Society)

Match Balls for todays game have been provided by Messrs. Hudsons Sports, Apperley and Sons, Stonehouse and British Telecomm.

10

11

Wales Youth players, including Richard Diplock, Steve Ford and Kevin Ellis, proudly wearing our club shirts at a training camp in Aberystwyth in 1983.

My collection of cups, caps and awards was growing.

My first taste of a rugby tour, with Wales Youth to France, where I broke my hand. I loved touring with my mates and Ron was such a good manager.
I was an Ironside through-and-through but the chance to play for Tredegar RFC was too good to refuse. Both my hometown clubs mean a lot to me.

MARK'S LATE TRY CLINCHES IT

Birmingham 18pts, Tredegar 24

A LATE try by ex-Welsh Youth back row prospect Mark Jones clinched a victory for Tredegar that midway through the second half they appeared to have let slip from their grasp.

The Gwent side had forged a 15-6 lead soon after the interval thanks to tries by newcomer Geoff Davies and the opportunist David Clarke, with Steve Giles's accurate kicking adding a penalty and both conversions.

Birmingham outside half Hemming-Allen, who had converted a try by Furze, pushed the home side in front with two penalties and two dropped goals, but then Tredegar mounted their victory charge.

First Giles levelled it at 18-18 with his second penalty and when Jones grabbed the vital try Giles did the trick again by adding the conversion.

My Wales Youth coach, Ron Waldron, also coached Neath and he obviously saw something in me that he liked. After a season with Tredegar I was invited to join him at the Gnoll, where I spent the next few years with the toughest, and most successful club team in British rugby – the Welsh All Blacks – scoring 61 tries in 168 games.

BRIDGEND were fed to the lions last night. A 6,000 crowd thronged the Gnoll baying for ammunition to fire at the beleaguered Welsh selectors, and Neath duly responded with a 49-0 victory.

Several of the Welsh All Blacks were out to prove a point. Mark Jones, anxious to promote his portfolio for the No 8 jersey, scored four tries in a match for the second time this season, two of them from a scrum as Bridgend squirmed in discomfort following the departure of prop Owen Reed after just six minutes.

Our dynamic and abrasive play drew huge crowds as we dominated Welsh club rugby, and more than held our own against touring teams.

THE selection of five Neath players for the Welsh World Cup squad delighted Gnoll supporters, but their pleasure was tinged with disappointment that Mark Jones was again overlooked.

He is an outstanding No. 8, and he showed on Wednesday at Cross Keys why Wales should make use of his talents.

He is an uncompromising tackler and the directness of his play disrupts opposition to create scoring opportunities.

At Cross Keys he picked up three tries with the simple philosophy that his job was to cross the line carrying the ball.

A hat trick of tries might be unusual for him, but so often this direct approach has created scoring opportunities for his team-mates.

Mature

Neath manager Brian Thomas has no doubts about his ability.

"He is one of the finest back-row forwards in the United Kingdom — and he knows his way to the try line.

"For a young man he is a very mature player and a bone-shaking tackler. He is a man, and there are not many of those playing in Welsh rugby at the moment."

The combination of an uncompromising pack of fierce west Wales farmers and hard-as-nails mining men, complimented by a back line of immense creative talent was irresistible. We all knew how to attack, and how to defend. What an honour it was to play in that team, and for the raucous 'Neath! Neath! Neath!' fans – great days indeed!

Neath players felt invincible. We knew we were fitter than any other team, and were united in the belief that our style of play was more effective than any other team. We played hard, and partied hard as well!

NEW NEATH No 8 Mark Jones has made such an impact during a handful of games for the Gnoll club that the WRU selectors last night named him in the Wales team to oppose France in the B International at St Foy la Grande on Sunday.

Playing well in an exceptional Neath team soon resulted in a selection for Wales B, against France, the first of my five Wales B caps. To receive a letter of congratulations from former Wales captain and British Lion, Alun Pask, who was head of middle school at Tredegar Comprehensive, was very special.

COMPOSITION ÉQUIPE DE GALLES

1
Brijan WILLIAMS
(Neath)

2
Mike RICHARDS (Capitaine)
(Neath)

3
Laurence DELANEY
(Llanelli)

4
David WATERS
(Newport)

5
Kewin MOSELEY
(Pontypool)

6
Alan HOPKINS
(Llanelli)

8
Mark JONES
(Neath)

7
Paul MORIARTY
(Swansea)

9
Robert JONES
(Swansea)

10
Geraint JOHN
(Bridgend)

13
David JACOB
(Neath)

12
Keevon JONES
(S.W.P.)

11
Arthur EMYR
(Swansea)

14
Ieuan EVANS
(Llanelli)

15
Paul REES
(Cardiff)

TRADE-MARK

20 year old Mark Jones, apprentice fitter/turner is off to Italy this summer — not for his holidays, but to play for the Welsh 'B' rugby team. Not that this is a new experience for Mark, he has already played for the Welsh 'B' team earlier this season against France 'B' and in fact he scored a try in that game.

Mark is now in the 4th year of his apprenticeship having started work at Ebbw Vale in 1982. Even in those days his rugby skills were recognised and he gained his first two Welsh 'caps' at Youth level early in 1983 with games against France and England.

Mark's home is in Tredegar and so naturally his first taste of senior rugby was with his home side, but at the start of the 1985/86 season he moved on to the 'All Blacks' at Neath where he came under the guidance of the legendary Brian Thomas. With his speed and 6ft 5ins frame, Mark is a natural No.8 and these talents are really taking him places. Not only is he a member of the Welsh 'B' team but he is also a member of the Welsh National Squad.

Surely it won't be long before he gets his first full Welsh Cap.

TREDEGAR COMPREHENSIVE SCHOOL
STABLE LANE, TREDEGAR, GWENT NP2 4BH
Headmaster: G. B. DAVIES, B.A., M.Sc., F.B.I.M., M.C.C.Ed. Telephone—3551/2/3

UNITAS

15th October, 1985.

Mr. M. Jones,
39 Walter Conway Avenue,
Tredegar,
Gwent.

Dear Mark,

I am writing to offer you my congratulations on your selection for the Wales B side to play against France. I was delighted when I heard the news this morning. To gain an International Cap at any level is a tremendous achievement and you now have two - one big step to go and to win a full Senior Cap - Good luck!

Your parents must now feel very proud of you. Although not directly involved with your rugby in school, I have followed your progress closely and have watched you move up through the ranks of Welsh Rugby.

The French match will be a difficult one for you but I certainly like the look of the Welsh B side - planty of talent and they should do well.

May I wish you a good try and a good game.

Well done!

Yours sincerely,

A.E.I. Pask
Head of Middle School.

Mark's glory proves costly

By ROBERT COLE

MARK JONES'S moment of glory in last weekend's Welsh trial, scoring the third try for the Possibles in their 17-11 win, has proved rather costly by putting the dynamic Neath forward out of action for a month.

His strong burst for the line not only took him through the last line of the Probables defence, but also caused him to break a bone in his left hand.

"I think I must have landed on it as I went over for the try and that seems to have caused the injury," explained the Neath and wales B No 8.

"I only felt a little bit of pain at the time, but after the game it began to ache. I have got a plaster cast up to my elbow at the moment, but that is due to come off at the end of next week.

"It won't stop me from training and keeping fit and I should be able to start playing again in about amonth. It is just a little bit of a setback, nothing too serious."

Almost there – from Wales B, I progressed to the Possibles team at a trial match in December 1986 when I scored a try as we beat the Probables 17-11. I'd shown the selectors what I could do and just needed to wait for my chance.

I also played for the Possibles in the January 1988 trial game (below), but they selected me out of position at second row. It didn't go well and I fell out of favour until the 1989 Five Nations.

From Wales Youth to Wales B and on the verge of selection for the senior team. My rugby life was better than good. On-the-field Mark was living the life he'd always wanted, but off-the-field Mark was battling his demons every day. All I wanted was to speak like everyone else and not to be tormented by my stammer, which I tried my best to hide from all those who didn't know me.

Kembers now moved the tablecloth to directly in front of himself. We all wondered what magic manoeuvre does this man have up his sleeve? As the beast got closer and closer, 'move ... move' shouted the, now worried, farm hands, but there was no movement. Kembers stood transfixed, rooted to the spot. The only flicker was Andrew's face dropping as he realised an impact was imminent.

'I'll fucking give you ole, ole' snorted the bull, as he flung Kembury into the air, spinning him, arms and legs all over the place like an 18 stone starfish. There were gasps and laughter from all around as he landed on his head several metres away. Fair play to the farm hands, they quickly jumped in to prevent the animal giving him a good goring. He was picked up and carried from the ring like Evil Knievel when he had just crashed his bike.

Neath's trio of farmers had seen enough. Kevin Phillips, John Davies and Brian Williams now stepped forward. 'The amateurs have had a go, now it's time for the pros,' Kevin said.

The three of them surrounded the cow. They took it in turns to distract the beast while trying to make an opening so one of them could grab its horns and jump round its neck. It was great to watch. After Kevin and John had made two or three attempts to distract it, Brian was on it in a flash. He dug his heels in and the cow took off, shaking and tossing its head. It wanted to go forward but Brian's heels in the dirt stopped it. I could see every sinew in Brian's body tightening, gripping on for dear life. It was a test of strength between a force of nature and the beast from Pembrokeshire. The snorting and grunting got louder, and that was just Brian! 'Go on Bri, go on.' We hollered and cheered.

He wrestled and squeezed, positioning his leg against the haunch of the animal's flank, and with one final super human effort he toppled the beast over his leg, keeping the horns gripped and forcing the cow's head to the floor. Kev and John leapt on as well and finally subdued the animal. The fight was over.

The Basque boys were dumbfounded. Now released from Brian's grip the cow was eased to its feet and ran off. I wonder if the creature was thinking, 'What the fuck was that?'

The Neath team went berserk, whooping and hollering, cheering and clapping, before Brian added the final verdict. In his Welshest of Welsh accents he quietly said, 'Fuck, I've hurt my fucking knee.' He was out for several months but became even more of a legend in my eyes.

When the Scarlets or Swansea came to town, the Gnoll's capacity would balloon to over 10,000. The hype would start on the Monday at training, building up through the sessions, picking out opposition players to take care of and building a game plan to take them apart. We knew the Scarlets would obstruct, lie on, and come round offside to slow the quick ruck ball we thrived on. Gareth Jenkins, their coach, was as much of a winner as Ron and Brian were, and certainly knew how to apply tactics to win games. They were coached to do anything (aka cheating) to win and that's rich coming from me. They would do anything to get one over on us and the feeling was mutual. They could soak up masses of pressure but as soon as you made a mistake, a stray pass or a knock-on – 'Whoosh!', they were gone. Down the other end as quick as lightening and scoring under the sticks. They were a crafty bunch, those Turks.

Some players would feign injury to gain an advantage. Rupert Moon had spent a time with us before he switched allegiance and we had played in the Dubai sevens together. Also, being paired at the back of the scrum, we had come to know each other's game quite a bit. Moonie never missed the chance to put in an Oscar-winning performance and there's a famous picture of him lying prone on the turf after Phil Pugh had clouted him – looking like he'd been shot by a bazooka. It was all a façade. Apparently, he opened his right eye and winked at Phil May. Even though I wasn't there, I had 'gone north' by then, it was the type of thing he did.

He tried the same with me when Ebbw Vale played Llanelli at Eugene Cross Park eight years later. He'd just put up a box kick and I brushed past him. Again, he went down as if he'd been shot by a sniper from the grassy knoll. Luckily Gareth Symonds was standing on the spot as Mooney lay prone on the floor.

I looked at Gareth and said, 'Have a word with Marlon Brando by there will you.' A wide grin came over the ref's face. He bent over the prone player and said, 'That's enough now, Rupe.' Rupert Henry St. John Barker Moon's eyes opened slowly, then he got to his feet with an expression of, 'Oh well it didn't work this time,' and he carried on playing. It was brought up later over a pint in the club and laughed off by all concerned. To me and thousands of other old school rugby players it's the exact opposite of everything we were taught.

All through my career, Llanelli were always up to their tricks. Players like Phil May and Russell Cornelius in the second row, and their prop Delaney were always killing the ball and just getting in the way. They were happy to obstruct and come offside, preventing the quick ball we lived off. This is where my life-long aversion to the Scarlets started. Don't get me wrong, I have nothing but admiration for the club, they are a fantastic advert for Welsh rugby and have a proud tradition of success, but try playing against those tactics. They really naffed me off.

Often, I would take the law into my own hands. In the 1989 Welsh Cup final I got sin-binned. The first player to ever be sin-binned in the final. The game was massive for us and we had lost to them in the cup the year before so we had scores to settle. I had scored midway through the first half and we were ahead. Laurance Delaney was disrupting, coming round offside and acting as if he had made an innocent mistake each time he got caught. So, I dragged him out of our side of the maul and threw him to the ground. Unluckily for me, I got pushed backwards at the same time, lost my footing and ended up blindly stepping backwards and unknown to me my foot ended up on Laurence, making contact with various parts of his person as I struggled to keep my footing. This for once was a genuine mistake, honest. Well, that was the official stance. If you were a Scarlets fan you would probably have seen that dirty bastard Mark Jones dragging poor old Laurence out of the maul, throw him to the ground and then stamp on his head. I'll let you decide which version you believe!

I was sent from the field. As far I was concerned, I had been sent off. There were no yellow cards in those days. I was gutted not just for me but for our team and supporters. I knew I had let them down. This was a cup final, against the old enemy.

On the touchline, I noticed something going on between the officials and our management team. More than the usual shouting and screaming. I was standing there, chest pumping, afraid to talk. Ron told me to sit down and relax. After a short while he told me to get warmed up. I looked at him curiously. I don't think anyone knew exactly what was going on. Ron sent me back on to everyone's surprise, including me. Even the players didn't know what was happening. I just shrugged. I didn't care what was said and by whom, I was back on and that's all that mattered to me. I played the rest of the game and we won. My Uncle Les (Les Peard) was ref that day. He wasn't really my uncle but when I was asked how I got away with that, 'He's my uncle,' I joked. Uncle Les got asked a few questions after that game but he answered them all perfectly. What a man!! What a professional. Thanks, Les.

At Neath we realised that to improve, we needed to match teams physically, but also to have bigger engines than the opposition so when they ran out of steam, we could turn up the heat and blow them away in the final 20 minutes of the game. So that's what happened, over the next season Ron and Brian brought in giants like Gareth and brother Glyn Llewellyn and Andrew Kembury who had physical size and total fitness. The juggernaut started to rock and roll and totally dominate everything and everyone before them.

7

Rockaway (Miami) Beach

'Mark was the best player I have had the privilege to play alongside, who executed the basic principles of rugby ... run hard and tackle hard! He could influence games just by being on the field as the threat of his physicality would create fear and doubt in the ranks of the opposing team. Above all, Mark is a top person. We were all aware about Mark's stammer but it didn't make a difference to me. He is a top bloke and a great rugby player, and to me that's perfection.'

Rowland Phillips

I was brought up on a council estate in the 1970s where the only car in the street was the Land Rover owned by the guy who worked for the gas board, and the furthest I had been before my teens was to Barry Island – on the social club trip on Whitsunday – with 50p in my pocket to spend on the fair.

I got my first one-year passport, aged 15, to go to Germany on that school rugby trip, run by Alun Pask, our deputy head and a legend of the game. We stayed on an army camp on the banks of the Rhine. All I can remember is all the boys getting pissed on the ferry going across the channel and spewing overboard. Next, I was picked for Wales under-19s and played away in France with the coffee incident.

So, compared to teenagers today who jet off to Ibiza or Faliraki at the drop of a hat, I wasn't very well travelled, plus I definitely had the Valleys mentality. At the end of my first season at Neath, they announced that we were going on tour to Miami, in America no less. I was a little excited to say the least. My head throbbed with excitement. 'Miami,' I kept saying to everyone. 'I'm off to Miami.' To be honest, a part of me wasn't sure if it really existed or had been invented for the cop show Miami Vice.

Over the following weeks, the club booked the tickets, sorted the accommodation and meetings were held to discuss the itinerary. I felt like that kid with the golden ticket sprinting off to visit Willy Wonka's Chocolate Factory.

Keiron Gregory, who had grown up near me in Cefn Golau, had also been coached by Ron Waldron at under-19s, and was invited to come on the tour with the hope of him joining the club the following season. Keiron and I had some history and had fought some battles – on and off the field – while growing up, but now that we were part of the same team, all of the small-town alpha male nonsense was put to bed. Tragically, Keiron – who toured Namibia with Wales in 1990 – died from meningitis, aged only 34.

The day finally came for us to head off to the land of sky scrapers, big cars and Dunkin Donuts. I didn't sleep the night before, scared I'd sleep through the alarm and miss my lift. Myself and Keiron were picked up from Cefn by my regular lift to Neath, Tex, a cab driver who was a massive Neath fan. He looked like Texas Pete, a character in *Super Ted*. He would pick me up and take me to the club for training and on match days. All his costs were paid by Neath and I had a free ride whenever, wherever. Somedays I felt like a king sitting in the back of his cab, leaving the estate on match days.

Heading off to America was a massive thing for me. Playing for Neath on tour was an honour, but I was looking forward to the trip far more. Like a dog on a lead being taken to a park for the first time, I was desperate to get there and take it all in. Anyone who's seen a dog's excitement as you turn the final corner and walk into a park will know what I mean. As soon as the lead is unclipped from its collar it rushes off like it's been fired out of a cannon – jumping in the air, pissing up trees, rolling in fox shit, simply enjoying its freedom. No matter how loudly and sternly you call it back, and no matter how many of those treats you wave at it, the dog just glances back at you with that look on its face that says: 'No fucking chance. See ya later!' Well, I was that dog and Miami was going to be my park. Look out!

Keiron and I sat in the taxi, smiles on our faces as wide as the river Howy itself. When we got to the clubhouse at The Gnoll, some of the guys were already on the beer. I wanted to join them but thought, 'No, wait. You've got to make a good impression. You're here to make your mark.' So, I stayed low profile, controlling the excitement bouncing around inside me.

We then had another team meeting and were told the do's and don'ts. The main message, which was stressed loud and clear, about Miami was: 'Don't go to the docks. Avoid the Cubans and don't do drugs.' This was repeated about a million times.

With that warning ringing in our ears we all got on the bus, a full-strength squad of Neath's finest players were on the trip. No one wanted to miss the trip of a lifetime.

The bus ride was eventful and a great laugh. Every time we played away, we always occupied ourselves by playing a game called 'Charge'. It started by pulling two names out of a hat. The two guys selected would assume their position in the bus aisle: one at the front of the bus, the other at the back, facing each other like two stags ready for a rutting. After a few minutes of the puffing out of chests and screaming like animals, someone would shout out 'charge' and like two stags they would run full pelt at each other. Whoever stayed in the aisle won. You can only imagine what went on when two guys like Brian Williams and Jeremy Pugh locked horns. It was fantastic but very x-rated, and all this happened before we actually got to the away team's ground.

However, you would have thought with a trip to America a few hours away, no one would risk the chance of getting hurt by playing such a stupid game. No, the leash was already off with some of the boys. The game went on all the way from Neath to Heathrow. When we arrived at the airport, we were lucky that no one was seriously hurt. Keiron couldn't believe it, but Keiron being Keiron loved every moment of it.

We also had a bit of fun in the airport before boarding the plane but I was still on my best behaviour. We were so close to flying away to freedom I didn't want anything to go wrong. It was the same old story with the safety demo from the air hostess who stood in front of us blowing in the tube. Her face bright red as a stream of raunchy comments came at her. There was uproar. We'd all had a few beers now and settled down for the flight, which surprisingly passed without major incident. Most of us slept for a bit so when the pilot announced that we were approaching our destination, everyone was ready and a few were loaded. We landed safe enough and the aircraft doors opened. We all rushed out of the plane like the Vikings, landing in the new world 1,000 years previously. 'C'mon boys,' was our battle cry. Then the heat hit us. What the hell! It slowed us up a bit. We were Welsh and lucky to see the sun from one year to another.

We all disembarked and boarded the transfer bus gasping like Nana Woodbine and sweating like a group of lazy students on results day.

I stood by the plane and took it all in. I'd made it. This was America, yeah, baby! We stayed in Orlando for a few days but this was no theme park leisure break – we had training and acclimatising to do. We ran each morning and trained with a few local athletes in the afternoons. In the evenings we met a few local wrestlers in the bars. There were a few superstars on that trip, Paul Thorburn being one. Paul is the nicest gent you could ever meet. The son of an army officer who was raised on military barracks around the world and he has the manners to match.

We all sneaked out one night and Paul let his hair down. There were 30 of us in a bar – beers and tequila shots all round. The format was 'follow me'. If one guy shouted, 'follow me.' and skulled his drink, all involved had to do the same. It always worked out that Thorby was involved in the calls and always had a double shot in his hand. I can't imagine how that happened! I didn't mind because it was normally me with 'one smart fellow', getting set up and totally mullered. After about six calls of 'follow me' Thorby was tanked up and getting into the beats being pumped out by the DJ. A few young ladies were positioned at different points up on the bar, dressed in their Daisy Duke clothes and cowboy boots, showing us their raunchy line-dancing moves to whoops and cheers of admiration from the lads. Then, what the hell? Thorby leapt onto the bar and, in perfect sync – like a scene from the Full Monty – he'd removed his shirt, swung it round his head before launching it into the baying crowd. He was having a great time, stomping his feet and clicking his heels like Michael Flatley in Riverdance, until the bouncers pulled him off the bar, all red faced and sweating, to cheers and applause from the boys. 'I don't know what came over me,' he was heard to say, as he was dragged along to the next watering hole.

After four days or so it was time to move down south. We rented cars, designated drivers were assigned and off we headed, down Alligator Alley, to Miami – arriving at the Holiday Inn on Miami Beach a number of hot, sweaty but humour-filled hours later. Bags were chucked in our rooms and then a quick team meeting held. The message was re-emphasised by the committee: 'No going to the docks. Avoid the Cubans. No Drugs.' We all had to repeat it parrot fashion back to them ... honestly!

'C'mon Keiron.'

'Where we off?'

'Don't worry,' I said as I opened the back door of the first taxi lined up outside the hotel. We piled in.

'Whara ya headed guys?' were the words I heard from the driver in his thick southern American drawl.

'Down the fuckin' docks drive,' I replied, 'and step on it.'

He smiled and we were off. All we could do was sit and stare out the window of the cab as we sped past skyscraper after skyscraper, all lit up like Christmas trees.

'Here ya are guys' he said as we stopped on the main strip. 'Six bucks.'

I paid and told Keiron that it was his round first.

We stood in awe, facing the sea. Here we were, two boys from Cefn Golau on Miami Beach. 'Yesssssss'. It was as if we had died and gone to Cefn, sorry, Heaven! Watch out Crockett and Tubbs – Jones and Gregory were in town.

We slid from bar to bar, passing all sorts of wild and wonderful characters on our journey. Flashing lights greeted us everywhere we went. The piercing noise of cop cars. The smell of food. Ladies in high heels and miniskirts throwing themselves at us. We both thought we must have been the two best looking blokes on the strip and we had pulled until we heard, '50 bucks an hour.'

'What do you mean 50 bucks?'

The night became a bit of a blur but I can remember jumping in a minibus with half a dozen Cubans in tow, and on the trip back to our hotel there was all sorts of stuff getting passed around in the back. 'When in Miami, do what the Cubans do' was my new motto. We arrived back at the Holiday Inn and I staggered through the door with a Cuban under each arm. Up on the pool deck, a load of my Neath teammates were having a cold beer and a soak.

'Where you been Scooby?' Alan Edmonds shouted.

'Down the docks,' I replied.

'Who are your mates?'

'Cu... Cu... Cubans.'

All the boys burst out laughing. A hushed Cuban voice came from my right shoulder and said, 'You wanna smoke, sweeties?' I grabbed a beer and joined the pool party. I vaguely remember 'wrestling' with one of the them, then it all gets a bit hazy.

I came round a few hours later, with someone looming over me, 'Scoob, Scoob, wake up. We got a team meeting.' It was one of our players. I squinted up through bloodshot eyes. It took me a while to focus and realise I was stretched out on the hotel beach. Waves breaking around my knees and the sun beating down on my bare torso. I felt like Robinson Crusoe on his desert island.

Then the panic hit me. 'My wallet!' I grabbed at my arse pocket. Thankfully, my wallet with all my money was still there. Phew! What a relief. I looked over, to Keiron who had been lying next to me, fast asleep. I woke him up.

'Whoow! What a night, butt,' I said. 'We went to the docks, partied with some Cubans, took some drugs and survived.'

'What's the plan for tonight?' he asked, 'A night out with Scarface?' We both laughed our heads off. The Valley Mongrels were definitely off the leash and it would be hard to tie them back up. He became a good friend and was one hell of a rugby player.

I nearly didn't make it back from that trip to Miami. On our last day I decided to lay off the grog. As we pulled up to the airport and started unloading the bags from the cars, someone mentioned passports and tickets.

'Tickets? What tickets?'

'The plane tickets!'

'What, I need a ticket?' They nodded. My memory flashed back through the beer-soaked archive of recollections of the trip. 'Ticket, ticket ... aarrrgh.' Oh no, my recall screeched to a halt. I could see it in my mind's eye, my ticket laying nicely on the bedside table of the Days Inn motel in Orlando, two weeks previous.

Bollocks! What could I do?

I walked sheepishly up to Ron Trimnell, the tour manager. I knew he was the only one I could turn to but I also knew that we, especially me, had tortured him for two weeks, and I mean tortured. We had bound, gagged and whipped him mercilessly. Unsurprisingly, he was in no mood to come to my aid.

'I've got my whiskey,' he smirked. 'You're on your own, butt.'

All sorts of stuff raced through my head. I pictured myself on the strip in Miami, dressed up in a suede, tasseled jacket, tight jeans, cowboy boots and a big Stetson hat giving it the Scooby strutt like Jon Voight in *Midnight Cowboy*. Well, I knew I'd have to make a living somehow!

Luckily, it turned out I wasn't on my own. A few of boys were in the same predicament. After it was confirmed that the club would reimburse the money for four new tickets, we had to find a way of paying for them. I was more or less skint. Luckily, Lyn Jones had a credit card.

A credit card!!! What was that?' The only credit card thing I had seen was the chitty my mother got from Rosie's shop on a Wednesday, when you went in for a tin of 'Pek' and 3lbs of spuds and your dad wasn't getting paid 'till Friday. All this was way above my head but Lyn delivered the goods with his cards. We had tickets and flew home, recalling all the stories – the good, the bad and the ugly – of the past two weeks, exaggerated in bucketfuls, after loads of free airplane booze. Fantastic!

The antics of the boys always made me smile. Along with Rowland Phillips, Lyn always kept us all entertained. I was still seeing out my time in Tredegar when Neath held a Christmas party. There was a fancy dress theme so you had big, hairy arsed forwards dressed in frocks and such like. The party was in full swing but there was no sign of Lyn or Rowland. Meanwhile, Elgan Rees, the famous winger, was there with his very glamorous wife. Elgan was a British Lion. The first out of Neath for a long while. He was a fabulous guy – very handsome, polite, immaculately dressed and a super quick winger. He scored the try that enabled us to beat Bath in the 'Battle of Britain' game, so he was held in utter reverence in Neath. Still is to this day. They were the glamour couple. The Posh and Becks of Neath.

Drinks were flowing with polite conversation mixed with some pop tunes in the background to add to the festive cheer. A lovely night was being had by all, but then ....

The door of the bar burst open and in bounded a caped figure in a black body suit and a black full-face mask, a shaving foam pie in each hand. The Phantom Flan Flinger had come to town, who then proceeded to splat a few of the players. Apparently, Lyn was dressed as the Phantom Flan Flinger (of *The Two Ronnies* fame) to raise money for charity and was sponsored to flan people all night. When the bar had been hit, he reloaded and proceeded straight into the lounge where a few couples had retired prior to his entry to enjoy a more intimate atmosphere. You can probably work out where this is going and you know it's going to end messily. Elgan and Mrs Rees were in there, enjoying the evening. Well, they had been up until this point. The offender ran in shouting, 'Who's first for the pie?' Splat! The treasurer caught one in the mush. Then the club doctor. 'Who's next? Who's next?' Lyn continued on his trail of pie destruction.

Yes, you guessed it. Mrs Rees copped it straight in her face. SPLATTTTT.

There was silence. People stood in shock. Others pissed themselves laughing. Elgan and his wife weren't amused at all. I'm not sure if they've spoken to Lyn since.

A quick, skilful and dynamic, player who also knew how to have fun, Lyn's ability to dream up pranks to surprise us with was matched by his innovative and unconventional thinking about how rugby should be played. Anyone who has been coached by him over the past 30 years will tell you the same.

He had arrived at Neath the season before me but we'd played together for Wales Youth and shared the Neath ethos. Playing in the back row alongside him was an honour.

Lyn was a highly regarded rugby player and many believed he had a very bright future, but the Welsh selectors never really thought so and kept saying he was too small for international rugby. Rubbish!

8

Anarchy in the U(Know who)

'On the field he was relentless, powerful, never took a backward step and maybe stepped over the line on more than a few occasions. Off the field, a gentleman. A kind, friendly, loyal man who liked nothing better than to have a laugh and a bit of banter. By the way, he took just as much stick as he gave.'

Allan Bateman

I knew Neath were the right team for me, and after just a few matches I was selected for Wales B (now known as Wales A). Making his debut alongside me was Swansea's outstanding young scrum-half, Robert Jones. Some would say that he went on to be a legend of the game, and I just went on!

The news of my selection was broken to me by my mother, when I was still in bed.

'You've got a letter, Mark,' Mam shouted up the stairs. 'It's from the WRU,' she added a few seconds later. 'Mark, Mark, you've been picked.' By now her excited voice was audible halfway down the street.

Still half asleep, 'Picked for what?' I yelled back.

'You've made the Welsh squad,' she shouted.

'The Welsh squad?' I said to myself. 'How does mam know that?' I leapt out of bed and nearly fell down the stairs in my rush to see the letter. 'Give it here, give it here,' I said as I grabbed the letter in the brown envelope with a WRU stamp on the front, turning my back to cover my modesty and showing her my arse as I ran back up the stairs.

Mam was nothing but inquisitive. Not a thing got past her. Like most Welsh mothers, it was her house and she was entitled to open any mail that came through the door, even if it wasn't addressed to her. It was a blanket entitlement of hers. It used to drive me crazy, but it was one of the things I had to put up with if I lived in her house. She would open bank statements, read my pay slips, the lot and not bat an eyelid if I kicked up a fuss. She couldn't help herself. Bless her.

Looking back now I can see how big an achievement it was, and is, to get selected. To represent your country at anything, any sport, is enormous but particularly for rugby, in Wales. It still didn't register, though. I had only just started my first year as a senior player, and only played 12 games for Neath, but here I was, getting selected for the Wales B squad – unbelievable! The disbelief continued when I was picked for the matchday 21, for the entire B-level Five Nations tournament.

As I couldn't drive, Pooler's John Perkins generously gave me a lift to the training sessions in his beloved Toyota. He loved that car and would promote its qualities, as well as the superiority of Japanese engineering, for the entire trip. This was a surreal experience for me as I'd been watching John play for the senior Wales team only eight months earlier, and now he was giving me lifts.

This was all getting very serious for me, but I loved it – both the recognition from the WRU and the media-driven public attention that came with it. That stammering boy from Cefn Golau now had his name in the paper each week, and for all the right reasons. In Tredegar, many of the boys of my age were only mentioned in the paper for appearing in court charged with causing mischief.

My memories of the first Wales B game I played are very sketchy. I think it was a bruising battle in France and, apart from Robert, the only other player I remember was Alun Hopkins. I was totally distracted by the occasion and nothing sank in: the score or the venue. I was living in the moment. Realising that international rugby was going to be a tough old nut to crack didn't take long, but I knew I could survive it.

My huge feet were now firmly placed on the international ladder and I was desperate to make sure that I didn't step on any snakes that would slide me right back to the start. I knew I had to tread carefully, both on and off the field.

Around that time, Dowlais RFC had become my favourite place to socialise and enjoy the craic. It was a wonderful, crazy, old place packed to the rafters with weird and wacky characters. People like Maxy, Gary Animal, the Bunko Brothers, Paul Barsi, Coughlan, Darren, Smithy, Mike, and Steve Fealey and his brother. God Save the Queen by the Sex Pistols was blasting from the jukebox the first time I walked into the bar. 'This is my kinda place,' I said to myself.

The boys accepted me from the off. They never ever took the piss out of my stammer. They took the piss out of many other things, but never that and they gained my respect right from that first punk-fuelled pint.

I was playing for Neath and Steve Fealey, who had also left Tredegar, had switched to Newbridge. We would meet up in Dowlais for a pint after our games and have a good laugh. Most of the time we would all end up in Fealey's parents' house, which became our unofficial party central, even though Ron and Mayo (his dad and mam) would be upstairs in bed. They put up with a lot. One drunken night I had headed off for a slash but took a wrong turning in the house and found myself bollock naked out in the street. Even worse – the front door had locked shut behind me. I knocked and knocked but the boys were all asleep. I stood there, a six-foot five-inch Wales B international, cupping my hands over the Jones meat and two veg, pleading for someone to open the door. Then I heard footsteps coming down the stairs. 'Please be Ron, please be Ron or please be one of the boys.' It wasn't. It was Mayo, Steve's mother.

Mrs Fealey opened the door, looked me up and down and hissed, 'Get in here you bloody big idiot.' Then clipped me around the ear and went back to bed. The next morning, she enlightened the boys with the story as we all crashed around the front room, drinking tea, eating toast and watching Tiswas. It was one hell of a mad place, but I loved it to bits.

A few years later when I was a member of the senior Welsh squad, me and Kieron Gregory were travelling back from training in Neath and arranged to meet up with the boys in the club in Dowlais. I think it was also someone's birthday or other special occasion. Our taxi dropped us off and after a few beers at the club, a gang of us headed down in Merthyr. Buffalo's, the wildest pub in the world, was the first stop and then we had a bit of a pub crawl through the town centre. It was rather a low-key event until around 11.30pm.

'Let's go for a curry,' Fealey announced.

'Yesssss,' came the replies.

The lads were hungry, not just for a meal but for a laugh. We snaked our way up the High Street to the infamous Taj Mahal Indian restaurant. The doors were locked but we could see the lights were on and we could hear voices inside.

Someone banged on the door. 'C'mon mun, we're starving.'

'No... no... no,' came the reply through the letterbox of the door. 'We're closed, we're closed.'

'C'mon, there's only a few of us.'

There were a few more knocks and maybe a few kicks at the door, each time firmly refused by the poor buggers inside the restaurant. It looked like there was no chance of a curry to end the night.

I turned to Keiron. 'Come on butt, let's go.' But as I was about to walk off, I heard shouting from behind me. 'No, don't.' Then... whoosh! I glanced back to see an empty milk bottle flying through the air and smashing through the window above the Taj Mahal with an almighty crash. Then came the tinkle of falling shards of glass.

'Run!' The shout went up and everyone scattered. This had nothing to do with me, so I didn't run far. I had no reason to run, no reason to hide in the shadows so, after a few yards I stopped and walked towards the taxi rank to get a cab home. Within minutes, I could hear the sound of sirens and screeching tyres. With an 'Oi you,' two constables leapt out of a car that was being followed by a police van. Without so much as a question, and despite my pleadings of innocence, I was bundled into the back of the van. Two of the Dowlais boys were also thrown in. I had only gone for a few beers on a bloody Tuesday night.

'Which twat threw that bottle?' I asked. They all shrugged. 'Boys, I really can't be dealing with this. I need to get to bed I have Wales squad training tomorrow.' The copper grinned as if to say, 'pull the other one sonny.' Someone said something like, 'Hey, the WRU will have to bail you out.' Everyone laughed, except me.

After a short time, another one of the boys was picked up and sat beside us in the van. To be honest, someone said something funny and we all started giggling and laughing out loud. Suddenly, there was a knock on the van door. The copper opened it. Steve Fealey stood there.

'I was there as well,' he said.

'What?' replied the copper.

'I was there when the window was smashed.' He then proceeded to climb in with us. He sat next to me.

'What the hell are you doing Jacques (Steve's nickname)?' I asked.

Smiling like a Cheshire cat, he said, 'It sounded like you were having fun in here so I didn't want to miss out.' The van shook from the laughter. I think even the copper was laughing.

With a full van, we were driven to the station. By my reckoning I was innocent, so after the interview I would be let go, maybe with an apology and if my luck was in, a lift home ... as if! The scene at the station was like a gangster movie with shouts across the cells of 'say nothing' and 'they can't charge us all.' Again, another misconception.

After all processed and locked up we bedded down to the sounds of muffled conversations and drunken renditions of songs reverberating round the cells. Every so often the door would open and I would get prodded by a black size 12 boot. 'You okay butt? You ok?'

'No, I'm bloody not,' I said. 'I want to get out. I've got Welsh squad training in a few hours,' but they just smirked and walked off. This ritual was repeated throughout the night until early the next morning when the day shift came on and we were given breakfast. If you call cold beans, concrete toast and a sawdust sausage – breakfast. It looked and tasted like Ghandi's flip flops.

Then the interviews started. One by one, we were escorted to the interview room and quizzed about the happenings of the previous evening. Again, shouts were heard of, 'Don't say anything. They've got to let us go by tonight.'

A copper said to me, 'Mark, we know it wasn't you. It's Fealey we want.' Like he was one of America's most wanted. Pablo 'Fealey' Escobar of Penydarren. 'Now tell us what happened. We need evidence.'

There was no way was I going to sing and land Steve in it. To be honest, I didn't know who had thrown the bloody thing. I said that I saw nothing. It got to midday and no one had said anything so we were still there clogging up the cells. I was panicking now. I had to get out. I had to sort myself out. I had to get to squad training. I didn't want the press to find out. I rang the bell. When the officer came, I told him I wanted to make a statement.

'Say nothing Jonesy,' someone shouted as I was led to the interview room.

I sat down and asked how was I to get out.

'Someone needs to be charged and as of now no one's admitted to doing it which means we ain't letting anyone go until someone makes a statement,' the copper replied.

'Ok, I'll make a statement,' I said. His face lit up. 'And if I do, you guarantee I'll be out when I make this statement and a person is charged?'

'Yes.' The copper sat there with his pen at the ready.

I started talking. He began writing. 'We were out ... blah blah blah ... and at approximately 11.30 we ... blah blah blah. We were turned away from the restaurant.' Then came the bombshell. 'I was hungry and peeved at this, so I picked up a milk bottle and threw it at the window and then ran.' His face dropped.

'We know it wasn't you, Mark.'

'It was.'

'It's Fealey we want.'

'Let me sign. I've got to go.'

Hesitantly, he handed it over. I signed the confession form and was returned to the cell. Within minutes I was let out. I was free and so were the boys. I flew out of the station like a swallow in Spring. I didn't have a clue what would happen, I just needed to get to squad training – at Waterton Cross in Bridgend, the HQ of South Wales Police!

I walked in that evening to be greeted by Rod Morgan, chairman of selectors – the infamous 'big five' – and David East, secretary of the WRU. They were both chief inspectors of the South Wales constabulary. How ironic?

'Hi gents,' I muttered and got on with the session.

I can imagine the backlash in the media if that had happened now. Someone would have probably have recorded the incident on their mobile phone and it would have been all over social media in the time it took to launch a milk bottle through a window. My career could have been over just as it was taking off.

As it was, I heard no more about it. I was very lucky. After that I got my head down for a bit, didn't go out as much and concentrated more on my training. It definitely served as a wake-up call. Things could have easily turned out very differently. This was another instance of when things I had been involved in could have blown the wheels off my bus. I've been very fortunate and lucky. My old man had another saying, 'When the beer is in, the wit is out. Remember that son.'

That night had been a great laugh to start with but sense goes out the window when you've had a few, and people do things that, when seen in the cold light of day, just aren't funny. Scoob was a lucky boy, and so was someone else.

I was as fiercely protective of mam as she was of me. My old man always said you can have five dads but you will only ever have one mam. Being protective of things that were important to me comes from my childhood. I didn't behave; I was disruptive and a bit out of control. I was totally irresponsible.

That changed when, in the cubs, two new kids joined. They were young and tiny, and the Akela (adult in charge) asked me to take care of our pack's new recruits. From that moment my behaviour changed. I would show them where to stand, how to tie a reef knot and make sure their woggle was in position. They were on my team and I reckoned I had a duty to protect them. That's probably why I had a tendency to stand up for teammates on the rugby field.

Mam's protectiveness towards me and my sister was astounding. One Sunday, not long after the trouble at the Indian restaurant in Merthyr, the boys from Dowlais had planned to travel over to get me out on an all-dayer, but I didn't fancy it. I'd decided to cool down a bit. I had a lot going on. I had upped my training and wanted to keep my nose clean. On that particular day I had already been up the tump for my run and been to the gym. I just wanted to eat then have a nap.

The Dowlais boys arrived with a sharp knock on the door and a huge craving for an all-day session. We had a bit of banter as I tried to politely refuse but they were having none of it. Finally Mam stepped in. 'He's not coming out to play. He's not going. He's said he's not, so he's not.' Now remember mam was about five foot three, and only six stone. She couldn't stand up straight and used a stick to walk. It was like the scene from *The Life of Brian*: Mark's 'been a very naughty boy' and is not going out.

As the boys looked at her, then at me, Gary winked at them and said: 'Quick, jump him, Jacques.' The three of them piled on me, laughing, and tried to drag me to the car. We were wrestling in the garden like schoolboys. All I could hear through the laughter was Mam screaming, 'Get off him, leave my boy alone. He's not coming.' She was waving her stick, taking air swipes at the Dowlais boys. They could see she didn't find this funny so it quickly calmed down.

'Mam mun, calm down,' I muttered, 'it's ok, they are only messing about.'

'You're not coming then?' Gary added.

I looked at Mam, breathing heavily as if she had been in the tussle herself. 'Nah, I better not.'

'OK. Bye Mrs Jones,' they all shouted, then jumped in the car and drove off. She saved me from what could have been another disaster. Bless her heart.

With a couple of B internationals under my belt, I was selected as a replacement for all of the senior 1986 Five Nations matches. Much to my frustration I didn't win a full cap, but I was getting closer. It wasn't like it is today where almost all the subs get a run out. Back then you had to be more or less pronounced dead by the doctor to be replaced.

While I was gutted I didn't get a minute on the field, it was great to be part of it and I wanted more. You can't imagine how it feels when you are so close to achieving your ultimate goal, so close you can almost touch it, almost smell it, but it's still just out of reach. It was so frustrating. I desperately wanted to do my bit for my country, not just for me, but for my mam and dad. It was so disappointing going home to them after each game, to be told 'don't worry, son, your time will come.'

It was still a great experience for me just being in the squad. The highlight was watching Paul Thorburn convert the longest penalty in rugby history – 64-metres. 'What a belt he's given it,' said the great Bill McLaren on the BBC commentary. 'That is amazing. I've seen all the great goal-kickers in the world over the last decade but I've never seen a kick like this one.' Enough said.

After the tournament, we all picked up our goodie bags, an Adidas holdall full of some of the most garish sports gear you could imagine: a tracksuit, T-shirt, trainers, and shorts. That was your reward for representing your country back then.

If you were really lucky, you would go on tour at the end of each season. That year Wales were going to the South Seas islands to play Tonga and Fiji. I had been on the bench all season so, naturally, I thought that I'd be going to an island paradise in the Pacific. I couldn't see any reason why I wouldn't be, no reason at all, but they didn't pick me! From what has been written about that tour, the Fijians and Tongans were unbelievably ferocious and incredibly violent – I would have fitted in quite well, and had a great time!

Instead, I got selected for a Wales B tour to Italy. At first that pissed me off. I should have been on the senior tour but, I thought, 'I'll show them. I'll make my mark in Italy. They'll regret not picking me.' I was obviously upset, but I was still representing my country. I would give it my best. I would work hard. I wanted to get back in the full squad. I wanted to play for Wales.

We played a couple of games in Italy but the wheels came off. I was hung out to dry and kicked all over the park. My only on-field back up being Ray Giles, the scrum-half, with Dai Joseph shouting from the dugout as the entire Italian pack kicked lumps out of me. I was escorted from the field by the Red Cross feeling like I had been in a scene from *Apocalypse Now*.

After being confined to the hotel for three days under concussion protocols. I started light training but was forbidden from contact and playing for two weeks. This was 1986, so when I'm being told that players are claiming there were no concussion protocols and they are claiming for negligence, I beg to differ. They have always been there. I had first-hand experience of it. The coach on that trip was Ieuan 'Compo' Evans, a proper headmaster-type. He told us he'd be writing a full report of the tour and submitting it to the powers that be. I would have loved to see what he wrote. All he could write about me was I had taken an old-style kicking! This wasn't positive and couldn't have helped my case.

However, my form for Neath did the talking and I made the initial squad for the 1987 Five Nations, but was left out of the matchday 21 for the first two games: an away defeat to France and a home win against England. Tulip (Phil Davies) had the number eight jersey and was established in the team. Fair play, he was a really good player and the physique and playing style the selectors preferred. He was a big old unit who could pass and carry well, so I had no issue playing second fiddle to him. It was something to aspire to. I knew that if I wanted the jersey, I had to outplay Phil. We had played his Llanelli team the previous October, at Neath, beating them 11-10 – the Neath juggernaut was only a 4x4 then – and I'd played well, but Phil was still ahead of me in the Welsh pecking order. He'd played the first two games of the 1987 Five Nations but got smacked by Wade Dooley (a policeman) in one hell of a violent international against the old enemy, in Cardiff. His face was busted up badly and he'd miss the next game.

I was watching on TV in the Ironsides club. As Phil was being wheeled off, one of the boys shouted, 'That's looking good for you, Scooby boy.'

'As if,' I said, shrugging it off. Then something triggered in my brain. I began to think, 'What if? What if?' But my heart was telling me I didn't stand a chance.

That night and all day Sunday, I kept my eye on the TV and scanned the papers. When it was announced that Phil had a fractured cheek bone and would be out for the next game, my hopes started to rise. I assumed they'd have to rearrange the back row from the 21-man squad and I may get a place on the bench.

I can't remember if I had a phone call or if we had squad training when I was told that I was in. I don't want to make it up, but I can remember it felt like I was on a Waltzer ride in a fairground. I was walking around in a daze, my head spinning. My parents were floating on air.

This was it – not the A team or the B team or the Z team, this was the W team, the Wales team. At last! The week leading up to the game was mental. Phil Davies was declared unfit to play on the Monday and it was announced I was in. I was going to start against Scotland. I was 21.

My dream had come true. This was the pinnacle. The guys I watched on our little black and white TV every February and March in the Five Nations were superstars. Heroes of our time. With the likes of Gareth, Barry, Benny, JPR and Gerald, Wales were invincible. Every kid wanted to be like them. All playing in the street, side stepping and scoring wonder tries. They weren't my idols, though. I'd always had an attraction to the players who were more rugged, the ones who did the donkey work and the ones who went in where the boots were flying. Players like Clive Burgess, Paul Ringer and Geoff Wheel.

'Ooooft,' my father would say as he jumped up from the settee, 'did you see that, Mark. Go on boys, get stuck in.'

To me, rugby was always connected with emotion and the pride of being Welsh. My father would stand for the anthem before each game and make me sing along with the players. I didn't understand the words and made up my own version at times but, even then, I could feel the passion and it made the hairs on the back of my neck stand on end. Sharing those 80 minutes with my dad, a few times a year, both of us screaming, shouting and cheering at the TV was brilliant and something I'll never forget.

My dad was full-on patriotic. His emotion grew in me, getting stronger and stronger with each rung of the representative ladder I climbed. Although I must say, my pre-game nerves got worse and worse, and by the time I was playing for Neath, the anxiety would start on a Thursday. I'd have trouble eating, retreat into my own thoughts and could be very abrupt with people. I would wind myself up into a mental frenzy and the fear of not performing was definitely an underlying factor. I'd slam doors, shout, hit myself and head-but the wall, anything to trigger my temper so I could be aggressive in the game and play at my best. I think I was confronting the 'flight or fight' trauma from my youth and forcing myself to fight. My natural instinct to run would be no good to me or my teammates. I wasn't going to be the same person who got a kicking in Tredegar bus station. I needed to be the other Mark, the guy who took the fight to the opposition. I needed to be a warrior.

There are only certain things I remember from the games I played, and that's because I was too wound up to take anything in. I now realise this behaviour and state of mind was all linked to my stammer, but back then the penny hadn't dropped. Being picked for Wales simply doubled or quadrupled my inner turmoil – I got into a right state.

I had made it. The box room boy from a council estate. Me – Scooby. I was proud, immensely proud. People smiled at me, congratulated me. I was in the paper and got free pints everywhere I went. It was big news in Tredegar but I still drank in the same pubs, worked in the steel works and drove a Mk 2 Escort which was falling to bits. I must admit, though, that I loved my mini-celebrity status, receiving telegrams and well-meant advice from people who stopped me in the street. That week, before my first cap, I was working the day shift so I finished at 2pm, allowing me time to go home for lunch, have a nap and get to training by 5pm. My heart was racing all the way there and I arrived at Waterton Cross feeling like a rock star.

John 'Sid' Dawes welcomed me with open arms, then there were more handshakes with the 'big five' and the two coaches, Tony Gray and Derek Quinnell. Straight after that I was kitted out. They knew my sizes so all the gear was there waiting. Then came numerous photos. I still had the mullet haircut – longer in the front and back, shorter on the sides – and was wearing the punk uniform of a long coat, black studded boots, tight jeans and a cut off T-shirt. The first and last punk rocker to play for Wales – no wonder someone suggested that it may be better to get some photos of me in my works overalls!

Most of the team were there, already in the changing room. 'Congratulations, Scooby' rang out as I walked in, and there were countless pats on the back from the players. Kitted and booted in my new gear, out I went for my first training session. We warmed up, then the forwards went off for scrumming and lineout practice. During this session, Stu Evans pulled up with a foot injury. He was quickly ushered off and someone else filled in, I can't remember who but I could see the worried faces of the selectors.

The interest went off me a bit which was a good thing and was all centered on Stu's injury, and if he wasn't fit, who they were going to bring in instead. The news quickly emerged that Stuart had broken his foot and was ruled out. I could hear the collective groan around the training ground.

The session continued without further incident. I caught a few balls at the back of the lineout, learned the calls and got involved with the forwards. There was no opportunity whatsoever for me to get out with the backs and run lines off Jiffy into the opposition's backs, like we often did in Neath. It seemed the tactics were 'catch, drive, kick'.

Maesteg's Peter Francis was drafted in to replace Stu, and what a tall order that would be. The cornerstone of the Welsh pack, Stu was also a rough, tough hombre who would be sorely missed at Murrayfield. I think everyone, including Peter, knew he wasn't at Stu's level in the scrummaging stakes, but no one imagined what was to come.

Training ended and I went home quite happy with what I had done. I was up for work the next day and had a photo shoot with the works manager and some of my colleagues. Later, a TV crew arrived at the steel works to film me at work. I didn't say much. They interviewed the works manager, who was a bit of a header. 'It is an honour for the steel works and an honour for Mark. The great Denzil Williams was the last employee of this steel works to be capped and its good to see the works being represented again.'

The reporter then asked, 'Are you going to Scotland to see him play?'

'Yes,' he replied. 'I need to go Scotland because I never see him in bloody work.' Everyone burst out laughing. That still tickles me to this day.

I was too nervous and too afraid to speak on camera. I didn't want the world to know I stuttered. I didn't want everyone laughing at me. I was now Mark Jones, the Wales international, and I needed to hide the other Mark, the stuttering Mark. Put him firmly in a box and hide him under the bed.

As the game approached I was being asked for interviews – to be filmed and recorded speaking to journalists. This was a nightmare scenario for me so I requested the questions beforehand and rehearsed the answers I wanted to give. I kept my responses as short as possible, to two or three words I knew I could say. I didn't want the nation to know. I didn't want to be the laughing stock. It was bad enough my teammates knowing, let alone the opposition and the watching public. I think I was more nervous of that side of it than playing against the Scots. This was such a big worry to me that the anxieties it generated far overshadowed the pleasurable experience of being picked for Wales.

When the initial media circus had finished and things had calmed down a little, the enormity of what was happening began to sink in. We arrived for training on the Thursday morning before flying to Scotland. Peter was there and going through all the same newby stuff I'd done a few days before. It was his first cap too.

Stu was there on crutches and we heard he was coming on the trip. Great news! I was 21, this was my first cap and I desperately needed guidance. Stu was my unofficial mentor at Neath and whenever I needed advice or a confidence boost he was always there for me. Stu was playing up to the injury a bit and wanting to get pushed round in a wheel chair. I was happy to oblige. That shows I really was the rookie. At first, he was my mate and was happy to care for him, until the novelty wore off and I told him to get off his fat arse and hobble. Have you ever tried pushing a 20-stoner around on wheels? It's not easy let me tell you.

Our hotel was in Peebles, in the Scottish borders south of Edinburgh. It was the traditional HQ of the Welsh team and had a golf course. I loved going away with Wales. I would never have stayed in these places or been to the countries I have been without rugby. A cheap B&B in Blackpool was my limit.

There were more photos to be taken for the media. One of them was me holding a teddy bear. I'm still not sure why. To make matters worse, the snap was plastered on the rear page of a Scottish daily paper. That didn't shout hardman, did it? Not very threatening. I bet it frightened Finlay Calder and his Caledonian warriors ... NOT!

On Friday morning we travelled to Edinburgh and had a run out at Murrayfield to get the feel of the place. It was an amazing stadium. The grass on the pitch was like a carpet and the terraces went back for miles. I could imagine how that would look the following day, packed with 60,000 drunk fans singing *Calon Lan* and *Flower of Scotland.* Even now, all these years later, that pre-match memory send shivers down my spine.

During the buildup I had a few chats with Stu and also Rob Norster who offered me good advice and helped calm my fraying nerves. I rated him. I had watched him play for several years. My father rated him too. He was a natural jumper, unlike me, and a big handsome bastard ... unlike me!

Game day arrived and we boarded the bus. I had my gear packed, including my jock strap. A load of guys wore swimmers under their shorts, but I always wore a jockstrap. You could get some cool ones back then. Over the years I had all sorts: pink and black, lime and black, even a leopard print which became a bit of a statement from myself and always raised a few laughs in the changing room. My warm up has always been me standing on a small hand towel, wearing my colourful jock strap, then jogging on the spot and furiously lifting my knees as high as I could while zoned out in a world of my own. I must have looked a sight.

The trip from the countryside hotel to the city of Edinburgh took a while but I loved every minute of it. As we got closer to Murrayfield, we could see the Scots in their kilts and the Welsh fans in red jerseys and scarves. It really hit home. I had been a sub before so this was my first experience of seeing and hearing our fans, standing on the pavement as the bus went by, shouting their support for the team – knowing that it meant they were cheering for me. I didn't want to let them down. I had been one of those fans on the streets of Edinburgh the previous time Wales played in Scotland in 1985. I remember watching the team bus drive past as we cheered. I so wanted to be in that bus, on my way to play for Wales. I really did.

We arrived at Murrayfield, and the pressure really stepped up a gear. I didn't talk, I just tried to soak up the atmosphere as we had a pre-match walk around the pitch. Everyone else appeared so cool. Jiffy, Norster, and Devs all seemed to take it in their stride. The only other player who seemed on edge, like me, was Peter Francis. He looked like a rabbit caught in the headlights. I wasn't far behind him mind.

The ground still wasn't full but noise was incredible. I had a bit of a knee wobble, but pulled it together and focused on the rugby, on my first cap. The next hour or so were a blur.

Every player has their pre-match rituals and I was no different. The final part of it was putting the jersey on and then the Elastoplast head band, followed by Vaseline to my eyebrows, nose, ears and shoulders. Next was the gumshield. I spewed three times and, when the gumshield was finally settled in place, I slapped some Vic to my nose and inhaled some smelling salts. I was now ready for war. My senses were tingling and everything seemed louder, brighter, and more intense. We had our last '1-2-3-4-5' in a group and then walked out. The roar of the crowd hit me – I immediately felt taller and heavier. 'C'MON,' I screamed out to myself.

We lined up for the anthems – what an experience! I was like a fighting, snorting and contorting my face as *Hen Wlad fy Nhadau* started. I stood bolt upright, with every muscle and sinew in my body tensed to breaking point. My eyes welled up and I had no control as the tears of emotion raced down my cheeks. I bit into the gumshield as hard as I could to stop myself blubbing. I had flashbacks to the night in the cells and how I had vowed to myself, and to my dad, that I was going to do this. I was one day going to play for my country, and now here I was. I was doing it. I had achieved what many dreamt of but only the few get to experience.

The game kicked off and I flew into contact. This was my first release. To me, their players were just blue jerseys. They had no features, there was no Finlay Calder, no Gavin Hastings, just a shirt that had to be hit. As always, after the first bumps and clangs and five minutes of intense action, things started to clear in my head. I had got into the game and things were going well. The pace of the game was astonishing, I didn't have time to be out of breath, it was too fast for that.

Their back row were Calder, Beattie and Jeffrey – all British Lions. They were the leading players in their position at the time in

Britain. If that wasn't enough, they also had Roy Laidlaw and John Rutherford at half back, the Hastings brothers in the backs and the pocket rocket known as David Sole in the front row. A team crammed with superstars.

Our side wasn't lacking in talent, mind you. We had Jiffy, the best outside half in the world, Robert Jones, Devs, Bob Norster, Paul Moriarty, Dai Pickering and then there was little old me, little old Scooby from Tredegar. I was certainly mixing with the *crème de la crème*.

The game shot by in the blink of an eye. There had been a few scrums where we had struggled, to say the least. David Sole gave Peter a torrid time. The Scots were causing havoc on our put-in and we were going backwards on theirs. The ref was getting annoyed by our inability to keep the scrum up, or straight, or anything. It would only be a matter of time before he'd penalise us. They would kick deep into our half and we'd be frantically defending again.

After about 20 minutes there was another scrum in midfield. We formed up and I thought, 'C'mon Peter, big effort with this one.' My fists grabbed the shorts of our second rows – Steve Sutton and Bob Norster – and took a quick glance around the ground. In that split second I saw the crowd and reconnected my brain with the enormity of what was happening. I breathed it all in – a deep Vic-fuelled breath of pride and determination.

The scrum hit. The pressure came on. It went down. It formed again, the Scottish pack hit, the pressure came on again and Peter's head popped out. The Welsh scrum was demolished and we all finished up in a heap on the turf. They formed again, they hit again, the pressure came on again, and Peter's head popped out again.

I'm no expert on the niceties of front-row play and would never want to play there myself – it's a jungle up there – but something was clearly not right and the Scots were destroying us. The ref stepped in. 'Right, this has gone on long enough. Reds, I'm not happy with your tight head,' he said.

Within a second, Rob Norster could be heard from the bottom of the pile of bodies. 'You're not fucking happy with him? How do you think we feel?' Cue giggles and guffawing from two sets of gruff forwards. I had to turn away before my laughing spat out my gumshield. Welcome to international rugby, Peter. I hope they weren't so scathing about me.

The game carried on but we were retreating all match and trying to combat the Scots enthusiasm with calls of *Ymlaen* (Welsh for 'forward' or 'onwards'). It wasn't working, though. They were everywhere. Their back row got amongst our backs and stopped any forward momentum. As the game went on, the pace slowed and we came back into it but we were down and out, and deep into injury time. We were playing for pride, and we had plenty of that.

Awarded a penalty ten yards from their line, we went for a quick tap to the forwards. Following a bit of interplay between Steve Sutton, Robert Norster and Dai Pickering, Robert Jones popped the ball to me about six yards from Scotland's try line. The space seemed to open up and my heart started banging madly in my chest. Realising my life-long dream was there for the taking, I gripped the ball like it was made of gold and charged for the line. Two Scotsmen grabbed at me but I was in no mood to be denied. Finlay Calder may have been a British Lion but he couldn't stop me. This Tredegar boy was going to score a try for Wales.

'Yeeeeeeeessssss.' If I could have done a somersault I would have. My dad had always said it's bad sportsmanship to celebrate a try so I tried to contain myself. Paul Moriarty pulled me up and Devs gave my back a pat as I threw the ball in the air. Inwardly, I was beaming. I wanted everyone to run on the field to congratulate me. I wanted to revel in the glory. Instead, I got polite handshakes from Robert Jones and Dai Pickering as I ran back to the halfway line. 'It's a try for Mark Jones in his first international. The big lad from Neath is simply overjoyed,' said Bill McLaren in his commentary. I'll treasure those words forever.

Wales lost. I was gutted, but I'd scored on my debut and not many of the lucky few can say that. As the whistle went and the players came together to shake hands and exchange shirts, John Beattie came over and signalled to me to swap shirts with him. I instantly declined. I didn't want to come across like a knob, but this was my first jersey. I was keeping this. No way was I giving this away. I pictured my old man sitting on the settee wearing it. Fair play to John, he shrugged his shoulders, removed his shirt and gave it to me, saying 'You keep yours, Mark, and well done today.' What a gesture. His words made me feel 50 foot tall. Thanks John.

I was stunned. I had done it. I had played for Wales. I had scored a try for Wales. Cefn Golau would be proud. My parents would be the proudest parents in the world. I hoped Tredegar, my work mates at the steel works, my mates in Dowlais and everyone at Neath RFC would all be proud. My heart was bursting.

We may have lost but, back in our despondent changing room, I was walking on air. After a quick debrief, a shower, and transfer back to the Edinburgh hotel, we dumped our bags in the room and reassembled for drinks and then the big gala dinner. Then more drinks with both sets of forwards mingling and really enjoying themselves. That's what I love about rugby. As soon as that whistle goes, its friendship all around. No looking for 'afters', no looking for revenge, just a bucketful of beer, a few laughs and a sing song.

'Benghazi' was the call. That was the Scottish version of the 'follow me' game we played at Neath. The players mixed, talked, ate and drank, and drank some more. Then came the speeches. The two presidents went about their business talking their normal formal bollocks. Next were the captains. Dai Pickering spoke very well. He expressed how disappointed our team were, but gave all the credit to the opposition.

That was David's final involvement as a player for the national team. He became the fall guy for that defeat, which was wrong. He'd finished his speech by saying 'Rugby was the winner', which some saw as a deflection from a poor performance. The big five clearly weren't impressed, and he was dropped.

I thought I had done enough to keep my place, but I was promptly dropped when Phil recovered in time for the next game, at home to Ireland. Oh well! It was back to St. Mary Street for me, with the boys and the beer and a seat in the West Stand, courtesy of the WRU as a capped player.

I hated the experience of sitting there, watching that particular game, more than any other I had ever watched. Seeing the team on the Arms Park, without me. I was wearing that jersey just days before at Murrayfield and I wanted to wear it on my home ground. I wanted to play for Wales, in Wales, where so many great players had played before me. I wanted my dad to be there. I can remember choking up as I stood for the anthem in row 14, seat 43 of the West Stand. As *Gwlad! Gwlad! Pleidiol wyf i'm gwlad* [(My) Country! (My) Country! I'm loyal to my country] hit its crescendo, I promised myself, 'I'm getting back out there. That's where I want to be. I'm no one-cap wonder.'

I may have been sitting in the stands, angry and frustrated, but I also had to be positive. The inaugural World Cup was coming up that year in New Zealand and Australia and I thought I was in with a chance of making the squad. That was my aim, and for the remaining

10 weeks of the domestic season I trained harder and played harder than I had ever done, but our 16-6 Welsh Cup semi-final defeat to Cardiff at Swansea probably ended my claim for a spot in the squad. I wasn't selected and didn't get to go. I was gutted.

What's more, Wales did very well and came third after beating Australia in the third and fourth place play-off match. That was an amazing feat. The main thing I remember about watching the World Cup that summer was when Wales played New Zealand in the semi-final, and Huw Richards punched Gary Whetton after a bust up at a line-out. Buck Shelford, probably the best player in the world, knocked Huw spark out with one hell of a punch. Huw lay unconscious on the ground, water was thrown on him, and when he woke up, he was sent off. Buck should have been sent off as well, but wasn't and went on to lift the cup in the final. There was no video ref in those days (thank God!).

Playing in the 1987 Rugby World Cup would have been a remarkable experience, particularly as I didn't know it would have been my only chance. Signing for Hull RLFC before the 1991 edition meant the Rugby World Cup passed me by, which is something I really regret.

The 1987-88 season was my third in senior rugby. I'd trained like a demon in the summer, bulked-up a bit more and was well up for it. I played well for a strong Neath team and was rewarded with a place in the match day squad for the 1988 Five Nations. Wales had a great season and won the championship but I got no further than the bench the whole campaign. I still hadn't played for Wales, in Wales. It was so frustrating.

The end-of-season tour was a three-Test series in New Zealand, the world champions. Having made the 21-man matchday squad for every match of our championship-winning, Triple Crown-winning, triumphant Five Nations campaign, I really hoped I'd be on that plane to the 'land of the long white cloud' (*Aeoteroa* in the original Māori). I wasn't.

I've often thought, and been asked, why I wasn't selected? This was the days of the big five when the selection committee picked the team, but the coaches had a big say in who they wanted. Neath were dominant and I'd played well all season so I assumed it must have been something else. Was it my character? Did they think I was an idiot and couldn't be trusted? Or was it that they preferred other players? Only they knew. Back then no one knew the workings of the big five. It was very much a cloak and dagger process. They were all-powerful and couldn't be approached. You really had to watch you didn't upset anyone and I guess my face and my attitude didn't fit.

As a player, selection decisions can really mess with your mental health but, as my career developed, I did learn to rationalise things. I came to the conclusion that selection is only an opinion. One man's meat is another man's poison. I needed to keep working. To keep the faith I had in myself and know that my time would come.

In New Zealand, Wales got absolutely battered 52-3 in the first Test. A few guys got badly hurt after that first outing and I was flown out as a replacement. By then I had left the steel works – after my apprenticeship had ended only a few were taken on and I missed out, but those other guys were better than me so no hard feelings – and was now unemployed, spending a lot of time with a pal of mine, Bulldog. He had a car repair business and I would go there to as sheer escapism with no pressure to speak. I would just hang around in the workshop watching him doing his stuff. One day I was there having a cup of tea when the phone in the workshop started to ring.

'Who's this now?' I thought but I didn't bother to answer it.

Bulldog (Tony) eventually dragged himself away from a bit of welding and picked it up. A few seconds later he shouted, 'Yes, you beauty.' I assumed one of his bets had come up trumps but he yelled across to me: 'It's Ben, you've been called up for the tour and you fly out tomorrow.'

'What?'

'Get yourself sorted butt, you're going to New Zealand!'

'C'mon!' I punched the air, raced home, packed my bags and, along with Nigel Davies, I flew to New Zealand.

We landed in Auckland and joined up with the squad in Hawkes Bay. The first two days were a blur – trying to cope with jetlag for the first time was a bit strange. Waking up at 2.30 am and going for a run is odd. It really messed my system up.

I had no idea what to expect, but when we began to travel out of the cosmopolitan area it was like traveling back 20 years. I can't put my finger on it, it was just very rural. The amenities we had in towns in Wales weren't available in many towns in New Zealand. Things were a little different. It was very much like the farming communities in the west of Wales, and this clearly had an influence on the physical condition of their players. They were all lean, sinewy, hard and naturally athletic – clones of Brian Williams – and when this solid farming stock was combined with the natural flair and brutal brilliance of the indigenous Polynesians, the All Blacks were unstoppable and streets ahead of European rugby.

In Wales our style of play was more 'kick and clap'. It was slow and pedestrian and not free flowing, open rugby. This was reflected in the sort of players who were picked for Wales. By that I mean 80% of the Kiwi forwards were in better physical shape than the Welsh boys. We just couldn't compete. This wasn't so evident in the back line where Jiffy still showed his class, but up front it was patently obvious. All their forwards could scrummage, maul, tackle, catch, pass and run. There weren't many in the Welsh squad who had all those attributes. Neath embraced that style and dominated Welsh rugby for a few years. It was all about supporting the ball carrier: hit, spin and offload. The way the Kiwis played was an eye opener for me. The game was expansive, with forwards running in the back line. It was brilliant 'heads-up' rugby with backs and forwards playing what was in front of them. Welsh rugby could be dour at times, more thud and blunder than blood and thunder.

My first game was against Hawke's Bay, selected at six. It was an odd decision as I'd never played at that position before and I was given a crash course during the previous day's training session. Wales has a bad habit of selecting players out of position, and it never works because the player will always be found wanting in those crucial situations when experience and positional know-how is so valuable.

The match was, more or less, just a big scrap from kick off to final whistle with skulduggery going on all over the pitch. They had a big Māori playing at lock who had a head like an October cabbage. He was putting it about and our forwards, including me, spent a bit of time dealing with the trouble he was causing. We won the game but Kevin Moseley got smashed and Jeremy Pugh had his eye shut for him.

We won and, after the game, the boys got patched up (which took quite a while, let me tell you) by the medics and we all jumped on the bus to go back to the hotel. A rustic hunting lodge, it had the stuffed heads of all sorts of animals on the walls: stags, deer and wild boar. Jeremy had a dressing on his eye and wasn't happy, telling us repeatedly that their second row had booted him. He hadn't – I saw it from the side line. Mr Pugh and their loosehead had squared up at a scrum and Jeremy had been hit four times by his opposite number before he had time to blink. We've all been there once or twice in our careers.

Arriving back at the hotel, Mark Ring and Glenn Webbe bolted off the bus, which looked odd. The rest of us all picked our bags up and walked in through the entrance into the main hall. Within seconds everyone was laughing. There in front of us, taking pride of place on the main wall, was the enormous head of a wild boar that had been adorned with a surgical dressing, covering the same eye as Builth's finest, Jeremy Pugh. By the time he'd walked in we were all in hysterics. 'Ringo, you bastard,' he shouted as he looked up at the eye-patched stuffed boar. The boys then proceeded to chip in with comments: 'Looks like you, Pughy'; 'Jer, it's your twin.' Even the people working in the hotel couldn't help but see the funny side of it.

That set the tone for the next two weeks. The boys were getting beaten heavily and beaten up badly, and needed a release from the torture they were being put through on the field. We actually won one other game but got hammered in the second Test in Auckland. We didn't stand a chance from the start. We were being intimidated into a losing mindset before the game even started. It was amazing watching the All Blacks perform the Haka and laying down the challenge. We could match them physically but it was the fitness and psychological aspect where Wales were defeated. They just kept coming. After 30 minutes we were spent and they were running away with things. Someone went off injured and I got the nod. I ran on like a banshee to win my second cap. The red jersey meant as much to me as the silver fern did to them.

The game was lost by the time I got on to play. Yet, I was going to do as much damage as I could. I was going to hit as hard as I could. They were going to know that Mark Jones was on the field. No way was I going to lie down like a fat Labrador and have them rub my belly and play around with me. Lots of the boys had been given a real kicking, and knocked about mercilessly. Bollocks to that. I was about to give a bit back.

I didn't touch the ball much. I just hit things, kept running and hit more things. I was penalised for careless feet a few times and was absolutely knackered by the final whistle but I think some of them have memories of me. I walked off with my head held high. When Neath gave a warm Welsh welcome to the All Blacks the following year, they certainly knew who I was.

Even though we lost that Test match 54 – 9, Jonathan Davies was given the man of the match award. That just shows the pure class of the man. Jiffy was still a revelation on tour. He was on their wavelength, but not many others were. The New Zealand players and the country's media loved him.

The All Blacks were hard, skilful and intelligent rugby players. Fair enough, they wanted to beat you and rack up huge scores, but didn't try to rip you limb from limb then enjoy grinding you into the ground, like the French or South Africans. To them this was in their rugby culture – all-out, on-field war and they had absolutely no interest in taking prisoners. The French boys could play as well and back then only the French could match the Kiwis. I am a big fan of French rugby. It's got the lot: intimidation, aggression, pace and sublime skill. I've been on the receiving end of a few absolute maulings from French teams and, to me, they are the best. They have issues with their motivation sometimes but if they could control their mentality which sometimes lets them down, they would rule the rugby world.

Wales have been stung by this approach a few times when playing the island nations, like Samoa and Fiji. If you are getting clattered continually, it's human nature to either avoid that situation or give a bit back. It's often said by coaches in pre-game interviews, 'we need to match their physicality.' To me, if you don't match the opposition, if you don't give a bit back, they are going to get over the top of you and grind you into the ground. This lack of willingness to get involved has cost coaches their jobs. You could have the 15 most skilful players in one team but if they are not prepared to man-up, they are going to get their pants pulled down and their arses smacked. It's not necessarily the best team that wins a contest, it's the team that wants it the most.

The mood flying back to Wales from the Southern Hemisphere was sombre, but I believed I'd done enough to keep a place in the squad. When called upon I had played well on the tour and put myself about, so despite the poor results I had something to positive to report. We had a month off, before pre-season training started with Neath, so I concentrated on getting as big and horrible as I could. I went straight to the gym and running up to the tump of stones on the mountain nearly every night. Maybe if I had worked on my ball skills, and learned how to channel my aggression, I would have put myself ahead of the pack, but I wanted to improve my physicality. I wanted to be the biggest and toughest I could be. There was a volcano building up inside me and I was trying to control it from exploding.

For the autumn internationals, the squad was called in and we trained to prepare for these games. Neath were rampaging through all who stood before them and I was scoring a few tries. My role was running at the back line and, admittedly, I didn't pass much. I would, though, break open defences and if I didn't score myself, I'd set up the ruck and the back line would have a walk-in at the corner. On the back of that I was certain I'd be in with a chance of starting the upcoming internationals.

'Arrgghhhhhhhh,' I was left out of the match day squad for the two games against Western Samoa and Romania. Why?

I was picked for the B international, against France at Parc de Pugh in Brecon on 29 October. This was the first of the games that autumn and some of the guys who had gone to New Zealand were in the squad. Determined to show the selectors that dropping me from the senior squad was a mistake, I was well up for the match. I was playing at eight with Mike Budd at seven. I don't have a clue who was in their team except for the monster known as Olivier Roumat playing same position as me.

I thought I had served my 'dark arts' apprenticeship playing against Gareth Williams, John Scott and Dai Arthur, who had exposed me to all the tricks at the lineout, and I was going to use them all in this B game in Brecon. I won't describe the ground and the atmosphere, just to say there was a 2-inch diameter hemp rope that skirted the pitch to separate the crowd from the players. We were so close to the crowd that we could taste the beer in the air as they swayed behind us.

In one such lineout, on the French 22 metre line, I called a ball to the back. Olivier had a couple of inches on me, so I knew I had to use some smoke and mirror tactics to get the better of him. Thinking back to my first training session with the Ironsides many years before, I thought I would use the same underhand tactics that Ian Price had used on me, before I'd thrown a punch at him. So, I set up, bouncing up on my toes. The ball left our hooker's hand and I dummied forward then stepped back a yard. As I went back my right arm went out and shoved Roumat in the back. He was gone. The ball came over. I leapt like a salmon, all of about 4 inches off the turf and claimed the ball, setting up a bit of a maul. The ball came out the back and our backs were on the attack. I had outplayed the famous Olivier Roumat. One nil to me.

The maul broke up and Roumat squared up to me. There was instantaneous grabbing of collars and a bit of pulling and pushing. He glared at me and I scowled back. Two fighting cocks shaping up for the off. In broken English with a Gallic accent he grunted, 'Push me again and I will punch you.'

You can imagine my reply. I had grown several inches since the last lineout and I was buzzing. I looked back with disdain. 'Fuck off, you French knob.' I ripped his hand off my shirt and went to join the next ruck in hot pursuit of Mike Budd and looking for a blue jersey to smash.

The game went on for a while, to'ing and fro'ing. A few scrums, a few rucks, a stamp here and there. Both teams still just weighing each other up. Then came the next lineout. I was confident. I told our scrum-half that I wanted it, so let's do same call as before. I got myself prepared. I knew what I was going to do. A little set up, a dance up on my toes, a little faint step forward, a step back, a push in the back, and up I go. 'Yes, I'll do him like a kipper again.' Or so I thought. There I was, all set up, dancing and waiting for the dummy forward then a step back and a nudge for Roumat. The dummy completed, I began my step back only to see the huge French forward turn round and smack me right between the eyes – BOOOOSHHHH!

Everything started to sway. I could feel my body going soft, my head spinning and my leg twitching like I was getting 5,000 volts shot through me. I was still on my feet, but only just. I looked to my right and Mike was there. Before I could think, I grabbed his arm and was clinging on him like Nana coming down the steps at bingo. 'Don't move, butt, don't move. My legs have gone.' He burst out laughing but took care of me. After a bit, I managed to regain my marbles and let him go. I'm sure Mike must have thought, 'have a bit of your own medicine, Scooby boy.'

Was Roumat sent off? I have no idea. My head was in Disneyland!

In addition to the B international, the WRU held a Possibles v Probables trial game and I was picked in the second row. I wasn't happy. What made it worse was I was jumping against Dai Waters of Newport. Dai was 7ft 3 with a huge reach. Even if you managed to outmanoeuvre him and get to the ball in the lineout before him, his hand would still come through and pinch it. That drove me mad and happened a few times. I'd had enough.

A few weeks earlier I'd played against Dai at the Gnoll, where he had dominated and scored a try directly after a catch at a line-out. I knew how effective he was and that I needed to take action or face being humiliated again.

'You can either let this happen and resign yourself to the fact that you haven't got a chance to get picked or you can deal with it.' I said to myself. I chose the latter and, at the next lineout, I called for the ball to be thrown to me. As it came in, Dai's extending arm came through and the ball ended up on their side. As it was passed to their outside half and I saw the ref, the legendary Clive Norling, following the ball, I turned and gave Dai a right belter, sitting him straight on his arse. I sprinted away and dived into the ruck. When the game was stopped, I made sure to get up last. Clive and the medics were tending to Dai. He knew something had happened but hadn't seen it. He was fuming. His tight shorts had pushed his nuts up into his throat and he was bright purple. He glared at me. 'Jones,' he bellowed, beckoning me over with his outstretched finger. 'Here. Now.' He really did take things personally did Clive.

'Hold on a minute Clive,' I thought. 'I'm not 14 and back in school. So, bollocks to you.' I sauntered over, playing all bemused. 'Yes ref.'

He pointed his finger in my face and said, 'I know it was you.' Then glanced down towards poor Dai Waters.

'What do you mean?' I shrugged.

'I didn't see it, but I know it was you. I'll be watching you for the rest of the game.'

'Watch away Clive,' the voice in my head silently replied.

Dai was patched up and two huge wadges of cotton wool were shoved up his nose. Fair play, he played for a few more minutes but couldn't continue and hobbled off. That was over 30 years ago and Clive hasn't said a word to me since. I went okay after that, but I still didn't get picked. So, it wasn't just one incident that was keeping me on the fringe. There was a catalogue of things.

After the humiliation in New Zealand, the coaches were under a bit of pressure. There were players like Jiffy, John Devereux, Dai Young, Rob Jones and others who were all expansive, quality players who could influence a game, but the style of club rugby in Wales was inhibiting how the other guys played. Wales were getting left behind. The way forward was to play expansive and fast but most of the pack just wanted a kick into touch, and slow the game right down. The Welsh teams being selected were neither one or the other and were playing disjointed rugby. By that time, a team selected by a committee was doomed to fail, but the coaches paid the price. They were sacked after an embarrassing defeat to Romania which shocked the world, and Welsh rugby to its core. I'm so glad I hadn't been selected to play in that one. The most unfortunate casualty was the one player who could have put Wales back on the journey to greatness. Jiffy was vilified. He was better than that and he knew it. He packed his bags and headed north to a massive fanfare. It was the beginning of the end. The plug had been pulled out of the bath and the water was about to escape.

9

Psycho (Thriller)

'Neath became one of the most revered club sides in Britain, with Mark being one of the pillars of that success. A rugged and integral member of the Neath team and pack of forwards, one of the highlights was when he rocked the New Zealand All Blacks with his phenomenal ball carrying abilities. Off the field, Mark's a gentle giant who became a great friend.'

Paul Thorburn

After the debacle of the loss to Romania in Cardiff, Grey and Quinell were forced out. The previous regime had tried all sorts of permutations in the back row for 18 months and had avoided picking me, ignoring my club performances and keeping me just out of reach of the starting lineup.

On saying that, there was one hell of a crop of talented backrows around at the time and some great open sides: Dai Bryant, Richie Collins, Dai Pickering, Lyn Jones (who never got a look in), Mark Brown, and Martyn Morris. Then there were the rest who could play eight and six, such as Rowland Phillips, Paul Moriarty, Owain Williams, Gary Jones, Phil Davies and Stuart Davies. I was in direct competition with all of these so there was never a lull, every game was important and you couldn't afford to have a bad weekend.

Looking back on those three seasons, it's obvious to conclude that the coaches didn't think I was up to the job. They didn't think I was worth more than a fringe spot. I've ignored this until now. Nevertheless, being involved in the squad, being on the bench and getting two caps in three seasons was still a proud achievement. This goes back to my roots in Cefn Golau and to my self-doubt. I was getting experiences I'd never have got any other way and I was grateful for that, but I was still massively disappointed when I didn't get picked and was left out of the tours. This manifested itself in my resentment of the coaching set up and my indifferent attitude after games and on tour. I could keep it under wraps for official functions but instead of being the model player and trying to ingratiate myself I rebelled a bit, as I'd done in school. Yes, I was loud and always up for a laugh and, yes, could sometimes be led astray by others, but I wasn't going to lick boots to get selected so, I can't really complain. I wasn't acting like a Wales international, so being omitted served me right.

John Ryan was appointed as Welsh coach and I was picked for the next game and many others after that – selection is just an opinion.

The following two seasons became a blur. I was riding the wave and living in the moment. I was the Welsh number eight, Neath were destroying everyone and I was enjoying all the notoriety that it brought. If you ask me to tell you what happened, I can only recall snapshots, as if I'm looking through a big photo album: part of a game here, an incident there. Internationals were just a haze. I'd experience the anthem head-on but couldn't take in details. Memories are vague.

The first match of the 1989 Five Nations saw me returning to Murrayfield to play Scotland, where we were taken apart by Calder, White and Jeffrey – their brilliant backrow. We were on the back foot all day. I tackled someone in the corner, the ball got recycled and they dived over three metres from me. As I sat there despondently, John Jeffrey ran past and rubbed me on the head

'You cheeky twat,' I thought. 'I'll have you for that.' I spent the rest of the game chasing him for retribution. I never caught him. They stuffed us 23 - 7.

Next, we played Ireland at home. As now, the Irish were tough. They strategy was 'kick ahead, kick any head.' They were banshees, proper kick and rush. Back then, we all believed that no one would be sent off in the first 10 minutes of a game, which gave us a window to set our stall and put markers down. A few warnings for overly robust play came my way in several games, but never a sending off, which seemed to prove the point and act as a green light to getting stuck in early. I scored in this one from about eight metres, but it wasn't enough. Noel Mannion, the Irish number eight, ran in a try from his own half to seal Ireland's 13-9 victory, and yet another Wales defeat. Off we then went to face France at Parc des Princes. It was our third match and I can recall motorbike outriders leading us to the stadium, sirens blaring and kicking people out of the way as they rode passed. The French supporters were always very passionate in that cauldron: their berets, drums, scarves, trumpets, cockerels and thousands of black moustaches. I always wondered what they did with the cockerels after the match. Eat them I suppose!!

We only saw or touched the ball in the warm-up. I chased shadows all game. I would hit a ruck or make the first-up tackle from a set piece yet, when I emerged from the bottom of the pile of bodies the ball would be gone, flying through the hands of the French backline, finishing with Blanco touching down under the sticks. They performed like a dance troop with well-rehearsed routines and exquisite timing. It was sublime. Our backs made about four tackles all day. We lost 32-12 and were taught a lesson in how to play the game.

All the international rugby arenas are steeped in history. They oozed emotion and atmosphere, but Cardiff, in my opinion, is the king of them all. Located right in the centre of the city, you just can't escape the atmosphere. Every home supporter is shouting for you, and die-hard club stalwarts from across Wales put their local allegiance to one side, all united with the common goal: 'C'mon Wales!' This reaches stratospheric levels when Wales play the English, and in 1989 it was no different, in fact it was more intense. We hadn't won a game and England were our final opponents. On that day it felt as if the whole nation was praying for the same result, for us to beat England in Cardiff. There was a whole two weeks of intense media scrutiny and national anticipation before this encounter. As is now, the London-based press were salivating over England's supposed superiority, saying Wales were on for a drubbing. The scene was set. My teammate Hugh Williams-Jones remembers that game well, and the hype that preceded it. Unbeknown to me, the coach and the other players had been playing mind games – not with the English, but with me. I was totally wound up when I took the field, and this is why:

'The England team of 1989 were very, very good and Mike Teague who had been crowned the man of the series for the Lions the previous year was their hard man. John Ryan, our coach, told Mark that Mike was his man. What Mark didn't know was John had told the rest of us, to keep onto Mark about it. All the team kept reminding Mark of this during the week. You could see him getting wound up. We shouldn't have but we kept on and on. Come match day, Mark was like a bottle of pop ready to explode.'

The boys really did do a job on me. That week, every time I closed my eyes, the only thing I saw was Mike Teague's face. The normal ritual I followed each week would start on Thursday after training. I would have a beer with the lads and 'Rugby Mark' would leave the club. I would go home and retreat into my world. I'd start putting on my invisible suit, my game persona, and the buzz would start in my head. I'd try not to speak to anyone. If I did, or had too, it was just pleasantries – 'Hi' and 'bye'. The mixer was in my guts all day, slowly churning the concrete. I'd get through the day, just, then in the evening I'd go to the cinema. I wasn't a massive film buff, but in the darkness of the picture house, I wouldn't have to talk to anyone. It didn't matter what was showing. I didn't care as long as I wasn't forced to speak. I would be visualising the game on the Saturday, building the hatred up inside me. The rage would be increasing slowly, and I could feel it. I'd get home to bed and dream about the game.

Saturday morning was an experience. Game day. I have read about and spoken to numerous sportsmen who have felt this as well. Overnight, I had fully morphed into 'On the Field Mark'. Nothing else in the world mattered except the game. I wasn't a nice guy on game day prior to the match. I was best left alone. I would play music at full volume: Pretty Vacant by the Sex Pistols rattled the windows but I didn't care. The feeling was extreme. I would be strapping on bits of the imaginary suit: click, clunk, crack, snap.

By now I'd also have the 100-yard stare. Everything about me was burning aggression. I would travel to the ground with my forehead pressed against the cool glass of the vehicle window, trying to ease the buzz burning inside my head. The bus would be parked up and we'd get off. No speaking from me on the way in, just nods, or a quick 'Hi', keeping my interactions plain and simple.

Then came the team meeting and more bits would be strapped onto the suit. The buzzing in my head was, by now, continuous. I just wanted and needed to get out on to the field. I craved that whistle so I could end this feeling and release the anger I felt about my stammer.

In the changing room it was jockstrap on and a ridiculously vigorous jog on the spot. Stretch, jog, stretch, jog, socks, shorts, boots, warm up, shirt on and out for the warm up. Still buzzing, devouring in the atmosphere, feeling the energy coursing through my body.

The warm up over, I'd now be in the toilet, spewing. I was full to the brim with nervous energy. My special suit was nearly all on by then. A few more smashes with the ball on my chest, then tape my head and fingers before 'Vasing' up. Finally, some Vic and smelling salts to clear my brain.

I would always sit down for about 20 seconds before the final piece was put in place. The gum shield fixed into my mouth. I'd spew again. The suit was on. It was time. I was ready.

There is a song by Indie punk band, Carter U.S.M, with the line: 'Just about to take the stage, the one and only, hold the front page.' That was me.

I would be talking to myself all the time. Others were talking about moves, offloads and such like. I wasn't interested. I just wanted the kick off. I just wanted to get rid of this horrible feeling inside me. Whether we won or lost the toss, I was going to be the first to wherever that ball landed. It was my first opportunity to smash something. To ease this pain that had built up all week.

Every time I had to pick up the phone, every time I ordered a meal in a restaurant or takeaway, every time had to ask for help in the supermarket. All those grins and sniggers about my stammer were stored up to be released at that moment when the whistle went on a Saturday. I made the kick off my thing. The chase or the catch. I wanted that ball. I wanted that smash, that release. It was the first chance to do damage. The first chance to hurt. After that came wiping out someone at the rucks. I'd just line up a shirt and hit it. Time after time. I didn't care if Mother Theresa was standing there. She was having it: slam, slam and slam.

In the Wales changing room in Cardiff, I was more than ready to face the old enemy. This was my moment. I raced out to the roar of the crowd, the pouring rain, and the expectations of a nation. I thought I was going to burst when the anthems played out, tears rolling down my cheeks. I thought of my parents, my mates, the whole of Wales.

'Teague is yours, Mark,' someone whispered to me. 'Don't get sent off.'

We won the toss and were kicking off. This was it, let battle commence. That ball was mine and I chased it like a lunatic. I could see 'Iron' Mike Teague's number in front of me, ready to catch the ball. I set the target and fixed him in the cross-hairs. As he caught the ball, he moved a little to my left. I was fully committed. 'I can't miss this,' I thought as I threw my left arm out, my upper arm, my bicep. It smashed into the back of his head. The whole nation was watching as I caught him a peach. I hit him with all I had. He took a few more bumps in the ensuing melee but I knew he was gone before he hit the deck. He cut his eye badly and was taken off after eight seconds, badly concussed. 'I think he got caught going up for the kick off, said Bill Beaumont in the BBC commentary box, 'and I think it was Mark Jones the Neath number eight who caught him.'

We ended up winning 12-9 after Mike Hall scored a great try with the rain lashing down. I didn't care who had scored, or how. We had won. We had beaten the team everyone said would smash us.

I felt on top of the world. I'd been given the jersey and I intended to keep it. They could have dropped me for lack of skill but there was no way they were going to drop me for lack of endeavour, lack of hwyl or lack of aggression. I won 11 straight caps which back then was a good run in a losing side. Considering there were only four to six international games a season, and the team around me had changed a bit, I was doing well.

After the game, we headed back to the Angel Hotel for a quick drink, along with what seemed like every mad Taff in Wales. It was fantastic. All the applause. All the slaps on the back. I was loving it and wanted to stay but we had all the formal stuff to do. So, it was up to the hotel room for a quick change into my penguin suit for the after-match dinner. I walked down the grand staircase feeling ten feet tall. I was flying, we all were. We'd beaten England. Nothing else mattered to the whole of the Welsh nation. The country was in party mode.

Both teams and the invited dignitaries made their way to the bar adjacent to the dining room. The mood of the two teams couldn't have been more different. They looked like they had lost a pound and found a penny. Absolutely gutted. Most of our lads, like Jeremy Pugh, Rob Jones and Mark Ring loved mixing with the England players and enjoyed chatting with the likes of Will Carling, Brian Moore and the mighty Mike Teague (who didn't look too good to be honest). Most of the boys loved the talking, the banter and the networking, and many a life-long friendship began over post-match pints. There was a mutual respect among the players and all barriers were broken down. That's the best thing about rugby, once the game is over the beers, singsongs and piss-taking unites players whatever team they represent.

Not for me. Those events brought back memories of school. Feeling like the outsider, I kept my conversation to a minimum. I wasn't going to speak. I wasn't going to expose my inadequacies. I wasn't going to let them see I stammered and give them an opportunity to laugh in my face. I didn't want to show any weakness. I was Mark Jones, the rugby international. I wasn't going to be stuttering lanky Jonesy, again. My fear inhibited me, made me defensive, held me back from enjoying the company of fellow internationals and forming friendships with some top blokes. I bet they thought I was just being a big, arrogant thug, standing in the corner itching for a scrap, but that couldn't have been further from the truth. I wanted to join in. I wanted to talk, to joke, to get drunk with them all, but my affliction was holding me back, controlling me. So, I just stayed with the Welsh boys, wrapping myself up in the comfort of the people I knew and where I felt more at ease.

I didn't speak to Mike that night. I'm not sure if he wanted to speak to me anyway after what had happened. We played against each other a year later, Wales v Baa Baas, and all through the game I was a bit wary that he was going to deal me some retribution, but it never came. Fair play to him. I'm not sure, if roles had been reversed, that I would have done the same.

It wasn't until 2012 that I finally spoke to Mike. This was when the British Lions toured Australia and I was playing for the Baa Baas Vets against an Australia Vets XV. I bumped into him in a bar in Brisbane. It was full of ex-Lions and Aussie players letting their hair down and talking about old times. We were all loving the atmosphere. Across the room, someone shouted, 'Hey Scooby, look who's over there, It's Mike Teague.' As he turned round, I caught his eye and we stared at each other for a second or two, like two gunfighters, and then we both cracked a smile, greeting each other with an aire of mutual respect. As the beer flowed, some good-natured banter was exchanged between the two of us. He didn't take it personally and joined in the craic. Mike was no shrinking violet and played by the same rules as I did – hard as nails on the pitch yet friendly and welcoming off it. He was a top player and is a top man: total respect to the fella.

I knew my style, being rough and aggressive, worked and playing for Neath helped no end. I was on the front foot each week. This enabled me to gain an ascendancy in club games and shine brighter than anyone else. I was playing well, scoring tries regularly, and Neath won the cup two years on the trot.

There was a down side, though. The press. As 'Rugby Mark' took over and my on-field misdemeanors began to accumulate, there were many articles criticising my behaviour – that I was a thug and how I should be banned for life. I was amassing quite a portfolio of articles but my dad would always say 'No press is bad press'. I'd turned into the rugby psychopath. At the time my attitude was, 'what goes out there, stays out there.' I had no remorse. It was all part of the game, but even I knew this was going well into the red zone.

The Mike Teague incident was exceptional, even for me, but the lack of consequence made me think it was somehow acceptable or excusable. That it gave me the green light to carry on doing what I was doing.

Wales played New Zealand that autumn. Neath had pushed them all the way a week or so earlier so I expected us to come close, but New Zealand showed their class by changing up a few gears and beat us easily. We didn't show the same physicality that was needed to compete with the best team in the world. Also, it was a different stage we were performing on. You can get away with a lot more 'inside work' on the Gnoll than you can at the national stadium with the world watching from numerous camera angles! If you look at all the legends of rugby they had playing in that game, like Buck Shelford, Fitzpatrick, Whetton, Gallagher and Grant Fox, it was incredible. Proper superstars of the game. We were definitely out-classed, but didn't stop me climbing into them from the kick off and leaving my mark. Hands up, though, they were a brilliant team.

The game they played against Llanelli summed up how great they were. Facing a gale force wind in the second half and only in front by a point, Shelford and the forwards stuck the ball under their jerseys for 40 minutes and didn't let the Scarlets have it. That's what is so great about the All Blacks, they can adapt their game and always have a plan A, B and Z if required.

At the end of the season, we travelled to Canada for a month-long tour. We traveled across the country from Nova Scotia to Vancouver via Ontario, Toronto and Banff. It was a fantastic trip in an amazing country. I loved everything about the place, the food, but particularly the people and their refreshingly laid-back attitude.

The standard of rugby over there was well within our comfort zone, compared to the All Blacks, so we had a successful trip. However, in the first Test, a week before the end of the tour, I was sent off in the second half. It was harsh to say the least and even Gerald Davies, who was commentating on the match, said he was none the wiser as to the misdemeanour I had supposedly committed. The dismissal meant

I missed the second Test, the final match of the tour, in Vancouver, which incidentally was more like a boxing match than a rugby game. The Canadians loved a good punch-up.

Again, the press slated me with headlines like, 'Mark Jones is the scourge of Welsh Rugby.' They hated me. Portrayed me as a monster and some again called for me to be banned for life.

Luckily for me, with a week to fill before the flight home, there was a lot of other things to do in Vancouver besides playing rugby, so I went shopping, enjoyed the baseball and put in a lot of training. As we had been doing quite a bit of travelling by road and air, there was of course lots of drinking and amusement. The highlight for many of the boys was a bar in Halifax called 'My Apartment.' It was just up the street from the Holiday Inn and became our party central with lots and lots of things going on there.

The Canada tour also, finally, helped me inflict some retaliation on South Wales Police, well, on Hugh Williams-Jones, our prop, who was also a copper. It was during one of our flights between cities. Huw takes up the story from here:

> *We'd had a heavy session on the beer the night before and were flying to Vancouver early the next morning. We were all worse for wear and I decided to pass the time by catching up on some shut-eye. I was fast asleep when I felt someone shaking me awake. I opened my eyes and Scooby was standing by me. 'You OK Hugh?' he asked, 'do you want a piss?' 'No, Mark,' I replied and went back off to sleep. Ten minutes later, another shake of the shoulders and the same question, 'You OK, Huw? Do you want a piss?' 'No!' I said. 'Mark, I need some sleep.' Five minutes later, the same routine. I snapped. 'Mark, what are you doing?' He smirked and replied, 'I... I... I just wanted to get my own back for every time I've been in a police cell, when they woke me up every 15 minutes to ask me if I was OK and ... did I want a piss?' The plane nearly tipped over from all the laughing. I think even the pilot joined in. That was Mark's sense of humour and sense of fun.*

10

'A' Bomb in (Twickers)

'Mark is a diamond of a person and someone I think of as a very good friend.'

Iestyn Harris

We started the 1990 Five Nations with high hopes. Having beaten England in Cardiff in the final game of the championship and a decent tour of Canada, we were on a roll. The least said about the New Zealand game that November the better.

The first game of the tournament was France at home. Arriving in Cardiff with world class players like Berbizier, Champ, Camberabero, Roumat and the brilliant Sella in their lineup, I knew it was going to be tough. As ever, we needed to match France upfront if we were going to triumph and it was all going soundly until Kevin Moseley let loose with his boots and got sent off. From then on we were doomed, losing 19-29, and it could have been – should have been – more.

England were up next at Twickers, a match that resulted in a massacre for us and the end of the journey for our coach John Ryan. To put it in plain English, we got battered and he resigned after we were defeated by 34-6. It wasn't a pleasant experience. After the incident the previous season with Teague, they did their homework on me, and us, and as Jeff Probyn comments in his autobiography, 'They had to devise a system to deal with hit men like Mark Jones.'

They sure did, I couldn't get within range of anyone. They ran shield lines all match – illegally I may say – protecting their catchers and play makers. Obstruction was the focus and I got really frustrated. At one breakdown, in my over eagerness to get my hands on the ball, my fingers found their way to the vicinity of Jeff Probyn's face as I grappled blindly for the ball. The next second, I felt pressure in my gonads. I couldn't find the ball but someone had found mine and they were both cupped in his clenched fist. As my fingers pushed deeper into Jeff's face, the pressure on my nuts increased. So, I ever so slightly withdrew my fingers and the pressure eased. I was thinking in slow motion and couldn't understand what was going on. I pushed deeper again and the pain I was feeling in my bollocks increased to white hot. Then the light bulb came on. I looked down and saw Probyn peering through my fingers, with the look of a Staffordshire bull terrier on his gnarled face. It was a proper Mexican stand-off. There could be no winner. We were both on a loser. The stakes were high but hands were even and so it ended. We released and played on. Thankfully, I went on to have four children and he can still read the newspaper each morning.

The game was a full-on humiliation and the brutal reality was that we were totally out-played. I think we only won three scrums all game. It was our worst defeat to England for over 30 years. We travelled to London with high hopes but it wasn't to be. What put the tin hat on it was when Will Carling danced round me late in the second half to score in the corner. Fair play to him, he would have got full marks on Strictly Come Dancing for the hip shimmy and the pirouette that left me grasping at thin air, on my knees, while seeing him prance to the white wash. To be thrashed 34-6 at Twickenham is too big an embarrassment for no action to be taken. It was a proper battering and seeing and hearing the English fans gloating and singing was something I never wanted to hear again. When asked, Paul Thorburn said that we were lucky to come second.

Fair play to the English, they were a great team. They were bigger, stronger, faster and more organised and should really have won the World Cup the following year, except they played into the Aussies' hands by trying to play an expansive game to please the crowd. I bet Carling still has nightmares about it.

John Ryan's tenure as Wales coach ended immediately, which was a shame. He was a top coach and a top fella. He was working towards a style that would have brought success, but time is something you don't have when coaching at the highest level, if results are poor.

Twickenham was an incredible place then, something from the Victorian era, with racing green picket fences and wooden duck boards. I could sense the history in the place as I walked through the gates. Very different to the next time I played there in 2010 for Ampthill RFC. They were being coached by Stuart Evans and he roped me in to play a few games that season including the final of the English Division Three play-offs against Jersey Rugby, who beat us that day, but it was special for me to be able to bow out playing at a major sporting arena like 'HQ'. Now aged 44, I played for 60 minutes before coming off, knackered but feeling self-assured that I had contributed to the team's efforts. It wasn't enough to win but I left the field knowing that a few people apart from just myself would certainly remember the final time I played at Twickenham.

So, with John Ryan gone, the national structure in disarray and players jumping ship to head north, Ron Waldon, the Neath coach, was asked to take over the reins.

A quick search on the internet reveals that Ron Waldron built a team of internationals at Neath from a band of nobodies. With all that success, he was appointed coach of Wales in 1990, but it was short lived because some players found his training methods too physical and he was forced to resign in 1991 – and people ask why Wales went through a slump in the early 1990s?

Although there had been a swift exodus of top players to rugby league, there were still some really good players in Wales. It was a shame, however, that a number of the seemingly entitled ones didn't see eye-to-eye with Ron. Nothing less than 100% commitment is required when aspiring to wear that red jersey. Playing for Wales in an honour, not a privilege.

When he was coaching Neath, Ron gave me a chance. I was just 19, and one of the kids he picked up and moulded. He threw me in at the deep end and I swam. A lot of boys went under. Ron knew what it took to succeed and demanded two things: we had to be fit and able to play how he wanted, that was the prerequisite. Lads would turn up and depart two sessions later with a single phrase ringing in their ears, 'Get fit!'. The players who had a wider skill set thought they were entitled and didn't need to go through all the hard graft. Some thought they would be treated a little differently. Not with Ron. He knew that if you dipped out at training, took an easy option, you would do the same in a game when things got tough. He knew they would go missing in action. Knew they would let their teammates down.

Neath was built on that, but it didn't sit right with the prima donnas at other clubs when he attempted to deploy the same principles with the Welsh squad. I find it a little ironic that the principles Ron wished to instil with Wales were identical to those demanded by Shaun Edwards when he coached the national team with Warren Gatland. Ron was just 25 years too early. Also, the exodus to league left repeated gaping holes in the squad and many of the players who were quickly drafted in to replace them weren't all up to the job at the time – for many it was simply too early in their playing career to step into the boots of a British Lion. A lot of them grew up quickly and matured into world class players, some did become better players than the ones they'd replaced, but that didn't help Ron.

He was blunt. He was a little left of centre, but his methods were years ahead of their time. He loved Scott Gibbs. He loved Allan Bateman. So, he was a good judge of a player and a good judge of character. He had a certain way of expressing his thoughts. He would put things in their simplest forms, 'steelworks speak' which often got lost on those from more genteel and sheltered backgrounds. 'Shit, or get off the pot,' being one of his favourite phrases.

At half-time in the Wales versus Barbarian game, we had all traipsed into the changing room. Ron was waiting. 'Right, where do I start?' he said. 'Jones – stop posing. Second rows – bloody do something. Props – first ten minutes, great, after that, gone to shit!' Which in Ron's language all meant, 'Boys, you need to get involved and do a bit more in the game.' That was Ron.

Earlier that summer he had taken a young Welsh squad on tour to Namibia. A tour in which we had been successful, winning all our six games. It was essentially a flag-waving, goodwill tour to forge links with that country and Ron had selected a squad to fit that criteria. Some players had opted to stay at home so it was a fairly new, unfashionable, squad with players like my good mate Steve Fealey and Alan Reynolds getting rewarded for their great club form. Both were gutsy, honest and hardworking. Exactly the qualities Ron admired. We trained hard, Jeremy Pugh had another bad case of jogger's nipple, but most of the players got through the punishing fitness regime.

Namibia was very rural. The only city was the capital Windhoek, and that was no bigger than Neath, so there were not many distractions for the players and we had to make our own fun. We travelled out to the Skeleton Coast, went on safari and experienced the charms of an old German colonial mining town. For the history buff, it was a fabulous trip but for most of the players it was hard work, socially. It's said that the devil makes work for idle hands and this was so true of this trip. Rowland Phillips and Steve Fealey, like two wicked twins, were always up to no good.

I took to reading, believe it or not, and was engrossed in James Herbert's novels. Namibia, or South West Africa as it was previously named by colonialists, was built by German settlers 100 years ago on the back of the wealth generated by diamond mining. When the diamonds became harder to find the rush eased and the Germans left, leaving the country to its own devices. The architecture of that period still remained, and looked amazing, but the décor was a bit dated! The electricity supply wasn't the best and the generator kept tripping out. This all added to the atmosphere of the novels I was reading, particularly *The Dark*.

On the eve of the first Test, we had the usual team meeting. The playing squad then retired to the team room for the evening to watch a film so Ron could keep his eye on the others, who had been taken to a reception evening with local dignitaries at the town hall. At about 10pm I'd had enough of Gremlins II so I went back to my room to read. Situated right at the end of the corridor, on the right-hand side, my room was next door to the wicked twins, Rowland and Steve. I settled down and was right into my book, which was about the dark engulfing places and devouring everything. It was a great book and the tension was rising. I was gripped. Then, all of a sudden, the lights went out. I was in total darkness, engrossed in a book about people being killed, by the dark! My heart bounced out of my chest.

I went cold. My mind started to panic. 'This is really happening. I'm going to die.' Regaining a semblance of composure and knowing who was next door I shouted, 'Rowland. Fealey. Stop messing about.' Silence. Then I then realised it couldn't be them because they couldn't get in the room. My panic returned. I leapt off the bed and looked out the window. All I saw was blackness. The town was black, not a light anywhere. My thoughts went straight to the book. 'Shit, the dark is coming.' I actually pinched myself to see if I was dreaming. No, I was awake. The story was true. I was a dead man, devoured by the dark. By now I'm seeing all sorts of shapes in the shadows. I was throwing my arms out in front of me like I was throwing punches. Then the lights start to flicker as the generators kicked-in. The room lit up and the lights of the town twinkled again. I was saved! I sat on the bed, relieved to be alive. I know now it sounds very dramatic but I guess you had to be there to feel the fear.

A few minutes later there was a knock on the door. 'Scooby. you awake?' I ran to the door. Steve and Rowland were outside. Still a bit hyper, I jumped into the corridor, naked, and began to offload my scary story to them. They were both pissing themselves laughing. I saw the funny side of it until I was about to go back in to my room and I heard a click behind me. Rowland the rat had nipped into his room closing the door but not until he had shut my door, locking me out. So, there I was stood in the corridor, bollock naked, apart from a pair of flip flops.

I could hear him and Steve laughing from behind their door. I shouted for them to give me a towel so I could go to reception and get a key. 'No chance' they replied. I pleaded about five times. Each time the laughter increased and the answers became increasingly unprintable. Where was Mayo Fealey when I needed her to come to my rescue? I was already a little wound up after the darkness incident and was getting more and more irate as the time went on. I was purple with rage. I asked one last time and then my internal switch was flicked.

Version One: I walked back up the corridor and turned to face the door. My head by now had totally gone. I had lost control. I crouched like a sprinter, heard the starting pistol and I raced down that corridor like a man possessed (which I was) launching myself at the door. Crraaaasssh! I went through like Jack Regan in the Sweeney, the door bouncing twice and hitting the back wall. I looked in and saw the look of 'what the ...?' written all over their faces.

Version Two: As I walked to the reception to get a key, concealing my modesty with a plant pot, when my flip flop got caught in the carpet and I tumbled towards the door. My shoulder made contact with the door and it gave way. Total accident.

Within 10 seconds the corridor was crawling with people and I was being interrogated by Ron and the WRU officials. I told them version two and that's the version I'm sticking to. Only Rowland and Steve could confirm something different.

It was a great tour, one that I'll remember for the rest of my life. We played two Tests in Namibia but didn't cover ourselves in glory. They were both quite close affairs. We won the first one 18-9 and the second one 34-30. Nowhere near good enough for us.

Ron tried to make the Neath way, the Welsh way, but it didn't work. We only won two games out of ten during his time. He also became ill during one of the worst tours in Welsh history to Australia, where we got hammered by the regions as well as the national team. Ron retired. By then, I too had left the nest of the valley's and flown north to the promised land.

When I first got called up to the Welsh squad, I hoped I was there for life and it would never end. It was an honour of a lifetime, even though we had some bad results. I loved the attention and I never wanted it to end. I was someone. I was 'Mark, the Wales international', not 'Mark the Stammerer'. Between matches I would pop over to Merthyr to see the Dowlais boys, and my mate Gary Morgan, who ran Buffalo's in the middle of the town. It wasn't a place for the faint hearted, or the boys in blue, but when I'd walk in, all I'd hear was, 'There he is, the best in the house,' being bellowed from Boucher the fruit and veg wholesaler who drank there. Who wouldn't enjoy that type of banter from my type of people?

My five years with Wales was like riding the Waltzers at the fair. You get in the carriage and they slam the bar down. You can see all the faces around you with flashing lights and hear the music blasting out of the speakers. The fair boy spins the car as the floor starts to rotate and your head snaps back against the padding on the inside of the carriage. That's how it starts. Then the car spins uncontrollably as the pace picks up. You can hear the music but all you see is a kaleidoscope of lights and a face or two perched on the barrier on the outside. All you can really recall is how tight you are gripping that bar and how your own body is coping with that nauseous feeling. You try to overcome the inertia and pull your head off the back of the seat and you can see individuals if you focus, but that doesn't last and your head snaps back again and you continue to spin around uncontrollably. That's how it is the first time you're picked, you're spinning, catching snapshots and just concentrating on what you've got to do to get through that ride.

As with everything, the more you do it, the better you cope, the more confident you feel, the more you can enjoy the experience, the more you take in and the more you remember. So, the collection of memories builds. Well, that's how it was for me. I enjoyed the ride but I knew it would stop, and when it did, I walked away slightly dizzy but a better person for it.

11

Working for the (Let Down)

'I'm assuming people who didn't know Mark assumed he was just an aggressive thug. But if they knew him, they would have found him to be a kind-hearted, gentle and compassionate man. Everyone I know loves the real Mark.'

Bryon Hayward

In the 1980s, all you got for playing for Wales was the honour, your cap (one cap only, no matter how many matches you played), your kit, a blazer, trousers and shirts. Maybe an Adidas bag of assorted kit at the end of each season. To me, and the others, that was enough. It was the privilege of playing for Wales which was my motivation.

There were always rumours flying about, like plates at a Greek wedding, that players sold their free tickets for prices way over the odds for some extra cash. Rumours of players car sharing and still claiming travelling expenses to and from training. There was even an instance when thieves got into the changing rooms and stole the wallets of the players. When the claims were put in for reimbursement, a number of the players allegedly were carrying large sums of cash in their wallets and expensive watches. Rumours that some people had their mortgages paid for them. Some reportedly had a share of the car park takings. I'm not sure how many of these rumours were true but I didn't see any of it!

The reward for my first game for Tredegar RFC back in 1983 was £1.25 expenses, and six beer tokens – and it was only Allbright bitter. The benefits had increased to £3.50 and six beer tokens by the time I was approached by Neath, who offered £4.75 and eight beer tokens. The £4.75 was a flat 'petrol money' benefit even though I was getting a taxi organised by the club. It wasn't about the money, it was kudos. There were other benefits that playing for Neath brought. For a boy from Tredegar, Neath, with its bright lights, nightclubs and pats on the back from admiring fans was more than enough

I started receiving invitations to attend presentations at rugby clubs, and other players were speaking at dinners – getting a bit of cash and lashed up for free. With my stammer I couldn't do the after-dinner speaking and I had anxiety attacks even doing the simplest club presentation night if I knew they wanted me to speak. I'd tell them beforehand that I wouldn't be saying anything. They must have thought I was a right diva. I hated it. I felt I was letting the clubs and their brilliant players down by refusing to speak. It was at that time that I began to realise that my stammer was a major issue. I loved the attention, but I hated being caught off-guard and having to speak to people off the cuff in the club or in the street. I had played for Wales. I was so proud, but inside I was fighting to keep up the 'Rugby Mark' persona I had created for myself.

Growing up, we are led to believe that getting a Welsh cap was the ultimate. It was the holy grail. Well, that's what my father instilled in me. It was the ultimate. He held Welsh international players in reverence. I inherited his adulation of all those who wore the red jersey of Wales. It was, and still is, an exclusive club and I wanted to be part of it. Getting a cap certainly opens doors for individuals off the field, and because the game was amateur, capped players received certain perks. Who can really blame then? No one was paid for playing but often opportunities of work were made available. Many capped players were given opportunities as company reps and salesmen and were allowed certain privileges such as paid leave when going on tour. After winning three or four caps, and not being considered a one-cap wonder, I started to get job offers from club sponsors.

After I was laid-off from the Ebbw Vale steel works I took a job in insurance for a year. I then trained as a financial advisor and, after passing my exams, was all set to sell their products through a brokerage in Tredegar. However, in my first six months I think I only sold two mortgages, and they were to friends. I knew deep down that I didn't have a hope in hell of it working out. I couldn't communicate well enough to sell drugs to an addict. Similar to when I was at school, I'd rehearse what I needed to say the night before. I'd stand in front of the mirror and visualise possible scenarios and situations until I was confident. Then, the next day, reality would kick back in.

'Hello. I'm M... M... M...' That's as far as I'd get before picking up my coat and leaving. How could I sell insurance? How could I represent a company? How could I create a good impression for a client when I couldn't even introduce myself? I couldn't communicate. I would have an introduction written down by the phone so if it rung, I could simply read off the piece of paper. I even found it hard to do that. I tried all sorts of ways to speak clearly and devise different tricks to bypass certain words or to get over the first letter block that all stammerers fear. My main escape word was 'it's'. I knew I could say it easily so 'it's' was inserted before any word I came across that was giving me a block: 'It's... I'm... it's... Mark. I'm representing ... it's... G...'

Even that didn't help me get past the first ten seconds with most people. Around 90% of the time they'd hang up, and my would heart sink every time I heard the 'click' as they ended the call. Some were kinder and said, 'I'm sorry Mark, it seems to be a bad line,' before putting the phone down.

My weakest link was what I now depended on for income. This nightmare scenario increased the pressure and deepened my anxiety. I was constantly on edge and my mind raced as I desperately searched for different words to help me string a coherent sentence together. On the plus side, it definitely expanded my vocabulary. I learnt 14 different words that can be used instead of 'philanthropist'! Annoyingly, though, I could only say about 4 of them out loud.

Like so many others who suffer the same affliction, I'd be thinking four or five words ahead while having a conversation. I was constantly planning what I was going to say next and trying to avoid the words which would cause the blocks. It was mentally exhausting.

Every day was a car crash in my head. I couldn't face work. I'd be sweating and on edge all the time. All this because I was trying to hide my stammer, trying to not let it be noticed. Constantly fighting it and determined not to let it win, but it was an unfair fight and I knew I had no chance of winning.

In the same way I'd built myself up before going to the shop on the way to school, thinking 'today is my day', I would convince myself I could beat the stammer, but outcome was always the same. Humiliatingly and without remorse, no matter how much I'd planned my spiel and carefully considered the words to lead with, the stammer would land the killer blow and knock the stuffing out of me.

If I was sat at home and the telephone rang, the fear and anxiety would kick-in immediately. I was, quite simply, terrified of such an ordinary thing that everyone else does without thinking. It's such a debilitating condition. Thank God for supermarkets. You just put groceries in a trolley, then load them on to a conveyor belt before sticking your card in a machine and typing your PIN without saying a word to anyone. They've saved me a hell of a lot of anguish and anxiety.

Those without stammers just can't imagine how it feels not being able to function in everyday life – in front of your spouse, in front of your kids. I would see a job advertised in the newspaper which really suited me, but how could I contact the company and sell myself over the phone. I clearly had some decent attributes as I was invited to be interviewed for most of the jobs I applied for, but that's where it all fell apart. Jobs that involved public interaction were a 'no-no' so I'd only apply for jobs that didn't involve any verbal communication.

I became a landscaper just so that I could avoid communicating with the rest of the world. Landscaping gave me the opportunity to escape. I'd talk to myself, the slabs and the fence posts. It was perfect. If I was feeling angry, I could shovel tons of chippings to purge myself to get rid of the anger and frustration. With no one else about, I was at peace. It was a strange kind of heaven. A million miles away from my usual state of purgatory.

Trying to get a proper job became a real issue when I failed in the insurance arena, then as a sales rep, and other white-collar jobs. This added to my frustration and so wrapped myself in my safety blanket, rugby, where I was known and respected. It was ok for my ego and enabled me to hide, and conceal my stammer, but it wasn't great for my bank balance. Then, out of the blue, a saviour appeared.

I met businessman Ray Griffiths through his son Damien who had been in the Wales B squad. Damien was a very fast winger who had been a sprinter and schooled at Millfield, one of the elite public schools in England that excelled in sport. He was earmarked for big things. Very quick, with great balance, he would have been a superstar now. He also had fantastic hair, straight out of a Duran Duran video, but in the late 1980s when the game could be gruesome, his talent didn't get the recognition it deserved.

Ray was a big pal of John Dawes, the Wales team manager, and I got involved with a sevens team he sponsored. To be truthful, Ray owned the team and dug deep into his own pockets, spending a lot of money and putting a lot of work in. I could tell he really had the players' wellbeing at heart and loved rugby. Ray was passionate about Welsh rugby and Welsh rugby players.

By then four or five of the Welsh squad had gone north. The floodgates had been opened, especially after Jiffy had signed for Widnes, and lots of the boys were selling their rugby skills to the highest bidders along the M62. No-one could really blame them.

Ray was passionate about keeping international players in Wales and had come up with a sponsorship scheme operated via his company, XELL – a computer and telecommunications business. Their contract offered a decent wage and a car, in return for which I would be used to promote the company when required. I would also be put on a training programme and continually monitored from a base in Cannon's gym in London, which I would be required to attend for testing at given dates and times. The contract could also be terminated by XELL if I did not comply with their requirements. It was an annual rolling contract, and if I was dropped from the Welsh squad I would have that season to regain my squad place or I'd lose the sponsorship deal.

This was an amazing opportunity and I almost pulled Ray's hand off when we shook on it. It was years ahead of its time. It would have put Welsh rugby back on the map and was definitely a forerunner to professionalism. I would have been a full-time sportsman but under another guise, which was no different to what players in the southern hemisphere had been doing for years.

It was shamateurism but I didn't give a toss. I was the first to sign. Next came Paul Thorburn and then Mark Ring. I was given a brand-new azure blue Sierra sapphire with my name and the company's branding on the side. When I pulled up outside mam's council house I felt like Billy Big Bollocks.

We all assumed that Ray had done his homework. That he had canvassed for like-minded individuals whose businesses were willing to become involved and invest an agreed amount to the fund and in return could use the player to represent them at functions, product launches and similar promotional activities. There must have been a positive response from the rugby-minded commercial world or Ray wouldn't have launched the programme.

The sponsorship contract was signed and it just felt too good to be true. I visited Cannon's gym four times using a pre-paid, first-class rail ticket from Cardiff and received one-to-one strength and conditioning coaching from a personal trainer, Dave Crotty. This was fantastic. I was totally pro but still amateur. I had no need to go north and play league. This was perfect. I was 24 and knew that as long I kept training hard and performing on the field I'll be secure for a few years. I started to dream of moving out of mam's box room, buying a house of my own and be a proper grown-up. What could go wrong?

On month five, my pay cheque didn't materialise. I rang Ray straightaway. 'There's been a clerical error,' he assured me, 'nothing to worry about.' He promised a new cheque would be sent asap. I rang Thorbie. He'd had the same issue.

A cheque duly arrived to my great relief. The clerical error explanation seemed to stack up, until it bounced. I was now suspicious and tamping mad. Paul and I travelled to London and had a face-to-face meeting with Ray. I could sense something wasn't right. He told us that things hadn't turned out how he had hoped. Supporters had reneged on their pledges and had left him high and dry. This news pierced my heart. I knew it wouldn't be so bad for Thorbie because he was well educated and could easily find a new job but this had really put a spanner in the works for me. Ray gave us a new cheque each and we headed back to Wales.

Paul tells a story in his after-dinner routine about how, for the first time ever, when we got off the train in Cardiff, I actually beat him in a race and got to the bank first and cashed the cheque. Part of that story was right. I did beat him to the bank, but for the second time the cheque bounced. Mark Ring had also been short-changed. I knew it was the end.

Someone contacted the press – it wasn't me – and they went looking for Ray. I think a Welsh TV programme, possibly HTV Wales' *The Ferret*, ran with the story and tracked him down. We all gave interviews for the programme and, of course, mine was a utter car crash. I only gave one-word answers and couldn't express my true feelings. The programme painted Ray in a bad light but he was trying to do the right thing – halting the exodus to league and investing in the players.

The WRU didn't have a clue how to stop their best players from going north, and didn't seem to care. At least Ray tried, and if the support he'd been promised had been delivered, the scheme would have been successful. In England, there were millionaires linked to many rugby clubs who used various methods to support their players financially. Not many English players went to league during that period but in Wales it was an exodus that ripped the heart out of our national team.

Wales had its millionaires and benefactors but there weren't as many of them as over the border, and the amounts ploughed in struggled to keep pace with the sugar daddies in England. Cardiff had Peter Thomas, and Tony Brown later pumped millions into Newport, but that was about it. Rugby may have been an amateur game, officially, but all sorts of behind-the-scenes shenanigans were going on back then and many blind eyes were being turned. It was, though, very piecemeal, disjointed and club-orientated. Ray was the first to try and centralise in order to support the national team. It was a great idea but I don't know if it would have complied with the strict amateur code of the time.

All I can say is a big thanks to Ray for attempting to bring an amateur game into the 20th century. It was ground breaking and visionary. I had received the full hospitality of Ray's family at his home and am grateful for that. As I said, Ray took a proper kicking off the press and it also affected his family greatly. I just regret that I didn't and couldn't fight his corner. I should have spoken up when interviewed. This has been with me for over 30 years. I don't know if Ray is still alive or if any of his family will ever read this, but I just want to say thanks – you were a real visionary and a top guy.

12

Looking After Number (8)

'Mark is a unique character and was a unique rugby player. Often misunderstood, he was one hell of a tough old cookie on the field, but a true gentleman and good family man off it.'

Stuart Evans

Stuart Evans joined Neath during my first season at the Gnoll and I soon latched onto him, both on and off the field. As wide as he was tall, Stu was a big boy and loved throwing his weight – and opposition players – about. He was Neath's 'enforcer', a role he also ably fulfilled for the national side and I saw myself as his apprentice.

In 1987, Stu signed for St. Helen's and went north to play rugby league. It was a shock to everyone, including me. We kept in touch, though, and would always meet up for a pint and a chat when he popped home to visit his family. The conversations would obviously include his experiences of life in the north of England and his new career in league. One weekend, Neath played Sale away and after our game in Manchester we made a detour to Merseyside to watch Stu play at Knowsley Road, the home of St. Helens.

We were very impressed. The set up was amazing, the atmosphere was electric and the fans were proper working-class people, down to earth and full of passion. Hairs stood up on the back of my neck while watching it all. It was like Neath but on a much bigger scale. After the game, Stu came to find me and said the chairman, Joe Pickavance, would like a word. By then I'd had a beer or two, so I walked into the board room with a bit of a swagger, but that was just to hide my nerves – firstly, talking to a rugby league chairman was forbidden and secondly, I'd have to control my stammer and talk to someone I didn't know, which got my heart racing. We went through all the polite chit-chat and then got down to business. He told me Stu

IF THE Welsh back row play at Murrayfield a week tomorrow like a Neath back row at the Gnoll, Scotland's rating as favourites is going to look rather overvalued.

That, of course, is the opinion of Neath supporters and a view that has a great deal of support from other parts of Wales.

So the announcement yesterday that there will be one of that renowned Neath trio winning his first cap at Scottish HQ will be welcomed warmly in all quarters.

Mark Jones, the 21-year-old No 8, is the man called up to take the place of the injured Phil Davies, and the choice is a popular one. The former Glanhowy Youth starlet has grown to manhood in a magnificent Neath pack after an invaluable apprenticeship with Tredegar.

The ultimate polish has not yet been applied, of course, because there is still a long way for such a young player to go; but Mark has matured sensationally alongside such back row stalwarts as Phil Pugh, Dai Morgan and Lyn Jones in Neath colours.

Murrayfield, 21 March 1987: my first senor cap, against Scotland. It was a tough introduction to international rugby and we were beaten 21-15 by the better team.

Losing is never a good feeling, but we didn't give in and five minutes into injury time at the end of the match I managed to score a try, thanks to a pass from Robert Jones. 'The big lad from Neath is simply overjoyed' said Bill McLaren in his commentary. How right he was.

I always gave everything for Wales, and sometimes I gave a little bit more! In 1989 I gave England's great back row forward, Mike Teague, a very warm welcome to Wales. It was the first time I'd played against the English at a senior level and had been told in no uncertain terms that nullifying Mike's power was my responsibility. The kick off went straight to him and I charged towards Mike with everything I had. His match ended after just eight seconds. We met years later and my overly robust challenge was long forgotten. He was a great player and is a lovely guy.

Wales Red Jerseys, White Shorts		Scotland Blue Jerseys, White Shorts	
15	**P.H. Thorburn** Neath	15	**A.G. Hastings** London Scottish
14	**M.R. Hall** Cardiff	14	**A.G. Stanger** Hawick
13	**M.G. Ring** Cardiff	13	**S. Hastings** Watsonians
12†	**A.G. Bateman** Neath	12	**S.R.P. Lineen** Boroughmuir
11	**A. Emyr** Swansea	11	**I. Tukalo** Selkirk
10	**D.W. Evans** Cardiff	10	**C.M. Chalmers** Melrose
9	**R.N. Jones (captain)** Swansea	9	**G. Armstrong** Jed-Forest
1†	**B.R. Williams** Neath	1	**D.M.B. Sole (captain)** Edinburgh Academicals
2	**K.H. Phillips** Neath	2	**K.S. Milne** Heriot's FP
3	**J.D. Pugh** Neath	3	**A.P. Burnell** London Scottish
4	**P.T. Davies** Llanelli	4	**C.A. Gray** Nottingham
5	**G.O. Llewellyn** Neath	5	**D.R. Cronin** Bath
6†	**M.A. Perego** Llanelli	6	**J. Jeffrey** Kelso
8	**M.A. Jones** Neath	8	**D.B. White** London Scottish
7	**R.G. Collins** Cardiff	7	**F. Calder** Stewart's-Melville FP
	Replacements		Replacements
16	**S.P. Ford** (Cardiff)	16	**P.W. Dods** (Gala)
17	**A. Clement** (Swansea)	17	**D.S. Wyllie** (Stewart's Melville FP)
18	**C. Bridges** (Neath)	18	**G.H. Oliver** (Hawick)
19	**H. Williams-Jones** (South Wales Police)	19	**D.J. Turnbull** (Hawick)
20	**I.J. Watkins** (Cardiff)	20	**A.K. Brewster** (Stewart's Melville FP)
21	**R. Phillips** (Neath)	21	**J. Allan** (Edinburgh Academicals)

Class show from Mark

By ANDREW BALDOCK

MADE in Tredegar, moulded by Neath, Mark Jones was unveiled as a back row forward of the highest calibre on his home international debut.

The 23-year-old No. 8 stood head and shoulders above a Welsh pack that battled hard in all phases but struggled particularly in the line-outs, losing the count 25-11.

His 66th minute try, Jones' second in four internationals, was the highlight of a storming display made distinctly memorable by two storming first-half runs into the heart of Irish territory.

"It was really enjoyable," said Jones.

"We had them on the rack for 60 minutes, but one or two mistakes were made and they cost us the game," he added.

The Welsh back row, under severe pressure following last month's Murrayfield defeat, at least answered some of their critics, but only Jones maintained a consistently high level of performance.

Rowland Phillips and David Bryant had their moments, although both were exposed for lack of pace, and not once did Bryant manage to disrupt Paul Dean's fluency.

Phillips gave Jones his scoring pass, and that injury-time flick to Carwyn Davies almost found the Llanelli winger's hands.

But he was anonymous for too long, and Bryant's pace, for an open side flanker, was exposed when Noel Mannion raced along the South Stand touchline for a memorable try.

Bryant was though in evidence as a good pack leader, and while this was an improved performance by the back three, it could be that Phillips will have to go.

Jones' pace and hunger for the game would perhaps be more suited to open side flanker, where he could get out into midfield and cause havoc of which he is more than capable.

Llanelli captain Phil Davies could be switched to No. 8, allowing a fit again Robert Norster to return alongside Kevin Moseley in the second row.

"It's going to be tough in France in two weeks' time," said Jones. "The forwards will need to get it together, and try and cut out mistakes.

"Personally I will take it one game at a time, but I enjoyed it on Saturday and was quite happy with my performance," he added. If Jones continues to reproduce that sort of form in Wales' two remaining games, a British Lions' place Down Under must be a possibility.

After a decent debut in 1987, and playing well for Neath, I didn't win another cap until being called up as a replacement on the 1988 tour of New Zealand. By the 1989 Five Nations championship I was back in favour and played every game that season. The emotional rush I felt when the anthem was being sung is something I'll never forget. What an experience, and what an honour.

The Committee of the
Welsh Rugby Union
has pleasure in informing

that he has been selected to play for
Wales against Ireland
on Saturday, 4th February 1989.

Secretary

Back then, the players received a note in the post informing us of our selection. Mine are treasured possessions. That Ireland game in Cardiff in 1989 was extra special as I scored my second and final try for Wales, and the only one I scored in Cardiff.

That summer I toured Canada with Wales B, where I was sent off in the game against Canada XV. I've done some questionable things in my career but that was a never a sending off! Even Gerald Davies, commentating on the match for HTV Wales called it 'An unfair decision'. We won 31-29.

Psyching myself up before the Wales v Scotland match in March 1990. Not only was I in my pre-match 'Rugby Mark' zone, I was about to shake hands with Princess Anne. As a stammerer, speaking to a stranger was almost impossible so my mental state at that moment is captured in this photo.

My final game for Wales in Cardiff, against the Baa Baas in October 1990, just days before I signed for Hull. After barely two minutes, I took out the brilliant French winger Dennis Charvet and was called over to the ref, Fred Howard. My belief was that no one got sent off in the first 10 minutes, and that was proved correct, yet again

ALEX MURPHY is poised to make an astonishing £½m raid on Welsh talent — with Mark Jones and Tony Clement his prime targets.

The manager of big-spending St Helens last night issued the chilling warning that the Saints have the ready cash to further deplete the stock of leading Union players.

"We are set to start recruiting very strongly and St Helens have no problems as far as money is concerned," he told me.

"We would love to sign Mark, a player I haven't hidden my feelings about, as I have long been an admirer of his play.

"He would be ideal for Rugby League and, I believe, a better signing than Paul Moriarty.

"I have watched Paul when the chips are down and, although he might do very well for Widnes, I rate Mark ahead of him as far as their potential is concerned.

Official confirmation of another St Helens raid — they already have Stuart Evans and Mike Carrington on their books — comes just a day after Widnes announced they were satisfied with their Welsh purchases.

On January 5 they swooped to sign Jonathan Davies in a record £200,000 deal and then last week came back to snap up Moriarty in another six-figure package.

That means in the last eight months various League clubs have splashed out over £½m on Welsh players, David Bishop joining Hull Kingston Rovers last July and Salford snapping up Adrian Hadley in September.

Now ambitious St Helens are threatening to match that spending spree in the space of weeks rather than months.

NEATH RUGBY FOOTBALL CLUB

President: County Councillor MARTIN THOMAS, O.B.E., O.St.J., J.P., D.L.
Chairman: Mr. R. TRIMNELL

Hon. Fixture Secretary:	Hon. Treasurer:	Hon. Secretary:
BERWYN DAVIES	JOHN PRICHARD	ALLAN BENJAMIN
20 Clifton Street,	8 Henfaes Road,	24 The Pines,
Aberdare.	Tonna, Neath.	Penscynor,
Tel. Aberdare 876857	Tel. Neath 635471	Neath, SA10 8AL.
		Tel. Neath 642172

11th Oct 9

Dear Mark,

Herewith your P45 which you will no doubt require. I'm sorry that you are leaving but wish you every success in your new career. I'm sure you'll end up as one of the Stars of the League Game. Your "favourite uncle" will certainly miss your winning smile!

All the very best to you.

Kindest Regards.

John

After much speculation, and a lot of interest from several clubs, a new career in rugby league awaited when I signed for Hull in October 1990.

Neath were brilliant about me 'going north'. I have nothing but huge admiration for the way they treated me.

HULL 30, FEATHERSTONE 14

MARK JONES blasted his way into the Rugby League limelight when he turned on an awesome display of power as Hull FC made it five League wins out their last six matches.

The former Welsh Rugby Union international put aside the horrors of last season's injury ridden nightmare and shot himself into prominence with a performance which could easily have rated 10 on the Richter scale.

Poor Featherstone were sent reeling as the massive 6ft 7in Jones punched holes in their defence with frightening regularity.

He had them clinging on for dear life and twice, in a ferocious final 20 minutes, he almost broke his senior duck by scoring, but was thwarted by four and five man tackles.

Jones' performance was the highlight of a magnificent display by Hull, who after a poor start to the season, are now beginning to click into top gear.

Injuries hampered my first season with Hull, but as soon as I returned to fitness, I gave 100% to prove myself at Hull and to repay their faith in me.

I played 68 times for Hull before moving to Warrington in 1995. I was so fortunate to have played for two such renowned clubs. League is a tough old game but I enjoyed it, and the fans were brilliant.

So many former teammates had also switched to rugby league, the Wales RL team was very strong. That team, managed so well by 'Big' Jim Mills, played some brilliant rugby and reached the semi-finals of the 1995 RL World Cup. Playing at Old Trafford in front of 30,000 fans was a terrific experience but we lost 25-10 to England.

Wales

Red, Green and White Jersey
Manager **JIM MILLS**
Coach: **CLIVE GRIFFITHS**

PHIL FORD (Leeds)

JOHN DEVEREUX (Widnes)
ALLAN BATEMAN (Warrington)
JONATHAN DAVIES (Widnes) Capt.
ANTHONY SULLIVAN (St. Helens)

JONATHAN GRIFFITHS (St. Helens)
KEVIN ELLIS (Warrington)

MARK JONES (Hull)
BARRY WILLIAMS (Carlisle)
DAVID YOUNG (Salford)
ROB ACKERMAN (Carlisle)
IAN MARLOW (Hull)
DAVID BISHOP (Hull K.R.)

ADRIAN HADLEY (Salford)
ROWLAND PHILLIPS (Warrington)
GERALD CORDLE (Bradford N.)
GARY PEARCE (Ryedale-York)

I never played in the Rugby World Cup, and was overlooked for the British Lions tour in 1989, so to be selected for the Great Britain RL team in 1992 was a great honour. Named as a replacement, I played for the final ten minutes and made a good impression. The fusion of experienced RL players from England and the former RU players like John Devereux, Allan Bateman and, of course, Jonathan 'Jiffy' Davies made GB a formidable team.

Jones gets good Mark in the Test

POWERHOUSE Welsh forward Mark Jones, a surprise choice for Great Britain against France, did *his* prospects of a summer tour of Australia no harm in Perpignan last week.

Jones, the former Neath and Wales union player, only rose from the subs bench 10 minutes from the end of the Test — but had time to scatter tacklers in one bulldozing charge and made "hard yards", driving the ball forward, on two or three other occasions.

And later Britain's coach Mal Reilly told Up North: "I like Jones's attitude and temperament and he has tremendous spirit.

Following rugby union's decision to allow professionalism, it didn't take long for me to return to Wales, joining Ebbw Vale in 1997. Led by the inspirational Russell brothers, Marcus and Paul, The Steelmen had a great set up and I spent five good years at Eugene Cross Park, playing over 100 matches, scoring 14 tries and captaining the club before moving to Pontypool whose charity work raised a few eyebrows!

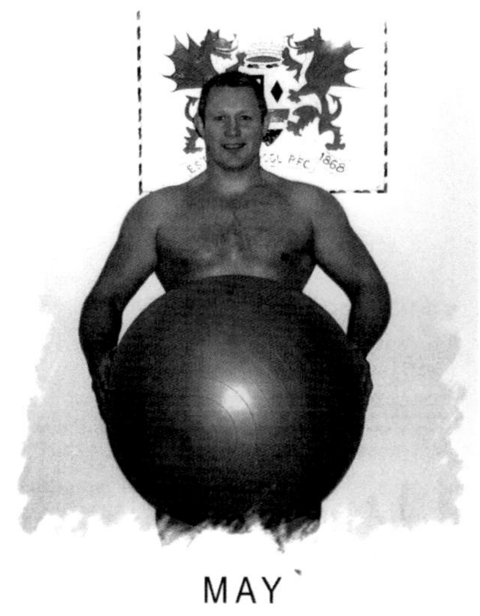

RUGBY UNION: WRU advised to think again

Jones delight as High Court judge lifts ban

Legal history was made in February 1997 when I successfully challenged the Welsh Rugby Union's handling of a disciplinary procedure after I'd been sent off for punching (my mate) Stuart Evans when playing for Ebbw Vale against Swansea. I've never tried to excuse what I did – it was totally wrong – but the actions of the WRU broke the law and all rugby governing bodies were forced to rethink and rewrite their disciplinary procedures.

Pooler's benefactor, Bob Jude, played a major in my decision to join the club as a player / coach. Not only did he offer me employment in his flooring company, but he was also responsible for helping to finance a speech therapy course which totally changed my life. I played 48 games for Pontypool, between 2002 and 2004 before being reunited with Neath for the 2004-05 season, and finishing my first-class rugby career with a season with Aberavon, and a summer with the local RL team the Aberavon Fighting Irish.

Although now retired from rugby, I still enjoy being involved with the game (and yes, lending a hand as referee now and again!), from the Alkhor (holics) team in Qatar, where I now live, to meeting up with former teammates such as Leigh Davies, Geraint Evans and Allan Bateman – along with fellow Celts, Ireland's David Corkery and Scotland's Derrick Lee – at occasions like the Lions tour to Australia in 2013. There is one thing I'll never do again, however, and that is boxing – even if I'm told it's for charity. Those three two-minute rounds in New Zealand in 2005 were terrifying!

Meeting Julia changed my life and I can't thank her enough for the love and support she has given me. I treasure our two girls, Izzy and Zara, and my two grown up children Osian and Manon – the four of them mean the world to me. My sister, Sandra, my Godfather, Arthur, and Julia's parents Pat and Malcolm, have all been so kind and generous. I love them all dearly.

For the majority of my life I've been anxious and angry because of my stammer, but the self-loathing that led to the frustration-fuelled on-field violence is well and truly behind me. I'm proud of what I achieved playing rugby yet openly acknowledge that my behaviour was, at times, unacceptable. The demons that dominated my life have been banished and I'm a happy, relaxed and positive person, determined to enjoy life with my wonderful family and friends. My stammer used to control me, but I've now learnt to control my stammer, which has been life-changing

had recommended me and they had sent scouts to watch me play. He then added that they liked what they saw and wanted to speak to me about a move north. A few weeks previously, a guy had approached me after a game at the Gnoll and asked whether I was interested in playing league, but I didn't realise he was a scout.

I was enjoying another win with Neath and looking forward to the post-match festivities so I brushed it off and thought nothing of it. This was different. I was standing in the boardroom of one of the most famous rugby league sides in the world. I was very flattered to say the least. St. Helens? Wow! I'd watched them win the Challenge Cup final many times on the TV when I was growing up. What a club! What an opportunity!

An offer to turn professional sounded great, and it was a real honour to be approached such a famous club, but my union career was really taking off. I was playing well for Neath and we were head and shoulders above the rest. Also, 'Buck' Ryan had taken over as Welsh coach and had given me the chance to claim the number eight jersey. It was the opportunity I'd been waiting for after warming the bench so often. My club were dominant and I was now a regular in the national team. All going great for me in God's own country.

Yet St. Helens were genuine about their interest. They asked me to pay a visit the following week to talk seriously. I agreed and a meeting was arranged. I shook hands then I returned to the Neath boys who were still down in the bar. When they asked where I'd been, I just said I'd gone for a quick beer with Stu in another part of the ground.

When I got back to Tredegar and spoke to mam and dad, telling them what had happened, they were proud but apprehensive. I got bombarded with a load of questions and reminded that if I went, there would be no coming back to rugby union. That I would be shunned and blacklisted, by Welsh rugby and many rugby supporters – I'd be regarded as a traitor who had betrayed rugby, and Wales. It all changed a few years later but at that time that is exactly what happened to union players who went north.

However, I'd agreed and was determined to go back to St. Helen's and hear what they had to offer. There was a certain draw about rugby league, a certain glamour. Going north was a dark taboo subject in Wales but I knew it would secure my place in an elite group of players who had played both codes. That was exciting. I made arrangements to travel up with a solicitor friend of a guy who ran the insurance brokerage I was working for. The plan was he would look over the contract for me and check the small print.

On the journey to St. Helen's we discussed different scenarios and how much I would be prepared to sign for. I knew I'd have to pay the solicitor for his advice – this wasn't a freebie – and I was also told that the brokerage was considering a change to my salary, probably due to my lack of success selling their financial products.

We arrived at Knowsley Road. It was a bit different on a wet Wednesday morning. Cold, damp and no fans, but it was still an imposing place. We were met by the lady in the reception and shown to the board room. The empty ground looked quite bleak, but you could still sense the atmosphere and the club's impressive heritage. It oozed tradition, history and success. I felt upbeat and was eager to sign. We first spoke to the chairman and I was given the full tour, including the accommodation they'd arranged for the first 12 weeks until I got a place of my own. It was in a flat above a pub. That would do for me I thought.

Then when we got back to the ground where we met Alex Murphy, the coach. He was the typical old school rugby league man. No nonsense, and as straight as an arrow. If you wanted warmth, you wouldn't get it from Murph. If you wanted reassurance, he'd be the last person to go to, as I later found out. I was a little out of my comfort zone. My personality needed a bit of warmth, someone to boost my confidence – wrap an arm around me and give me a cwtch. It was a massive move for me and I felt apprehensive. I was physically strong but, emotionally, I was fragile.

We went back in the board room where we started talking numbers. I was offered £120,000 for a four-year contract. It blew my mind. Playing rugby for £30,000 a year, plus a win bonus, plus an international bonus. That was more money than I could dream of. I simply couldn't believe I'd be getting paid such an enormous amount and have the chance to wear the St. Helen's shirt, in front of those passionate fans.

Yet, there was no real love in the room, it was all very matter of fact. No warmth, just business. I must have been in the board room for about two hours, discussing, thinking, and mulling things over. In the end I made an excuse that we needed to read the small print of the contract and I would return to sign.

I never did. I regret that. If I had manned up, taken the bull by the horns, accepted the challenge and gone for it, who knows what would have happened. I turned my back on a lucrative new challenge because I couldn't face leaving my comfort zone. St. Helen's hadn't done anything wrong. It was an honour to be approached. I think I lacked the vision and maturity to see the potential of what was on offer. I'd stupidly let a golden opportunity slip. Would I ever get a second chance?

Later that year, I met with Brian Smith, the coach of Hull FC in a pub in Tonna, a village in the Neath valley. He had come to Wales to sign a player to give his team a boost. I think Glenn Webb was the first name on his list. When that didn't come off, Brian called me about 11am on a Saturday morning. Neath weren't playing that day, and had scheduled a training session for 12 noon. The afternoon was mine. Me and Glyn Llewellyn had arranged to head out for a few drinks, but after training I told him we were popping up the valley to Tonna for 30 minutes, saying I'd arranged to meet Brian at 2.30pm. We got there and ordered a pint.

The Hull contingent walked in and I immediately realised that maybe this wasn't an ideal meeting place. A Neath player was meeting a delegation from a rugby league team, in a Neath valley pub on a Saturday afternoon – what was I thinking! This was a big deal for me but I really hadn't given the situation enough thought, or respect. After a short panic, we found a table in a quiet corner.

Hull offered me a potential £200,000 deal which would have changed my life forever. It didn't come off, but we parted on good terms. Brian was warm and full of love. He totally sold the club to me and made me feel wanted. My lack of confidence and vision, plus the fact that Neath were still looking after me, saw me turn down another amazing opportunity.

The previous season I'd been the first player to be sinbinned in a cup final and labelled a thug by the media. The attacks continued that season but I did nothing to quell the fury. In fact, I played up to it. Part of me enjoyed the notoriety and the calls for me to be banned. That was when I really began to realise I had anger issues. I was increasingly volatile, and found it almost impossible to control my on-field behaviour. The clamour in the papers for action to be taken grew and I knew I could be banned for a long time. Instead of tackling the root cause of my anger issues and focusing on my skills, I thought the best course of action was to escape the cauldron of south Wales. My inability to hold down a decent job and support myself financially was also playing heavily on my mind.

I had been approached by other Welsh clubs that had offered attractive financial incentives, but I was never going to leave Neath because they treated me so well and the team was successful. It was now obvious, however, that rugby league could be my personal and financial salvation. Allan Bateman and Rowland Phillips had both been signed by Warrington as had Kevin Ellis, so I wouldn't have minded joining up with them, but that didn't come off. Then another offer came in from Brian at Hull. I leapt at it. Wales were playing the Baa Baa's in October so I set a date to play that game and leave to sign for Hull the next day.

I hoped to go out with a bang. It didn't really happen. I got penalised in the first few minutes for a late shot on the brilliant French winger, Denis Charvet, and I played okay in a side that lost. That was it for me. The next day I packed a bag and headed off to Hull, via Warrington, where we watched the Welsh boys play on the Sunday, before travelling to Hull. Another new chapter was about to begin.

13

Highway to (Hull)

'Never mind Scooby. Mark was a cross between a Rotwellier and Lassie. On the field, he would chew you half to death. Off it, he would go out of his way to help. I can't speak highly enough of the big man. He brought so much to the team.'

Clive Griffiths

On Monday 8 October 1990 I joined many of my Welsh compatriots and went north. In the weeks before I signed for Hull my dad had been under medical supervision and was on the waiting list to see a specialist. During that time we discussed my likely defection and I told him the way I was playing for Neath kept getting me in trouble. Each game I was half-expecting to get sent off, and receive a ban. It wasn't sustainable. I knew it was only a matter of time until I got in serious trouble. So, he knew I was going. End of discussion.

'Another one gone, mass exodus' read the newspaper headlines. My decision to join Hull was a big event in Wales.

My first experience of rugby league came on a Friday night at the Boulevard, Hull's home ground, when I was selected for the club's A (reserve) team. It was a bit alien to say the least but I did okay. The coach and the lads gave me some useful post-match advice and I felt I was beginning to get a handle on the niceties of league. I needed to. I'd been told I'd have a few minutes in the senior team that Sunday.

Relieved to have completed my first game I grabbed my bag and headed back to my digs for the night. On the way I decided to stop for a pint on the city's Hessle Road and get to know that part of Hull. I parked the car, a big, black Renault 25 with power suspension, and because I only wanted a swift pint, I left my kit bag and £200 new leather jacket on the back seat. Ordering pints was tricky with my stammer so I went in and pointed to the beer pump. As the barmaid pulled my pint, I realised that all the eyes in the pub had focused on this big stranger. That made me feel good. Small talk and a few words with the locals was impossible for me so, after a few minutes, I finished my pint and left. I must have only been in there for ten minutes. As I approached the car, I could see the rear window was open. 'Bollocks,' I thought. I must have hit a button when getting out and dropped the electric window. I needed to be careful of that next time. Then the twinkling of broken glass caught my eye.

What the hell! Some little scumbag had done my car. I peered in through the smashed window to see nothing except broken glass. No jacket, no bag, nothing. The lot had gone including my new boots, gumshield, pink jockstrap, everything. I was gutted.

The next day I went to training a bit pissed off. We ran through a few things and at the end I was doing some footwork drills, stepping left and right to evade the big hit. As I stepped off my right onto my left, then tried to come back my ankle gave way and I collapsed in excruciating pain. I had I ruptured my ankle ligaments. It felt like a red-hot iron bar had gone through my ankle. What a start, robbed and crocked all within 24 hours. Welcome to Hull, or was it Hell!

Recovering from my injury, finding a place to live in a new city and dealing with the robbery, I become engrossed in my own issues and my dad's illness was put on the back burner. That didn't last long. A week later, Mam phoned me. I knew when I picked up the phone and heard her voice that it wasn't going to be good news. 'Mark, your dads got brain cancer. He's going to have an operation.'

I froze, not knowing what to think or say. How can you prepare yourself for something like that? Even though he was unassuming, he was a tough 5'10 Welsh miner who'd worked at the coal face for 40 years. He had numerous 'blue scars' (cuts on the face or hands where coal dust had infected the wound) and a couple of crushed fingers, but would take pride in saying he'd hardly missed a day's work.

I rushed back home to see him at Llandough hospital, just outside Cardiff, limping into the ward to see my dad, sitting up in bed with a heavily bandaged head and tubes everywhere. He was a bit dazed but tried to put a positive slant on things. At least he was talking, although he couldn't find certain words. It seemed as if there was a bit of him missing. I spoke to mam and Sandra later who said the operation had been successful and they had removed the cancer. 'It's just a matter of wait and see,' my sister said, tears rolling down her cheeks.

I went back to Hull and carried on with my rehab with the aim of getting fit enough to start in early December. With the daily physio and gym sessions, I put all I had into getting back on the field. Johnny Whitley, a rugby league legend, who owned a club round the corner from the Boulevard took me under his wing. He let me use his gym and personally treated my ankle to get me back on the field. It worked. After about six weeks I was ready for another run in the A team. I knew my ankle wasn't perfect but the pain was manageable and I thought I needed to repay the club so I got out there. The first game back went well, and I played again the next week with an aim to make the match day squad for the senior team the following Sunday. All was good until ten minutes before the final whistle when some little half back was hanging onto my leg as I was carrying the ball and he decided to crocodile roll my ankle.

A white-hot pain shot through my lower leg and I collapsed again – out for another 12 weeks. Holy shit! what a great start to my league career. It was going from bad to worse.

During all this my father was still in hospital, working towards a coming home date and a few more years of him potching about in his garden. This is how I pictured the scenario in my mind. I was oblivious to the truth. Mam and Sandra had kept me in the dark about it being a lot more serious than I had thought.

It only really hit me when I went home for Christmas and saw my dad again. I knew then it was only a matter of time. I just tried to act as if everything was normal, but the knowledge of my father true condition was always in my head. Back in Hull, I got straight back to rehab – wearing an inflatable boot for most of the time. There were also twice-weekly sessions in a hyperbaric chamber which enriched my blood with oxygen and enabled me to heal quicker. The physio 'Cheggars' was superb and treated me well. He saw more of me than his wife.

The boot came off by mid- January and I started jogging again. After a series of x-rays and scans, the news came through that I had a Lisfranc (foot) injury and was lucky not to require surgery. This diagnosis gave my plight some credence and reduced any sceptical thoughts among the Hull fans about me having a genuine injury. It was serious, but just bad luck.

Phone calls to my parents became more frequent than previously as I checked on both of them. Then, one evening in January about 8 pm, I had the dreaded phone call. There were no mobile phones back then, and there was a message for me to ring home on the answering machine. My heart was thumping and I was instantly drenched in sweat. I dialed my parents' number.

'Mark, you need to come home quick, dad has taken a turn.'

'Mam, I'm coming,' was all I could muster.

I was in Hull, though, a four-hour drive away from Cefn Golau. I threw some clothes in a bag and rang 'Crusher' Cleal, Hull's coach, to explain what was going on. A combination of my stutter and my heightened emotional state was probably impossible to decipher but he got the gist that my father was at death's door. Crusher fully understood, told me not to worry and to get home safely. At that I jumped in the car and headed back to Tredegar.

It was mid-January and the east coast of England was freezing. Storms from the North Sea had brought Siberian weather to East Yorkshire. Within minutes the road was two inches deep in freezing rain, with me bombing down the motorway at 90mph. It was time to slow down a bit. I touched the brakes and I could hear the tyres crunching the fresh ice on the road. The speedometer began to fall back but this was still too fast. I applied the brakes again and the car slowed further, until the tyres caught in a rut of ice and with a violent jolt the car began to spin and I lost my grip of the steering wheel. Now total out of control, the car slid around the dual carriageway and came to a stop facing the wrong way, back to Hull. Luckily there were no other vehicles around or mam would shortly have been burying the father and son.

I gingerly turned the car back around before any traffic appeared and continued my journey – hazard lights on and relieved to be alive. It took around an hour for me to fully regain my composure and for my body to stop shaking. Arriving back at my parents' house around 1am I noticed that lights were on. 'Mam! Mam!' I shouted as I hurriedly let myself in. The place was silent, so I steadied myself and walked in the living room. Mam, sitting motionless in the chair, just looked at me. 'He's gone Mark, he's gone,' she whispered. 'He went this afternoon. I couldn't tell you on the phone before you left. I just couldn't.'

I knelt next to her and gave her a massive cwtch, both of us crying. I plucked up courage and slowly walked up the stairs, my legs shaking with emotion. The bedroom door was closed. I didn't know if I could go in. I slowly pushed it open, half expecting to hear his booming voice saying, 'Is that you boy?' There was no voice, just an eerie silence, and the dim glow of the bedside lamp that cast shadows around the small bedroom. Then, on seeing a sheet covering my father from head to toe, I froze. I couldn't believe it. I didn't want to believe it but there he was. I sat on the side of the bed and started to talk to him.

'Dad, I'm sorry I didn't get back in time. Mam's okay. I'll take care of her, don't worry. If I'm not here, Sandra will be. Mam will be fine.'

My memories of that moment and what else I said to my father are very hazy, but I knew I had to see him, so reached over and pulled the sheet off his face. I had never seen a dead body before. His face was pale and he had an indentation in his head where they had operated. His eyes were closed. He looked like he was sleeping. I looked at him for what seemed like ages, then with tears falling down my cheeks I leant over and kissed him, and whispered, 'Dad, I love you.' I touched his face as my tears fell onto his skin. He was cold. It was the first time I had ever kissed him and told him I loved him. I should have done it sooner. I should done it often. I should have kissed him until my lips were sore. I should have told him I loved him until my throat was hoarse.

Over the years I'd felt a bit of resentment towards my dad. Disappointed that, in my view, he hadn't watched me play often enough, or followed my career close enough, I assumed that Sandra was his favourite. Now I'm older and have kids myself, I realise that was all utter nonsense. Dad couldn't travel to watch me because mam wasn't well enough. He didn't drive and was too proud to ask for lifts. He also told me he didn't want to live off my reputation and be known as Mark Jones' father. He was his own man. He didn't want to be a 'hanger on'. I realise now that all the little things that hurt or frustrated me were things that were out of his control. He never did anything deliberately or without care. Stupidly, and immaturely, I blamed my father for dying and leaving us to pick up the pieces. How stupid of me? I was a true idiot. This was highlighted by a mate of his over a pint. I was whining that dad had left mam on her own. 'How could he?' I hissed.

His mate Bernard snapped, 'For God's sake, Mark. Wise up and grow up. Ben couldn't help that he died at 57. He cared for your mam, Sandra and you. He gave you everything he could. He gave your mam everything. He was so proud of you and he would be so unhappy to hear you now.'

Bernard was right. His words were a wake-up call. A hard slap in my face. I apologised and, feeling embarrassed, shrunk back into myself. It made me realise that while he may not have gushed affection, he may have been somewhere else when I wanted him to be with me, but he was the proudest dad anyone could have. I wished I could have told him how much I loved him when he was still alive. I love you Dad.

After the funeral I had to go back to Hull, meaning Mam was left on her own. It broke my heart to leave her but there was nothing I could really do. Luckily, Sandra moved in just three doors up from her, so she kindly cared for mam.

I was fully immersed into the life of a professional rugby league player now – training every day, and working hard on my skills, strength and conditioning. I would do extra weights and skills sessions, and most of my spare time was based around me trying to improve in my new sport. Plus, I would be playing on weekends. With Hull located at the eastern end of the M62, almost every away game meant a few hours spent travelling on the team coach, arriving home after 10pm. There were a lot of events at the club and we were all expected to be there, I was their employee, after all. This was the world of being a professional sportsman. I was with the lads at all these functions and, to tell the truth, I was loving it.

As my second season approached, I had a couple of warm-up games and played in the Charity Shield at Gateshead but was struggling to last the whole game and finding it difficult to come to terms with the pace of the game. The speed we were expected to play, charging in, getting tackled, getting up and running back into position was torture. I was getting there, but not fast enough. Also, when you hear things like 'Jones! You'll never make a rugby league player as long as you've got an hole in your arse' being hollered from the terrace, it makes you work that little bit harder

During the pre-season training at the Boulevard, we played a lot of touch rugby as part of the warm up. It was always played at pace, trying to throw all sorts of passes, trying to play like Harry Pinner and 'Knocker' Norton (two proper rugby league legends). As the game went on people were obstructing each other, pulling shirts – no holds barred professional fouls. I lost it and threw one of the guys out of the way. There was an audible intake of breath, followed by comments like, 'Woah! Woah! Easy tiger.' 'Simmer down Mark.'

After training, me and a few of the lads went for a beer. As we were walking up Anlaby Road with Rob Nolan, a 'cod head' (someone from Hull), the conversation turned to what had happened in training.

'What was all that about earlier, Mark?' he asked.

'My head went because that player was messing me about,' I babbled, 'I just want respect.'

Rob looked at me sideways as if I was talking Russian. 'Respect!!' He stopped dead in his tracks. 'You've done nowt up here lad. You've got to earn respect... earn it... understand?'

For that to come from a fellow player was a massive wake up call for me. Playing union for Wales, playing for Neath, one of the most successful club sides in the world, didn't mean anything to these guys. This was league, a completely new ballgame and past glories didn't wash. It was exactly what I needed.

The culture and attitude to rugby up north was intense – a fierce hunger to win and massive rivalries between clubs and intense competition between players. As professionals, we were getting paid and we all wanted the win bonus getting into the first team, and keeping your place was paramount. The player turnover in league was much faster than in union. In Wales, if you played well for a while and cemented your place in the team you normally had a decent run of games. League wasn't like that. There was a constant push for improvement from the coaches, and a constant expectation to perform from the fans. There was no sentiment about dropping a player if they put in two performances that were below par, below what was expected. They were dropped to the A team. If you were coming back from injury you had to prove yourself in the A team, whoever you were.

This was professional rugby, even though most of the Hull team still had full-time jobs and trained three times a week. It wasn't until my second season that the core players of the team were signed full time and expected to come in for training every day. The coaches were Aussie and implemented an Aussie model to the training regime. The lads were the same as lads in Wales – we loved rugby, loved a pint, and loved the craic – but we were employees of the club and were expected to behave accordingly. The threat of being sacked and losing your income was real and was effective in curbing bad behaviour. Rugby was a way to a good life with decent money, to be noticed around town and a way to be someone. If you were a 'cod head' and played for either Hull FC or Hull Kingston Rovers you had made it. You had kudos among your peers and respect around the city.

The verbal slap off Rob did the trick and after a few weeks of graft I had broken into the first team. Selected as a replacement for the next few games, which was fine by me, I got more and more game time under my belt. My rugby league career was starting to take off. One of those games was against Warrington, the team that had signed Allan Bateman, Rowland Phillips and Kevin Ellis. It was a team I'd fancied signing for because it would have been home from home with all the Welsh boys there, and closer to home, but no offer had been made. This was my chance to show them what a mistake that was.

The game was played at a hundred miles an hour. In one of my carries, two Warrington players tackled me and were clearly holding me down as I tried to quickly start the next phase. Hanging on, to slow down play, delay the ball being released and give your defensive line time to reset is a normal part of the game, but I found it very frustrating. On this occasion, Bob Jackson was wrapped round my ankles and I was kicking and flexing to break free of his grip. He finally released but I was riled. Lashing out, I caught him in the face with my studs, played the ball and the game went on with Bob left writhing on the pitch. The home crowd reacted and started shouting. The ref heard the commotion, stopped the game and the medics rushed on. Bob was escorted from the field with blood all over his face. I didn't know the full extent of his injuries, but I could see that Gary Tees, the Warrington enforcer, was incensed.

Gary was a big tough Cumbrian with a head like a bison. 'You're havin' it Jones,' he yelled at me. 'You dirty bastard. Just me and you.'

I was about 20 yards away and I gave him the talking hand back. 'Yeah, yeah. C'mon then you twat.'

We both growled at each other and carried on with the game, but it was obvious that some retribution was on the cards. Shortly afterwards a penalty was awarded and the ball was booted in to touch. 'Here we go,' I thought. 'Let's have it.'

It's all a bit sketchy now, being over 30 years ago, but as he approached the carry, Gary was shouting, 'Jonesy, I'm coming for you. I'm having you.'

The ball was tapped and Gary ran onto it like a runaway train. With the ball under his arm, he headed straight towards me like a rampaging buffalo. I wasn't backing down. This was the moment to prove to everyone I was born to do this. I charged at him as fast as he was running at me, both of us very wound up and seeking confrontation. By now everything was in slow motion – I could see the whites of his eyes and the spit coming out of his mouth. The crowd inhaled waiting for the collision.

The irresistible force smashed into the immovable object to the sound of the crowd exhaling a massive 'Oooooft'. I felt groggy but managed to get to my feet. So did Gary. 'That didn't hurt, you stuttering bastard,' he hissed. I don't recall the precise words he used but the red shutters come down hard. Only he knows what he said and I haven't seen him since to ask. Taking a step back, I cocked my right hand, pulled the trigger and let it go. My rage had been triggered, the red mist swirled and the next few seconds were a blur.

The ref saw it all and a red card was duly shown. Disciplined yet unrepentant, I was still furious as I made my way to the dressing rooms as the home crowd bombarded me with abuse, coins, cans and bottles. I didn't care. I had no remorse, no regrets. He deserved it.

I have spoken to Allan Bateman about the incident and here's his recollection:

> *'Warrington were playing Hull. His encounter with Gary Tees, a tough man, was legendary. Mark and Gary had been having a bit of a slanging match, until Mark at one play, allowed Gary to play the ball then knocked him out cold. The ref had no choice but to send him off, deservedly. He marched off blowing kisses to the crowd on the way. Typical Mark.'*

Even though I pleaded, via my representative, the legend that is Big Jim Mills, that I had been goaded through extreme provocation, the RFL's (Rugby Football League) disciplinary panel weren't impressed. They slapped me down with a six week ban and a hefty £600 fine.

Thankfully, I was slotted straight back in the first team when the ban was up. I'd trained hard and was fully fit but, it seemed to me, that it was my on-field antics that had helped put me where I wanted to be. I was in the Hull FC first team. One of the biggest and, strangely enough, proudest moments of my rugby career came as I ran out of the dressing rooms on my first game back at home. I took a deep breath and marched up through the caged area, then up the steps and across the dog track on to the Boulevard. I could see and hear the thruppenny stand in the bottom left corner of the ground banging the stand and chanting, 'Lennox, Lennox, Lennox.' It was aimed at me. Then I heard a massive cheer when they saw me, followed by more chants and louder banging. I felt 10 feet tall and totally bullet proof. Instinctively, I ran over to the stand, stood upright in front of the fans and gave a double fist salute. A huge cheer went up. Shivers rippled all over my body. That was it. I had finally done it. I was part of Hull FC. I had proved myself.

Brian Smith had gone back to Australia and 'Crusher' Cleal was now in charge. I was learning quickly, putting the work in and thoroughly enjoying the whole thing. Professional sport is superb if you are lucky enough to be part of it, but it has many pitfalls, so you can never rest on your laurels.

A lot of Aussie rugby league legends, such as Greg Mackey, Des Hasler, Ivan Henjak and Dave Ronson, had stints in Hull. All of them had reached the top in the NRL (National Rugby League) and passed on so much of their experience and wisdom to the squad and myself. When you're new to a sport and you have pros like that to learn from, it certainly makes things easier. Despite the six-week ban I played 19 games for Hull that season.

With so many great Welsh players now playing league, the Wales RL team took off again. We played Papua New Guinea in November 1991 and France in March 1992, both at the Vetch Field in Swansea. It was superb to get back together with all the boys who had gone north. Hull is as far east as you can go and was a bit isolated compared to the other Welsh boys who were mostly playing in the west. For me, there were no meet-ups and days on the piss with the boys from Wales. To cap it all I squeezed into the Great Britain squad and played against France in Perpignan in February 1992. This was the pinnacle for me, it was an absolute honour. The World Club Challenge was being played at the same time as this game so the Wigan contingent couldn't participate, meaning there were gaps to fill and Mal Reilly thought I was the right fit. I was a lucky boy but I didn't care one bit.

Four of the Welsh squad got selected for the game – Jiffy (captain), John Devereux, Jonathan Griffiths and yours truly. I really wish my old man could have been there to see it. We were right in the spotlight. It was bigger than big. We'd trained for a couple of weeks going through moves and plays and I'd worked my arse off learning all the plays and calls. I looked to players like Karl Fairbank, Paul Dixon and Lee Crooks for advice. Without a shadow of a doubt, Lee Crooks was to rugby league forwards, what Jiffy was to the backs. He was the best forward I ever played with. He had it all. What a player.

He could set you up for a tackle then spin out and offload. I learnt so much from those guys.

I'd found league a much faster game than union, but international rugby league was even faster. Even the training was three yards faster than anything I'd experienced previously. It came as a bit of a shock when, in the defensive drills, all I could see was the back of the players next to me as I struggled to get back onside at the same time as them. It blew me away and made me realise what a step-up Test-level rugby league was all about. Mal Reilly gave me some game time, off the bench, and it went well. I had a few good carries, made some yards and made my tackles. My league career was still a work in progress but definitely going the right way.

Mal Reilly held himself with such poise and dignity you could not fail to be in awe of him. He had done everything as a player and everything as a coach. He gave me the chance to represent GB and I am indebted to him. We won the game and what an experience it was.

Two weeks later, by which time the Wigan boys were available for selection, I was named as travelling reserve for the follow up game but didn't get on. This was the game that led to an incident that, I believe, sealed my fate with Steve Crooks, who later took over the reins at Hull.

Hull had a game the day after the second GB game against France but, as I'd aggravated a knee injury preparing for the Test match – it was sore as hell – I withdrew. In retrospect, I should have played, even if it was only for ten minutes. Having suffered a serious injury the previous season I was anxious and didn't want to do any long-term physical damage. Crooksy must have thought that I was unreliable. Why was I okay, the day before, to be a substitute for GB, but be unavailable the next day for my club. He didn't say anything at the time but it may have been a factor in a later decision that had a major impact on my career.

By now, Rebecca, my girlfriend, had moved up from Wales, I had bought a house in Beverley, a lovely market town north of Hull, and a wedding was planned for the following May. I was settled and happy, but that didn't always equate with me behaving myself.

The night before the wedding, in Tredegar, Glyn Llewellyn, my Best Man, came to stay at Mam's house, and the two of us headed off to a rugby dinner in Merthyr where Glyn was the after-dinner speaker. My stammer formed part of his speech, telling stories about me getting blocks, and instances in Neath when that had happened. It went down like a lead balloon. A few of my Dowlais mates weren't impressed at all, and were getting very agitated. I was totally humbled those guys were insulted for me and were willing to fight my corner. We all had a chat afterwards and I explained why I didn't take Glyn's attempts at humour as an insult. He was a very close friend and was just trying to be funny, not cruel. With my assurances fully understood and respected, the evening ended amicably.

At 7am the following morning, my wedding day, I was up and away to the tump of stones for my daily run. I offered, but Glyn wouldn't come with me. He was never one for running if it wasn't during matches. The three-mile run, up and down the mountain, then another two miles to include the recreation ground was partly to clear my head from the night before, but also to focus on what I was about to do – become a married man.

The plan was to have an endorphin rush to give me the feel-good factor, but it didn't work. Even as the car was heading to the church I was confused and had mixed thoughts. Everyone is nervous on their wedding day but my feelings were different – I had never felt so terrible in my life. I couldn't speak. I was drenched in sweat and my head was spinning. Glyn was talking to me, but nothing was registering. It was like the world was in fast-forward and I was in slow-motion. Seconds later I slammed on the brakes as the contents of my stomach exploded up to the back of my throat. Just in time, I jumped out and starting spewing all over the pavement, to the sounds of disgruntled drivers blasting their horns and shouting abuse as they swerved past. It took a few minutes but I sorted myself out. I got back in and drove on. 'I'm okay,' I said to Glyn.

I wasn't. We went another mile and my stomach exploded again. After that, I settled down internally and I managed to get to the church. I can't recall the details of the next 30 minutes, except I was like a cat on hot bricks. The church filled up and I took my place at the front. As the minutes ticked down to the start of the ceremony my anxiety heightened, causing that familiar burning, buzzing sensation in my head. When the music started, the sweats started again. I glanced back and saw the church was full of aunties, uncles, Mam, Sandra, my new in-laws, and my mates. Seeing all those familiar faces my stomach churned again and I felt my throat shut tight. Stupidly, it was only now that it hit me. I had to speak in front of a full congregation. How the hell was I going to do that? I was caught in a vortex I couldn't get out of. At that second, I was so terrified, I wanted to run, headfirst, through the church's thick stone walls and back up to the tump of stones to escape it all! To be on my own, to get away. Every time I looked over my shoulder I could see Mam, standing there in her new dress and hat. She looked so small and frail.

She must have known how I was feeling and how terrified I was. The ceremony started and soon came the marriage vows.

'Repeat after me ... I, Mark Jones ...'

'I... I... I... I... M... M... M... M...'

That was it. Nothing else came out. The harsh, blinding spotlight switched on. The spotlight of humiliation I remembered from school when instructed to read aloud. All eyes settled on me. Everyone waiting, holding their breath. Waiting for me to speak.

Fair play to Glyn, he gave my thigh a quick squeeze to reassure me that he was there for me, but my head was in chaos as I pleaded with myself to get those words out.

I could feel the heavy awkwardness rising like a tidal wave around the church. I looked at Mam again. She was willing me on with all her heart. I could hear her silently praying for me.

I tried again. 'I... I... I... M... M... ark J... Jones.' I spat it out – and so it went on, excruciatingly, for what seemed like hours. Every world block seemed to last for minutes not seconds. It was intense. I was trying to focus but felt I was being publicly humiliated like a freak in a Victorian side show. It wasn't nice for me. It wasn't nice for Mam, and I cringe when imagining what the others were thinking every time the vicar said 'repeat after me'.

I looked upwards towards the heavens. If there was a God hiding up there, somewhere, why did s/he have to put me through this? Didn't I deserve a break, today of all days.

It was all a blur after that. When you go through an emotionally, traumatic experience, which that was for me, it takes you a while to recover and to pull yourself together. As a kid I would lash out or run away. As a grown man, a professional rugby player, I had to get through it. So, I pushed on, knowing there was another potentially embarrassing experience waiting for me, the speeches.

The speeches are usually the fun time, after the formality of the religious ceremony, when the guests are relaxed and entertained with funny and revealing anecdotes and when the best man tells the world of your indiscretions and misdemeanours as a single man.

During Glyn's best man's speech, and the father-in-law speech, I was waiting in the wings, waiting for my time to go out and entertain. Watching the audience laughing and clapping at one liners and funny stories wasn't fun for me. I should have been enjoying the occasion and laughing along, but they just increased the anxiety.

Getting to my feet was hard enough, but then my legs starting to shake and I soon felt my whole body in convulsions. For all grooms, this is where you say nice things about your bride, thank the bridesmaids, the vicar and all the guests for coming. You attempt a few saucy anecdotes and say how this is the happiest day of your life. All married blokes know the score. All I could manage was, 'T... T... Thanks for coming. Hope you en... en... enjoy. S... S... See you later.' I then ran to seek comfort from my old flame, Stella (Artois). That day has been burned in my memory for 30 years, for all the wrong reasons.

I now know, of course, that everyone was willing me on with their endless love and unrelenting support but, as a stammerer, you think the world is laughing at you, ridiculing you, and unrelenting, deep humiliation becomes a close unwelcome acquaintance. The impact it has on your self-esteem is profound and I wouldn't wish that on anyone. A fist in the face or a kick to the bollocks on a rugby field is nothing compared to the gut-wrenching pain stammerers experience every day of their lives.

After the ordeal of the wedding, I concentrated on keeping my spot in the Hull first team. My on-field conduct, however, got me into a bit of strife, copping a few bans for shots to the head and one for bringing the game into disrepute by giving the main stand at Wigan the finger as I walked off. Maurice Lindsey wasn't happy! Other than that, the rugby was going quite well. There was also a baby on the way. This was the family life I think I always wanted, except that I'm a Cefn boy, and as my dad often said, 'You can put a pig in a suit, but it's still a pig.'

The rugby was kept totally separate to my home life. I tried to be the dutiful husband all week, but after the game on a Sunday I let myself go and it often wasn't very pretty. We had a few disagreements concerning Sunday and Monday, but I wasn't for changing. I had a totally boorish and chauvinistic attitude. I was bringing in the money. I was the one getting my head smashed in, so I was entitled to do very much as I pleased as long as it didn't bring trouble to my door.

Osian, my boy, arrived on 18 January 1994 and I was totally made up. I tried to be the best father I could. I gave him time and love, and thought I was the best dad ever. I'd push him around Beverley in his pram, I changed nappies, bathed him, and put him to bed. Having children is a life-changing experience. It's the most important day in your life when the first one arrives.

I was made up to be a dad. You have ideals how you want to bring up your children, and what you want them to do when they grow up. You want them to succeed, you want them to excel. When Osian was growing up, I had big plans for him. I wanted to do all the dad things with him, like play football, ride a bike, swim in the sea, and climb trees. When we were kids we did all that stuff with our mates because our dads were always working or having a pint. You would ask your dad for advice but that was it. You were generally on your own. You had to find your own way through life. Even if he wanted to be there, circumstances mostly prevented it.

I was a pro and being a pro came with a lot of responsibility and commitment. What the club said, went. Not turning up for training or at a function was sacrilege. If Osian was ill, I couldn't nip off and take him to the doctors. When I was working, I was unavailable for family responsibilities. There were no normal office hours. No 9 to 5. You needed to keep it separate. This worked for me but didn't work for my wife.

One of the greatest joys of being a parent is sitting on your child's bed and reading them a good bedtime story. To watch their little faces, light up as you engage them in some fictional adventure, with both of you feeling part of it. Then watching them yawn and curl up and fall fast asleep. However, even that small pleasure in life wasn't simple for me. It disturbed and affected me greatly that I couldn't read Osian a simple bedtime story. When I say I couldn't, I couldn't without stammering.

Whenever I did read to him, I'd make sure I was relaxed and totally focused. I'd disguise any blocks and keep the words short. Glancing ahead, I'd change any words I knew I couldn't say or would have problems with. So even something as basic as reading a short story to my child could be a nightmare and would need forward planning. At times it became like a major operation. On countless occasions, the words I'd read to him bore no comparison to what had been printed in the book. Often, I would just make up a story and pretend I was reading it from the book, praying that he hadn't really noticed how I struggled. This happened every night. It was exhausting but I was determined he would see me like any other dad and not notice the tension, fear and uncertainty I felt. It was an act – not to impress him, or me – just to enable me to be a dad, doing what dads do.

I harboured a great fear that I might pass the stammer on to him. Knowing of the acute personal embarrassment that accompanies a speech impediment, the thought that he could somehow inherit my stammer haunted me. Hearing him say his first words, his first full sentences, without stammering was such a relief that I broke down in floods of tears, knowing that whatever happened to him, at least he wouldn't have to endure the torment I'd lived through.

There are a few aspects of my story that I've avoided mentioning until the final chapters – this being one of them – because I was playing in Hull when it happened, and I only had snapshots of the devastating effect it had on people I loved and respected. I still don't believe it happened.

Back in Wales, me and Steve Fealey had struck up an instant friendship and bond when we played for Tredegar. I played eight and Steve played nine. We both liked the craic and a pint. I was 6'5' Steve was 5'4', but his personality more than made up for his stature. He was the cheekiest little bugger ever and for the next six years we got into some scrapes, more off the field than on.

I was in Hull when I heard he'd been involved in an accident at work and had suffered fatal injuries. I was utterly devastated. When Steve's family asked if I would be one of the coffin bearers at his funeral I was humbled and honoured. The number of fellow players who attended was testament to how much he was loved and respected. The procession of mourners following us as we carried Steve's coffin stretched back out of sight. I remember glancing back and feeling a surge of emotion as the sheer magnitude of the occasion and the amount of people there hit me. It was overwhelming. Hundreds of people had come to pay their respects to the man. He left a wife, Sharon, and two boys, James and Rhys, plus his parents, Ron and Mayo, and brother, Mike. It was utterly heartbreaking.

Moving to Hull helped me deal with the tragedies of losing my father, and then Steve. Being far from home I was removed from everyday reminders that they'd gone. I grieved, of course, but the true magnitude of their loss didn't hit me hit me as hard as it would have hit others. So, to me, they are still where they were, just like all my other friends and family.

14

Smash it Up (Bash it Up)

'Scooby arrived at Ebbw Vale, a dual-code international by that time, and had generated a great deal of respect in both league and union across the world as a tough, combative, no-nonsense player. As a relatively young and inexperienced coach, managing him – along with the rather rambunctious group of players we had at the club – sometimes felt like 'having a tiger by the tail'. I very quickly learned that because of the respect he engendered from his teammates at the club, if I got him on-side with ideas and tactics the sell was pretty easy with the rest of the group. It was the start of what I like to think of as both a great partnership and friendship, one that endures today. Scooby – a good man!'

Leigh Jones

Not everyone is paid handsomely to do what they love. Most people's reality is a life of going to work because they have to. I lived in a parallel universe where I played because I loved it, and I was paid for it. When I drove into the club car park each morning for training, the outside world of 'Stuttering Mark' was left behind and I was 'Rugby Mark'. At Hull, just as it was at Neath RFC and Tredegar RFC, people knew the score and accommodated me. They gave me the space I needed. I could live my other life, and I loved it.

Wherever I played, once everyone in the squad knew I stammered all my anxiety disappeared. It was out there, but it wasn't an issue. Some lads would crack a smile but I'd rip the mickey about how fat their arses were, or how squashed their noses were. We all have aspects of ourselves we're uncomfortable with, or that draw the attention of others. Mine was just more obvious. 'Those in glass houses shouldn't throw stones' is such an apt phrase.

Some of the guys were sharp as a knife, mind. I went to training one day wearing a new pair of expensive suede boots. They were noticed immediately.

'Nice shoes Taff,' Brian Blacker commented.

'Ta,' I said. 'Yeah, they're Hush... Hush... Hush P... P... P... Puppies.'

Quick as a flash, he replied, 'They're bloody quiet mate.'

There was uproar. I looked at him, a bit peeved, but I did see the funny side of it.

I found sport to be non-discriminatory as long as you can do the job you're paid for. Players didn't care about my personal inadequacies, just my playing inadequacies. If I couldn't catch, they cared. If I missed a tackle, they cared, because those things had a direct effect on them. When I stammered, it had no bearing on who won or lost or if I could do my job on the field. So, they didn't give a toss. It was all about winning.

Nothing was sacred, yet nothing was vindictive. No one said anything like 'You messed up, you stuttering idiot.' It was more like 'You were shit today, sort it out.' So, when I was in that environment nothing else mattered except my own performance – how was I going to play and the impact I could make. I'd concentrate on making sure I didn't mess up and that I did my job.

Being on the receiving end of a big hit is not pleasant. The bigger you are, the bigger the hit your opposite number has to make, so the harder you charge at him. Whenever you're trying to tackle a big ball carrier – like when Os du Rant attempted to tackle Scott Gibbs in that epic British Lions versus South Africa game in 1997 – or when you're carrying the ball and some fella comes out of nowhere and smashes you into the middle of next week, each occurrence can have a massive effect on your team. If you're doing the smashing, it lifts the team, lifts you and lifts the crowd. However, if you're the one being smashed, it can have a very negative effect on your team, and on the potential outcome of the game.

When I was playing in Neath, I craved hitting static rucks and doing a bit of damage. Hearing bones crunching and the roar of the crowd a split-second later was addictive. When I signed for Hull in 1990 and switched to league there were no rucks or mauls so I had to learn to hit a moving target. It was a new skill on my steep learning curve.

I was a bit naïve. I was this big Welsh guy and I thought that if I ran straight and hard, I would do okay. That wasn't the case. I was told I needed to develop my footwork in order to make more metres. However, after rupturing my ankle ligaments in that first training session I decided against the step and decided to back myself by developing my strength, hitting the ball on the advantage line, and running as fast and as hard as I could. This worked for a few weeks, as my tactics enabled me to get outside the first marker, but I soon came a cropper.

As I was still bedding in and didn't have a set pattern of play, I had some attributes that fitted the front row, but I also had a bit of pace and could break the line if I ran a bit wider so was sometimes placed in the second row. I was still a work in progress. Still trying to find my feet and understand the complicated world of rugby league.

Hull were drawn to play Rochdale in the cup and since they were a Division 1 outfit, a league below us, we were expected to win. As lots of first-class players have found out to their peril over the years, though, league status means nothing in cup competitions. If teams don't turn up, with the right attitude and perform at the highest level, they lose. Nothing is a given in sport.

Rochdale in February was cold, wet and the wind was blowing a gale, a big leveller. Plus, I could tell they were well up for it and their crowd were baying for blood, guts and thunder. For a small place the noise levels were incredible. I carried a few times, running straight with no fancy footwork and made a few metres. I thought this was going to be a good day. Then, the next carry, a 'nine' move was called, meaning a ruck play. The first runner was the dummy, then the ball would go, from the acting half back, to the outside runner. I was the outside runner for this move and got myself ready. The ball was duly played, the dummy runner did his job and I turned my body in and received the pass from the acting half. 'Here I go,' I thought. 'Happy days!'

Perhaps not. In simple terms I was absolutely smashed. The guy who nailed me, I was later told by Rob Ackerman, my former Wales international colleague who'd also turned professional, was the hefty Samoan Paul Okesene, brother of Hitro Okesene. That boy could hit. He wiped me out. My body may have been in Lancashire but my head was back in Yorkshire. I didn't know if I wanted a shit or a haircut. After being helped to my feet and led to the touchline, the physios sorted me out and sent me back out. Apparently – having consulted the internet – we won 28-32 and I played on until the 74th minute, when I was substituted. Not that I can remember it, the rest of the game was a blur.

The following Monday we all turned up for training, me still feeling a bit groggy, and a post-match team debrief which included a video session of the game. We watched, sitting back in our chairs, the play-back of the match but when the 'nine' call incident appeared, all 19 of us stood up and huddled around the screen. Then came the Jones - Okesene smash. We watched as I received the pass from Lee Jackson, our hooker (what a player). I had turned in towards the ball, as I was coached to, and had started to straighten up. Then, from my blind side, Okasene absolutely smashed me. I shivered just watching as his shoulder made contact with my torso, my head whipping back like I was in a car crash, and my legs buckling as I collapsed. I was out cold before my head hit the turf.

There were collective 'Ooooghh's,' from the boys watching and the odd comment. 'He caught you there, Taff. You need to get that elbow up. Where was your footwork?'

It was an instant 'Road to Damascus' moment for me. The boys were right. I wanted and needed some of that in my game. I didn't want and couldn't have survived many more of those big hits. I wanted to dish them out, not receive them.

I needed to work on my footwork and I had to get my elbow up. I got a copy of the X-rated video and took it home to study. After about 30 views I believed I had it worked out. How to avoid being smashed again. My plan was to receive the ball outside the chasing marker, and by extending my peripheral vision, I'd see if anyone was coming up on the blind side. The instant I caught the ball I also needed to switch it into my outside arm and raise my outside elbow, so if a human scud missile was coming in it would run into the Spanish archer ('el bow'). Instantaneously, I needed to use my inside arm to fend off the chasing marker while stepping in, back towards the play, off my outside foot, to change the angle so if I was clipped it would only be a glancer and I could spin out to avoid the full force of the contact. Also, if I managed to get down the back of the ruck there were easy metres – all that in just a split second. That's the level of technical know-how we needed to master to succeed at rugby league.

Women claim that men can't multi-task. We men know we can but keep it quiet, otherwise women would be having us doing more around the house. It's simpler to let them believe that urban myth.

However, it took me a bit of time to pull all that together. I'd run through the routine – stepping and lifting the elbow – every time I received a pass in training. I practiced that routine so often I know, if someone passed a rugby ball today, I'd do it automatically: step, tuck ball, lift elbow. It became an unconscious action. Eventually I mastered the technique. I had to. Sitting in a post-match briefing while my teammates watched me get destroyed was something I never wanted to do again.

Once it dawned on me that other players were doing the same thing – step, tuck ball, lift the elbow – it became essential for my self-preservation. Kelvin Skerrett, Paul Dixon, Barry McDermott and Karl Fairbank all had big elbows and running into one of them was no fun. I once cracked my sternum doing it and required cortisone injections to help it settle down. The needle was like a nine-inch nail. The medic drew a spot on me, exactly where the pain was, then 'whack' he stabbed the needle in. I bounced off the bed, sucking in air, like waking up from a bad nightmare.

I once caught another elbow right in the throat when I went in for a big hit in another game. It caught me directly in the voice box. I was talking like an asthmatic bulldog for six weeks. I still can't sing soprano.

My intention was to be the one making those hits, not taking them. Back then the shoulder charge was a big part of the game and hadn't been outlawed. You didn't need to hit and wrap your arms. You could annihilate someone legally with the shoulder. It was a great weapon.

If you got on the runner's blind side, just out of his peripheral vision, as he turned in to receive the ball you could rush up and wipe him out as he was taking the pass. It was all about timing: an early hit and it's a penalty to them, a late hit and you'd be eating an elbow, as I did a few times. Getting it right meant you'd do some real damage. Smashing your teammate in training wasn't an option so I'd shoot out of the line in a touch session but not make contact with the ball carrier.

Then came the big test. Attempting it in a game. Sometimes it worked and I got pats on the back and 'Ooooh's' from the crowd. Sometimes I ate an elbow. Sometimes, though, I conceded a penalty and was called a dirty bastard. There were other occasions when I'd miss the hit completely and go flying past, ending up face first in the mud with the players and crowd taking the piss.

It was very much a case of hit or miss. I was told not to go chasing the big hit. That the big hit would come to you. That was so true. Get it wrong and you did as much damage to yourself as to the opposition player, but when it came off it looked spectacular. There was a lad in Hull at the time, Rob Wilson, who had no fear at all. No regard for his own body. I dread to think the concussion issues he could have now. He knocked himself out more times than he did the opposition.

I fractured my left shoulder hitting Tim Street when we played Leigh. He was a solid as a concrete block. The collision tore the deltoid attachment right off the bone. Hull were so impressed they signed him for the next season! In another instance, I stormed out of the defensive the line and put a hit on Karl Harrison, who had just left Hull to play for Halifax. It rocked him a bit but he went on to get man of the match. Respect!! I once collided with Paul Carr of Sheffield Eagles, who ended up with a fractured cheekbone – I got stiches and a headache. It was a tough old game.

Later, when I was with Warrington, I clashed with Apollo Perelini of St. Helen's. We went long from the kick off and Paul Cullen pushed up outside as Perelini came charging back with the ball, stepping off his right foot, straight into my left shoulder. Boooom! The ball went into row four of the stand and he was upside down. My teammates congratulated me with 'Superb, Taff' and 'Great stuff, Mark.' I was pumped up and felt on top of the world. From the subsequent scrum, our centre dropped the ball and they ran in a 70-metre try. We lost 74-14 and the coach, Brian Johnson, was sacked. Without a complete team performance, a big hit is a mere sideshow.

Always looking to improve my technique I once, at Warrington, pulled our conditioning coach, Chaddy (Phil Chadwick), aside after a session and got him to hold a tackle shield for defensive drills. He was only a little guy with hair straight out of the 1970s and a big Zapata moustache. He would jog forward and I'd step either right or left, then hit him with either shoulder about 20 or 30 times a session. After four or five weeks of this he'd had enough. During training I asked him to pick up a shield. 'Not a chance,' he replied, 'you've loosened me fillings. Find someone else to smash.' A great fella was Phil. He had my utmost respect.

I was always treated with respect when I was playing for Hull by the players and supporters and most of the people I had come across, but it wasn't all smiles and taps on the back. After one game, I was in the club, just mingling with the spectators and the players and could see two blokes looking over at me. I assumed they were the £100 sponsor types, standing there in their open-necked shirts and Burton blazers. They nudged each other, walked over and introduced themselves. This was and still is a regular thing in all rugby clubs. Where, after the game, the players are told to act professionally and be accommodating to these people. Sponsors are normally good people who have the club's best interests at heart and give up their money and time to support the players. Clubs worldwide couldn't exist without sponsors and they deserve a pat on the back, but not these two.

When you stammer you develop an extra sense, call it the ridicule sense, when you just know they're looking to humiliate you 'for a laugh'. It makes you hyper-alert to idiots like these. I had never met these blokes before and never seen them around the club. They must have paid lots of money for the privilege of a beef dinner, some free beer, a ticket for the game and to mix with the players afterwards.

As they walked over, smirking and nudging each other, I didn't like the smell of them from the off. My stammer sense began tingling like an electric current running through my veins. The club was packed with over 200 people drinking, laughing, joking and discussing the game we had just played. These two sponsors slid across, all fake smiles and cheap shoes.

'Hi Mark,' one of them said, 'good game today.'

'Thanks,' I replied.

'How are you feeling?'

'Yeah... I'm... I'm... good ... I...' The blockage started in my throat and I started to sweat. 'I... I... I thought we pl.... ' Another blockage, more sweating. I felt as though I was suffocating, I felt as if every person in the room had stopped talking and was staring at me. My head filled up full of white noise. I couldn't hear anything else except what the two blokes were saying to each other. It was as if their little taps and nudges between them were audible.

'See. I told you...' one sniggered, grinning like a Cheshire cat. I hadn't expected that. The stammer sense was buzzing by now and the red shutter was about to come down. I can remember closing my eyes and breathing in deeply.

'What's so fucking funny guys,' I snapped. 'Why are you laughing at me? What's all this about?' There was a look of horror on their faces. They hadn't expected to be called out. 'So don't fucking laugh at me.'

'We're not.' They tried backpedalling, but their game was up.

'Just fuck off.' I downed my pint and walked off. It took me a few hours to calm down from that. A sea of rage overtook my body. I sat alone in a pub in Hessle and got shit-faced on Tetleys. The entire thing had knocked me a bit. I hadn't expected to be treated that way by our own sponsors. It made me even more insular, more guarded, but even more determined to prove myself.

This happened again when Wales RL played Australia RL in Cardiff and I was on crutches with A.C.L and medial ligament ruptures. I was hobbling down the stairs in the clubhouse at Ninian Park when two Aussie players came towards me. There was a nudge and the stammer sense lit up. We started chatting, just some small talk about my injury and a pity I wasn't playing. I was giving it my best shot. Trying to hide my stammer, trying to be normal. It wasn't working. I kept blocking, sweating like fuck and breathing heavily. I could see them tapping each other and not trying too hard to hide their grins.

If I had already met them and they knew about my stammer, or if it was to happen now, it wouldn't have bothered me, because rugby attitudes are the same the world over. If you can't take banter you can't survive in rugby, but purposefully demeaning someone because of an affliction or medical condition is just wrong. Even rugby has a line that shouldn't be crossed. I should have spoken up and said, 'Fuck off boys, don't take the piss.' That would have put it to bed, but I didn't. They walked away and I was left standing there, feeling humiliated.

Instances like that can have a profound psychological effect on you. It would be easy to spiral into depression but I didn't reach the depths that other people have. I could feel incredibly low, and complete despair was a regular visitor, but it never got as bad or as dark for me to descend into a state to consider ending it all. Perhaps it was because I had a release and I could vent my anger, but also because life is a gift I wanted to enjoy. You only get one chance and I wanted to make the most of mine. I was getting highs, endorphins surged through my body every time I played rugby to the cheers and the boos of the crowd. I lived for this. I embraced it. I loved it.

When things got me down, rather than thoughts of doing myself harm, my thoughts focused on escaping to a village in a remote part of Scotland where I could work as a landscaper or an odd job man and keep myself to myself. The thought of not needing to talk much, of living my life saying very little, was a recurring daydream. All the hassle would be left behind and I'd be free of anxiety, existing under society's radar. The thought of not having to communicate sounded like pure bliss, just walking along a beach and listening to waves crashing on pebbles, or hearing birds chirping in a forest. I escaped to these places numerous times, but only in my head. I never had the gumption to do it.

Why? It could have been because the headlines I was generating helped boost my self-confidence. Having my name in the paper, good or bad, gave me a buzz and kicked-off an endorphin rush. The buzz it gave me was more powerful than the anguish and humiliation. It made me feel like a somebody. It made me more than a stammerer. It felt as if I was sticking two fingers up to all the people who had laughed at me, who had made my life hell.

Like many people with mental health issues, I never spoke to anyone or shared my feelings. My life was a constant state of denial, refusing to acknowledge that my stammer was the root cause of my troubles. Thought would be closed down. My stammer was a taboo subject. It was never broached and I just got on with it, took the steps I needed to take to function in everyday life.

Hull was good for me. It's a top city, perched out on its own on the East Yorkshire coast. At first, it seemed a bit isolated, knowing that almost all of the other Welsh boys were with clubs in Lancashire, but Hull's a vibrant place with plenty of nightlife. LA's and the Tower nightclub were regular haunts, along with Pepi's and the Minerva on the waterfront. Hull was very similar in size to Cardiff but with half the population, so the streets in the city centre were never packed or overcrowded – there was room to breathe.

One fine Saturday afternoon in 1992, I was walking through the centre of the city. The place was bustling but not packed. I was feeling good. Now injury free, I had cemented a place in the first team, picking up some new skills and successfully perfecting my big hit technique. While enjoying the sunshine, I saw a young man about 20 yards ahead walking into an electrical shop. In a blink of an eye, he grabbed a video camera from the window display, which was no mean feat as the cameras were huge back then, and sprinted away in my direction, closely followed by the shop assistants shouting, 'Stop him! Thief! Thief!'

The distance between us was closing rapidly and the shoplifter was glancing over his shoulder at the shop assistants while shouting a stream of obscenities. As he came nearer, I remember lining him up as I would an opposing player. Shifting my weight to my outside foot, my newly honed rugby league skills kicked-in. Exploding back onto my inside foot and throwing my arm up I hit him with my shoulder, his head jolting back as if he had been hit by a dumper truck. His body buckled as he was thrown backwards, into a heap against a shopfront where he was quickly pounced upon by the shop assistants. I picked up the camera, dusted it off and gave it back to the shop girl. I imagined a scene from the end of a *Scooby Doo* episode, with the old villian cursing, 'I'd have got away with it if it wasn't for you meddling kids.' For once, my photo appeared in the local paper for doing something good! The police awarded me a commendation for bravery and invited me to an official function to receive it, which was a world away from the 'invitation' to the cells I'd been used to! Not sure what happened to the thief.

In late 1992 the wheels had come off at Hull RL. With only Weeks of the season remaining we were deep in a relegation battle and our coach, Noel Cleal, had been sacked, with the job given to Steve Crooks, the club's A team coach and assistant manager, until the end of the season. Hull through and through and a proper cod head, within days of taking over Steve invited me into his office for a meeting.

I wasn't certain, but the speed of his request made me think it wasn't going to be good news. Sure enough, he made it very clear that as long as he was in charge, I would never play for Hull again.

Surprised? Yes, I certainly was. I wasn't sure what I had done wrong or not done right, but he'd formed a sufficiently bad opinion of me during a couple of seasons with Hull to want me out as soon as he'd taken over. I'd be the first to acknowledge my limitations, I was a no frills and little thrills, straight up and down type of player, but I'd performed well when required. My 100-metre-a-game gain average was more than reasonable, and I had played at international level for GB and Wales, so I was delivering on the pitch.

Did he think I had a bad attitude or wasn't committed to the club? He had definitely been angry with me the season before when, on the morning of a game, I'd pulled out with a crooked knee after being an unused substitute for GB the day before.

Like any reasonable person, and professional sportsman, I asked him why I had no future with Hull under his leadership, but he wouldn't give me a reason. He just said he had no intention of picking me, and that was that. It was all very abrupt and without warning. So, I was destined to be the water boy until he left or I did.

Crooksy just wanted me out, there was no other explanation. He had his opinion and had made his decision. In many walks of life, a new boss strides in and makes changes. If your face doesn't fit, you're out. Your future is reliant on one person's opinion, from hero to zero in a minute.

Being shocked, angry and frustrated doesn't pay the mortgage so, until something changed, I just had to do what the club required. I continued to train with the team, go to games, carry equipment and help the staff, but I didn't play. As long as I kept turning up, I'd be paid, and with a young family dependent on me there was no short-term alternative. I wasn't disruptive or petulant, and I didn't throw my toys out of the pram. Perhaps he hoped, or expected, me to react badly so he could dismiss me and cancel my contract. Instead, I did what I was asked and gave the team support.

We played Hull KR that weekend and beat them to stay up. I was landed for the lads but gutted I hadn't been part of it. Luckily for me, the club then hired Royce Symonds as coach.

He was a top fella and when he came in it was clear my slate had been wiped clean. If a player performed on a Sunday you were picked for the next match, if you didn't you were dropped. Simple as. I developed under him and once again became a regular in the first team during the year at the club.

It all changed again the following year, my final season in Hull which was a bit of a 'mare just as my first had been. Our coach Royce Symonds had gone back to Australia and Hull had appointed Tony Gordon during the pre-season. Tony told me he wanted to try me out in the second row, running a bit wider and really showing my power and strength, and for the next few weeks I trained hard in that position. As promised, he selected me for the pre-season game against Bately.

The game started well, but midway through the first half I was caught in possession and twisted in the tackle to offload. As I did, a defender hit me at knee height and the force snapped my medial ligaments. An operation was quickly arranged but the recovery period was four months, meaning I also missed the Wales RL international against Australia.

By the time I was fully fit, we were languishing at the bottom of the table and were odds-on to be relegated. The club had also informed me that I'd be out of the door once my contract expired. The chairman, Steve Watson, informed me that other clubs had enquired about taking me on loan for a month or so but Hull weren't interested unless it was a full transfer. It was clear that the club wanted me off their books, but only in return for a transfer fee. It was restriction of trade, but it also gave me a boost. If teams like Wigan wanted me there was nothing wrong with skill-set or performances.

Two years earlier I had arranged to play in Australia during the British off-season, on a 'train and trial' deal with Penrith Panthers, but Hull blocked it. Also, the year before that, the same kind of off-season deal with South Sydney Rabbitohs had also been pulled by Hull. They said it was because I needed a rest but I wanted a taste of the NRL, as a way to enhance my RL skills and widen my playing experience.

In those circumstances it's vital to have faith in yourself and your ability. I kept myself fit and knew something would turn up. I knew I could move on and start again. The season ended, Hull got relegated and I got signed by Warrington. It's a strange old world.

Warrington had a hell of a squad but people came and went. Jiffy and Allan Bateman went back to rugby union but then in came Iestyn Harris, Leigh Briers and Paul Sculthorpe. They were all young men, only 17 or 18, and made an immediate impact. All of them went on to be legends of the game. Top talent but also salt-of-the-earth-boys: no pretence, no sense of superiority, just humble and brilliantly gifted individuals.

That was one of the biggest differences between league and union. Some of the guys I played with, but mostly played against, before going north had an arrogance that reeked of their own sense of natural superiority – striding around in their club track-suits, aloof and self-important. Many thought they were bigger than the game and could hardly find time to say hello. Hopefully, I wasn't like that. I never experienced that from a league player. It was just a different culture that reflected the society from where players were drawn. League is embedded in the working-class industrial culture of the north of England, while union remains, in many parts of the world but much less so in Wales, the sport of the middle and upper-class professions.

Another difference between union and league, in my opinion, was that in league, you can't hide. There was nowhere to go for a rest. On a good day, I'd be aiming for 10 to 15 carries a game, gaining

100 metres and making 15 to 20 tackles. The structure and rules of union, on the other hand, enabled players to go AWOL for minutes on end. I've known international players who have made a living from lurking at the side of rucks – either arriving just as the ball was leaving, or, if they've arrived too soon, binding on with no aggression and throwing an arm out in a token gesture to paw at an opposing player while they have a breather. That would drive me mad! As Ron Waldron used to say, 'either shit or get off the pot.'

I had big respect for Mark Hilton at Warrington. He was a 100%-er. He never gave anything less and wasn't called 'The Beast' for nothing. I respected him totally and would fight anyone for him – come to think of it, I did fight for him! In one mid-week game, away to Bradford, it had all kicked off minutes after the start. A few of the Bradford players targeted him and started giving him a pounding, so I dived in to the fray, throwing a few punches and connecting with a couple. It was my natural instinct but I was also new at the club and wanted to show that I would defend the shirt. What I lacked in rugby league know-how, I more than made up for when duty called. When I left Warrington to return to Ebbw Vale, I gave Mark one of my Welsh shirts as a token of respect to him. He was a one in a million.

Having missed out on the 1987 Rugby Union World Cup, signing for Hull in 1990 meant I missed out on the 1991 Rugby World Cup too. However, getting a chance to play in the Rugby League World Cup in 1995 was amazing. The tournament was held in Britain and we were able to base ourselves in Wales, which gave us one hell of an advantage. It would have been great to go to New Zealand or Australia for three weeks but being at home, in the rain, really suited us.

We were a team of union converts splashed with some quality league boys. Playing at Ninian Park in Cardiff and the Vetch Field in Swansea, which was considered by some as our home ground was an unbelievable experience. The atmosphere in the Wales RL camp was nothing like a WRU camp. There was no petty schoolboy discipline and no autocratic leadership. Clive Griffiths was the coach and Mike 'Nicho' Nicholas was team manager. That was it. The team, captained by Jiffy, policed itself. We were grown, professional men and knew the score. Plus, there were top class professionals like Kelvin Skerrett, Neil Cowie and Keiron Cunningham in the mix. These guys gave the Welsh team an edge and led the way. We turned up when we were supposed to and did what we were asked. Everyone had an input and everyone was motivated. Without exception, wearing that red shirt meant everything and we were determined to perform to best of our considerable abilities, so we all conducted ourselves in the correct manner and were all focused towards the same goal.

The relaxed approach united us as a squad and that atmosphere paid dividends. Clive could be intense, but he knew when to crank it up and when to ease off. If you wanted a crazy 30 minutes with him, you could arrange a one-to-one session and really go for it. Every time we trained, we gave it everything, because anything less wasn't acceptable.

The 1995 RL World Cup was the first time I had the experience of working with a sports psychologist, when Clive called in an Irish guy called Kieron, who succeeded to flick our switch – well he flicked mine. Through visualisation, relaxation and focus sessions, he gave us the mental tools to compete with the more favoured teams.

We reached the semi-final, which was an outstanding achievement, but lost to England at a packed Old Trafford. Walking out in that iconic stadium was an experience in itself, and I'm not embarrassed to admit that my legs buckled as I strode out for the warm up. The place oozed history and atmosphere. Without a doubt it was one of the best grounds I've ever played in. We gave a good account of ourselves and the English knew they had to give it 100% for the whole game, but their class and rugby league *nous* shone through in the end, winning 25-10.

15

(Hitting Rucks) and Alcohol

'When recalling Mark's impact at Ebbw Vale RFC – formidable is the first word that comes to mind. Or, put it this way, if he was in a rock band and not a rugby team, he would be defined as always having stage presence ... in spades.'

Marcus Russell

When I signed for Ebbw Vale I knew the club had big ambitions. The guys who ran the club were brothers Paul and Marcus Russell. Paul was a renowned corporate lawyer in London, while Marcus managed the world-famous rock band, Oasis. Paul was the public face of the club, a powerful and articulate public speaker who dealt with the WRU, the media and external matters. Marcus was quieter and liked to stay in the background. He worked effectively inside the club, and having dealt with the infamous antics of the Gallagher brothers, Liam and Noel, he sought to keep the players and staff happy and focused. There were other good guys there as well such as Patrick Harrington QC, Malcolm Shepheard and Bob Jude who player smaller but essential roles.

By this time, my stammer and my behaviour were both spiralling out of control and I was at my lowest ebb. League had taken its toll on my body and my mind, I couldn't string three words together and I seemed to be constantly angry. My stammer was having a huge effect on me.

However, rugby-wise, I still believed I was more than good enough to hold my own. To reassert myself in union, with both the players and supporters, was my primary aim, and also to reintroduce myself to the powers that be in the WRU and the head honchos in the Wales national team. I genuinely believed I could still do a job for Wales, but would they cap me again? I could only try my utmost to get back into the reckoning.

First up was winning a regular starting place in the Ebbw Vale XV. The Steelmen had a good number eight there at the time, John Williams – a powerful, muscular guy with a low centre of gravity. He was one heck of good ball carrier and as gutsy as they come. Saying that, I wanted that shirt. I wanted to play number eight, not be stuck in the tumbleweed of the second row. Switching over to blind side flanker was a huge no-no. To catch the coach's eyes, I was determined to stand out at every training session. Competition for places is healthy but John had been plagued by shoulder problems and the niggling injuries finally forced him to retire, leaving me as Ebbw Vale's undisputed first pick at eight.

The club culture was good but I was constantly reminded about my stammer via banter and ribbing from the players. I gave it back as good as I got but it did, on occasion, go right to the edge and make me angry. It could be brutal. Team meetings and video sessions were times when some serious piss-taking took place. Any player who took the bait and showed they were offended was done for. Every little mistake was highlighted and commented upon, and the offending player left in do doubt of the unacceptability of his misdemeanour. Everyone had a nickname, whether they liked it or not. There was 'Spotty', 'Mongo', 'Urcho', 'Bogsy', 'Sheep's Teeth', 'Planet', and 'Baby Dai'. No one was excused and it could get quite heated. A few guys got really pissed off and stormed out of sessions after an onslaught of abuse and childish banter directed at them. A few of them even left the club.

It didn't take me long to realise the game had moved on a bit since I'd signed for Hull. The tough old teams had gone and there weren't many fighters left standing. Union had cleaned up its act. Many would say for the better, and many would say for the worse!

There were still a few who would throw it about a bit like Dale McIntosh, but we only played Pontypridd twice a year. I vaguely recall playing against Dale when he first came over back in 1989. He was about 20 then but already as tough as old boots. We faced off again 15 years later and nothing had changed. He had certainly stood the test of time.

The teams in south Wales were full of good rugby players, but the emphasis had changed from intimidation to skill. The other league boys – Jiffy, Bateman, and Scott Gibbs had flourished after returning to Union, with several, including John Bentley, selected for the Lions tour of South Africa, the world champions, in 1997.

It's true to say that I'd returned to union as a bigger, fitter and stronger player, but my on-field behaviour had also worsened. Guaranteed to be involved in all the nonsense, I was sin-binned or sent off several times while playing for Ebbw Vale. With Spike Jones, the Merthyr boy from Cefn Coed, and Byron Hayward, the Ebbw side were no shrinking violets. Kingsley was more of a talker than a fighter but we also had Dai Llewellyn, Chay Billen, and Mikey Wilson who could all get stuck in if needed.

Ebbw was an old school style club. A club built on grit, heart and a never-say-die attitude. It was a privilege to play with those boys. As Leigh Jones our coach once put it, 'teams need ball handlers and man handlers.' That is so, so true.

During the first few months of my comeback, we played Swansea and I got into the ring with Big Stu (Stuart Evans). Mates for over 10 years, we were also near neighbours, and had worked and trained together. Nonetheless, on that day Eugene Cross Park, the shit really did hit the fan. My years with Neath meant any fixture with Swansea was always a massive game for me. There was a huge crowd and reputations were at stake. During the match, myself and Kingsley would sometime swop positions at the scrums, him packing down at eight and me replacing him at flanker. Every time the scum set in position, I'd pinch Stuart's stomach and whisper, 'Come on fatty'. Stuart, naturally assuming it was Kingsley, always grunted back that if he did it again, he'd take him out. To be fair to Kingsley, he didn't know what the hell was happening.

Like a naughty kid, I did it a few more times and it was really getting to Stuart. At another scrum, it almost kicked off. With fist clenched, Stuart popped up ready to smack Kingsley, but it was me standing there. Stuart didn't care by then and we stood toe-to-toe, eyeballing each other, adrenaline pumping, the crowd baying for a scrap. It was a moment that you can either walk away from or you can wade into. I waded in, right up to my head. The red shutter came down. I could hear the crowd and the ref's whistle, but I was totally zoned out. For the next ten seconds I launched into him with punch after punch, I then remember someone pushing me away. Turning to let one go at him, I realised it was Kingsley. Our eyes locked on each other, Stu and me were a split second away from heading into round two but other players intervened, pushing and shoving, and the situation calmed down. Unsurprisingly, we were both sent off. We were mates! How could this have happened? Regaining our senses, we shook hands as we left the field and had a laugh about it. There were no afters, just a few beers in the bar. We are still big mates to this day. We expected nothing else on the field of battle.

Nonetheless, someone wanted me to pay and I was automatically banned for six weeks, Paul Russell was incensed. He was having none of it. He came up with a plan to challenge the WRU's decision-making and the inconsistencies of the punishment issued to players who'd transgressed. Employing all his legal know-how, and using their own rule-book against them, he claimed their disciplinary system was flawed. Paul's interpretation of the WRU rule book, if I understood him correctly, was that each case had to be taken on its own individual merits, irrespective of past transgressions. He argued that the WRU were not following these protocols and challenged their decision in court. Over the next week or so, all the paperwork was prepared and presented to the High Court in London. I was told to keep training as normal.

There were a few day trips on the Intercity 125 (always first-class!) to the big smoke where, in the Wig & Pen near Fleet Street, I met Paul's team of lawyers. We discussed the legal details of the case at great length, well, the truth is I mainly listened to some very intelligent blokes talk about the law and how it impacted on my punishment from the WRU. It was truly amazing, and exhausting, to hear their views and strategies to try and win the case. When it was my turn to speak, to answer their questions or to try and explain mt opinions, it got tough. Every word, every sentence, had to be thought through and my breathing controlled as the legal battle became a very personal battle against my stammer. It was extremely difficult, not only find the right words to articulate my views and feelings, but also to find words I could actually say. The mental gymnastics I endured were emotionally draining and incredibly tough. Give me a two-hour fitness session in an actual gym any day. I tried to listen more than speak, so I wouldn't be looked on as an idiot and was glad to get back home to Wales and escape up the mountain with Charlie, my dog.

Finally, the day came when I appeared before the judge in the High Court. I must have done okay, and Paul's legal challenge had merit, because the judge found in our favour and decided the WRU's process was indeed flawed. It was big news and I even made the front page of the Daily Telegraph. The WRU were forced to reconvene their disciplinary hearing, and still banned me for four weeks, but Paul had given them a bloody nose, legally speaking, and he loved it.

In the weeks after the incident with Stuart Evans, I had a bizarre visit from my old pal and prankster, Lyn Jones, who was now coaching Neath and showed his serious side. We had played and beaten a good Neath side the previous Saturday. It had been a very interesting game and, let's just say, I had been involved in a few 'minor incidents', centered around the kick offs, lineouts and rucks. I had flagellated myself and taken my pain out on a few of the Neath players. All within the framework of the law, I must add – well, Mark's law. Others might disagree. Lyn definitely did.

I was sat in my house after coming back from training on the Monday, and heard a knock at the door. 'Bloody Jehovah's Witnesses again.' I thought as I opened the door.

It was Lyn. He only lived half a mile away and our sons went to the same school but he'd never popped around for a chat, even though he used to live next door before I moved in.

'Come in butt,' I said, 'you fancy a cuppa?'

'Yes okay,' he replied.

We sat down in the kitchen and I noticed he was carrying a VHS tape – you can see how long ago this was.

'Not another one, Lyn,' I joked. 'You normally drop those off in the dark. I can't let the Missus see that.'

'Yeah, very funny, Mark,' he said, looking me straight in the eyes. 'I may as well get down to it, Mark. It's about the game on the weekend.'

He then proceeded to say how I had caused chaos, damage and injury illegally in the game. He had examples on the tape and was going to forward it to the citing commission that night. I had never seen him this serious before in his life. He mentioned that if we couldn't reach a compromise, I couldn't really afford to be cited, what with all that was going on. It was just after the Stuart Evans incident and prior to the high court trial.

'Mark, you have a bad reputation and I could make it worse.' I was more than intrigued. 'What do you mean, Lyn?' I was expecting him to burst out laughing and tell me the punchline or stick a flan in my face, but it was no joke.

'Sign this letter,' he said, placing the document in front of me. He explained that the letter was a statement promising that I wouldn't play against Neath the coming season. He added, that he would destroy the tape and that would be that. A sort of written gentlemen's agreement. In a sick sort of way, I was flattered. He wanted to protect his players. Protect them from me.

'No way!' I thought. 'There's nothing on there that is in any way Incriminating.' I could have signed it and bluffed him and played. Our next game was weeks away, but he had sown a seed of doubt in my head. Would he? Could he? That he'd asked me not to play against his team because they couldn't handle me said it all. It gave me a weird sense of pride. I saw it as a huge compliment. Saying that, and knowing Lyn, he might have left saying, 'You stupid twat, it was just a tape of the Teletubbies.' I'll never know. As it happened, the ultimatum from Lyn was academic as I was injured and didn't play in the next Ebbw Vale v Neath fixture anyway.

Another prankster with a serious side was our club captain at Ebbw Vale, Kingsley, who was, and remains, a great friend, but his banter about my stammer really annoyed me at times. Back then he didn't realise the impact it had on me. His jokes and comments were never malicious and I do believe that, at times, he thought I needed it to spur me on and get me in the right frame of mind for matches. I tried my best to give as good as I got from him, which I did on occasions, but he's a sharp cookie and a funny bloke. Kingsley was the team joker and was always playing tricks on everyone. There were a few times, though, when he took it too far and I'd chase him out of the club, threatening blue murder, but by the time I'd caught him, we'd always end up laughing.

Once, when we were travelling to play in London, he arranged a print run of business cards in the service station when we stopped for a break. When we got back on the bus, there was a card on everyone's seat that read: 'M... M... M... Mark J... J... Jones, Speech Therapist, 34 Stammer Street, Stutterville'. I knew it was Kingsley but didn't say anything until later that night, in the hotel room we shared.

'I know it was you, spotty dog. I'll have you back ... goodnight!' I whispered as he switched off the light. He slept with one eye open that night.

My stammer had been an uninvited and unwanted guest throughout my life, and had intervened to prevent me living the life I'd wished for, but it hadn't stopped me playing rugby. Yes, it sometimes stopped me calling moves on the field but I was still a dual-code international who had earned a good living as a professional player.

Rugby was my safe haven, my stammer free zone. Now, though, I was approaching the latter end of my career and wanted to move into coaching. This was when my stammer became, for the first time, a big rugby problem.

Working with players, coaching them and developing their skills meant I had to communicate clearly and effectively. I had to speak and I had to explain what I wanted. Almost as soon as I started the WRU coaching course the problem was apparent. Organising groups of players and setting up drills meant I was required to explain the purpose of the drill, assess and articulate the outcomes and coaching points from the drill and explain how mistakes could be corrected. This is all normal stuff but I found it very tough. Knowing what I wanted to say, and believing I could really help to develop players, was a world away from actually opening my mouth and saying what was needed to be said. Determined to succeed, I battled away and jumped the hurdles the stammer put in front of me.

Over a couple of months, and despite a couple of awkward moments, I was awarded the Level 1 and Level 2 coaching badges. Level 3 came a couple of months later, just after I'd started my speech therapy. The course was scheduled over a weekend at Usk College and was an intense experience for all, for many different reasons, but particularly for me.

Acknowledging my stammer was a problem emotionally and psychologically, and then agreeing to a speech therapy course were two huge steps for me to take, but the therapy was a further ordeal I needed to battle through. I'll skip most of the fine detail but the details were organised and a therapist came to the house. I don't know what she had been told or expected, but she walked in equipped with toys, books and flash cards. Like a speech therapy Santa Claus in her Ford Fiesta sleigh. She was taken aback a little when I informed her that it was me who had the issue, not one of the children, but she was utterly professional and quickly switched to Plan B.

The first session started with me sitting nervously in a chair, feeling a bit of a fool, as she started off with breathing exercises, coaching me how to breath in and out correctly. 'I've been breathing since I was born,' I thought, what's was the point of all this?' However, she explained that we have two chambers and I was only using one. She taught me to breath into my stomach, to breath in and out and relax. This took a while – I needed to do something I'd never done before – but she explained how it would help me and I began to breathe correctly. Next step was the alphabet. I learned how to say each letter while breathing in, then out: breathe in, 'A', then out, 'A'; breath in, 'B', then out, 'B'; and so on to 'Z'. That was enough for the first session, and she told me to practice breathing whenever I could and do the alphabet exercise. To be truthful, it is something I still do, to this very day.

The second session involved more breathing, and more alphabet exercises but also re-learning how to speak again. Over the years, in order to side-step and escape from tricky words or phrases, I'd developed so many avoidance habits that I now had to strip everything right back and start all over again. We started with one syllable words – The cat sat on the mat – the Ladybird Book One-type sentences. That may be simple stuff to most people, but to me – saying each syllable on a breath – it was torture. Even though it took ages to read a sentence, I didn't care. The elation I felt when I started to reading whole sentences aloud, without a block, brought tears to my eyes. I was so emotional. It was as if I had been reborn.

With the help of the speech therapist my stammer lessened and speaking skills improved. It was horrible at the start – totally cringeworthy. I would have to listen to recordings of myself and watch myself on video. I noticed facial tics I hadn't previous been aware of and I'd watch myself fidget as I fought speaking blocks.

Watching my facial contortions as I tried to spit out a word made me extremely self-conscious and embarrassed, but it also made me more determined to beat my stammer. This was probably my last chance and I wasn't going to make a mess of this opportunity. I wanted to do it for myself, but also for those who'd been so supportive and kind during my life. I knew they were willing me on, with love and respect for what I was trying to achieve.

My gradual improvement boosted my self-confidence, and that, in turn, made me calmer and help me improve even more. It got to a point when I could operate in society and do things without thinking – answering the phone, asking for assistance in shops, reading aloud, and introducing myself to people I'd never met before. My fears and anxieties were still there but the breathing and relaxation techniques I'd been taught helped me to overcome them.

As this slow reconstruction of my speech continued, I'd take every opportunity to consolidate what I'd learned and not slip back. Every time I was alone, I'd practice the breathing exercises when reciting the alphabet. It's a constant feature of my life and I'll never stop. It's my 'go to' place. I still do it now. If ever I'm going somewhere where I know I'll feel uncomfortable, I'll start my drills – breathing in and out, and putting myself in a mental space that I'm in charge of. I owe that lady so much. She helped change my life.

There were about 16 of us on the WRU coaching course, a mixture of players and development officers, and we were lectured and taught in groups by rugby-playing school teachers who knew all the buzz words and coaching methods. We were put in groups, given a task and told to coach each other. This wasn't a problem. Being in small groups and knowing the boys made me comfortable and I remained in control of my breathing. We had homework each night, and I'd rehearse and visualise what I had to deliver. Not only was I mentally comfortable, I was also confident in my knowledge of rugby and my ability to coach what was required. Preparation is key to success and that was doubly so for me – ensuring I had alternative words and phrases in case I had a block. It's the same as everything else in life, if you try to wing it and don't prepare, your performance is likely to be poor. When I knew what I was talking about and had several ways to convey my point I felt good. Failure wasn't on my agenda.

At the end of the weekend, we were having discussions about the course and what would happen next, when one of the officials brought up my speech issues. The question posed was whether it would it have an effect on my coaching? Would I be effective or would I lose my credibility with the players?

The blood drained from my face, then returned as the rage burned inside me. Beads of sweat started running down my forehead, into my eyes, and I started blinking to ease the stinging. The atmosphere changed and the lads in my group went silent. That awful, stomach-churning, feeling returned. The same one I'd had all my life. The spotlight of humiliation was shone on me again, knowing I was the focus of everyone's thoughts and that my weakness was exposed. My mid started racing: 'You cheeky bastard!' I thought. 'Don't you dare question my credentials, my game knowledge, my suitability for the job. If you only knew how much work I had put into this weekend, and how much effort I've put in at home in my speech therapy sessions. I spend every minute of every day trying to speak like everyone else, but as a fella who finds that sort of thing easy you would never have spared a thought about what people who stammer go through every single day.'

I quickly ran through my well-used mental drill to restore calm and prevent me from losing it: breathe, relax, focus. I kept it very low key but I was furious.

'No. I'm sure I'll be fine. It's never an issue among the boys.'

Kingsley, who was also on the course, and the others could see I wasn't ok. The final part of the course was to be assessed in a training session at our home clubs. It had all been arranged for a few weeks later. I'll let Kingsley deliver the rest of the story. He tells it far, far better than I can.

'During our level 3 coaching sessions, Mark was doing quite well up until the point when the assessor gave him some feedback that his knowledge and understanding of the game were good but he could struggle to control a group due to his stammer. I could see Mark was spitting feathers and I tried my best to cool the situation before Mark threw the bloke over the fencing. I knew it was going to be a challenge for him, even Mark was aware of it but I knew he could do it. He just didn't need that added pressure.

A few weeks later came the practical examination. This was where the assessor came to the club to watch us take a 30-minute training session with a group of players. Fair play to our coaches and our players, we made a plan to make Mark look like Carwyn James in his prime. I explained to the guys what was happening and told them all to be on their best behavior. I helped Mark to practice what he was going to do and more importantly what he was going to say, down to the last detail. I told him to growl out the drills. I knew he had less of a stammer when he growled.

On the day, we all stood in front of him, the assessor with his clip board by his side. I could feel the tension and could only imagine how Mark was feeling. I could tell he was so nervous.

'Right boys,' he growled in his deep Welsh valley's voice, 'run across the field, passing the ball.'

Like a bunch of well-trained monkeys, we did what we were told. There was no back-chat, no piss-taking. We were all on our best behaviour as we raced off. The assessor turned and said, 'Good Mark, but you didn't tell them what type of passes you want them to do.'

Suddenly we could hear Mark bellowing out. 'Hold it. H... H... Hold it.'

We all stopped and came back. There was silence. No one know what to do.

Mark puffed out his chest. 'It... it... it's...' he couldn't get his words out. The boys started to glance at him with a look of, 'come on Mark... just say it... please.'

The assessor looked at him. We could all see Mark fighting through his block. 'It... It... It's... easier to... to... to... fucking do, than fucking say,' he finally blurted out. We all burst out laughing, including the assessor. It broke the ice into a million pieces and for the rest of the session, Mark was Carwyn fucking James.'

Ebbw Vale were a decent team and, in 1998, we reached the Welsh Cup final, playing Llanelli at Ashton Gate, the home of Bristol City FC. I've watched the tape a few times and we played well, but couldn't quite break them down. It was the same old story with the Turks – soaking up up all the pressure then pulling our pants down at the end. They really do my head in because they are so good at it.

Llanelli cited me for foul play after Iwan Jones, their open-side flanker, suffered a broken nose. He had tried to obstruct me and run across my line, so I belted him out of the way. At the disciplinary meeting, Stuart Gallagher, the larger-than-life Llanelli chairman, came out with a video nasty of all my misdemeanors during the game. Not only that, Llanelli had included clips from a game the previous season.

As with the previous WRU disciplinary, I challenged the video and reminded them I was answering one single citing, not 10. It hadn't escaped my notice that Ebbw were playing Llanelli on the second Saturday of the next season so I got the feeling they didn't want me to play in that game. The video didn't show any contact, just before and after clips of Iwan Jones' nose, but that was enough for the panel, who convicted me. It was purely circumstantial. Nonetheless, I received a three-week ban from the start of the next season and missed the Scarlets game. Llanelli had got their way.

I have been asked, many times, why I played the way I did, and I've given it a lot of thought. I'm under no illusion that it was all I had. There is no doubt that smashing someone and doing some damage gave me a buzz, but why? I believe it was mainly down to self-worth. It was the way I thought I'd achieved something. It could also be linked to the hurt and pain I had internalised in the days or weeks before a match, then wanting to inflict my humiliation and anger on to others. I've self-analyzed myself for many years, trying to find out why I've behaved as I have. Some just can't stand losing and go off their heads if their team doesn't win, but I've never been like that. Of course, I've always wanted to win and am gutted my team loses, but it was never about the team, it was about me. As long as I'd done my bit, as long as I could walk off having given 100%, I was happy. I didn't have the skill set to win a game on my own. I was never the one who could run 100 metres to score a wonder try or put someone through a gap. I always judged myself on endeavour, and effort. So that I could look myself in the mirror with pride, knowing I'd given everything to the cause.

By then I'd become deluded and behaved like an idiot. It wasn't a case of showing my skills as an attacking player, I'd descended into a person who was hell-bent on destroying the opposition, stopping them playing.

After about a year back in union, I was offered a sales rep job by one of the benefactors, a top guy, Bob Jude. He took me under his wing and we got to know each other really well. It was Bob who broached the subject of my stammer and over the next few years, Bob and his wife Sue, became like family to me. Bob encouraged me to have speech therapy and I can say, with total certainty, that he played a massive part in helping me conquer my stammer. Bob sadly passed away recently and his death hit me hard. What a lovely, generous and considerate man he was and I will always be grateful for what he did for me. Thank you, Bob.

The chance of me ever playing for Wales again at eight were non-existent. I had no illusions there. Scott Quinell was in possession of the jersey and was carrying Wales on his own, from what I could see. My only, slim, hope was in the second row. My work around the field was as good as any, but lineouts were another thing. Lifting was introduced and there were many young bucks who had way better aerial skills than me. Even I wouldn't have bet on myself.

A tour to South Africa had been arranged for the summer of 1998, which was going to be tough, very tough. Wales had a poor Five Nations, beaten 60-26 by England and 51-0 by France. Kevin Bowring was the unfortunate coach who was shown the door, and Mike Ruddock was pencilled-in as the new national head coach. In the weeks leading up to the tour, 18 players withdrew from the squad for one reason or another, maybe in support of Bowring, maybe they were injured, maybe they didn't fancy being annihilated by the Boks. Who knows?

Ruddock picked a squad from what was left and I got the nod. 'C'mon!' I was made up. It was obvious I was only there for one reason, and it wasn't my ball playing ability, but who cares! I was on the trip. I had been picked for Wales again. Former league stars Allan

Bateman, Scott Gibbs and John Bentley had played on the Lions tour the year before, and nailed it. In my deluded mind I thought I could do the same. My desire was still there – wanting to mix it with the world's best and challenge them face-to-face. To show what the boy from the box room was about.

Mike picked the squad but wasn't going to coach the tour. That unenviable task went to Dennis John and Lynn Howells. Advocates of old school values, and believers that hard work would lead to results Dennis and Lynn were top quality, both as coaches and men. Those values took Pontypridd to the top of the league, and their Sardis Road ground became infamous as the House of Pain.

When the squad finally assembled there were rumblings about money, with some complaining that English players were supposedly being paid far more for their summer tour. Player meetings were held and some threatened to withdraw. Me? No chance. I was going. I would have paid my own way to get there. Byron Hayward thought exactly the same. We couldn't wait to have our bags loaded onto the bus and take our seats right at the back. The payment row was eventually sorted and the tour party left the Copthorne Hotel in Cardiff but, with heavy Five Nations beatings, a new head coach, 18 withdrawals, two stand-in coaches and an unsightly argument over money, our preparations hadn't been the best.

Zimbabwe was our first stop and we landed in Harare in good spirits, ready for the first game. There was a confidence in the camp, we were expected to win and the atmosphere around the squad reflected this. There were more rumblings about money and whispers were heard that a few boys were going to play the first game, get the tour pay then bail out before we hit South Africa. This wasn't what I was about. Was I hearing right? FFS boys? This was the chance to play for Wales! Where had the pride in the jersey gone? Where was the honour of representing your country? Me and most of the boys were fully-signed up to the cause but it seemed like money had corrupted a small minority.

The team was announced and I was starting in the second row. I was flying. Hearing I'd won another cap, when I thought it would never happen again, was an amazing experience and I was determined do all I could to keep the jersey. My task was to hit rucks, push in the scrums, tackle ferociously and own the kick offs. Lineout ball would be fine as I'd perfected the 'number one – low and hard – ball' so I could secure possession. That was it, simple. Just work 'till I collapsed.

When I pulled the jersey on again, I felt 7 foot tall and bullet proof. A gladiator in my impenetrable red armour. The anthem played and the hairs on the back of my neck were standing up exactly as they had in Scotland in 1987. Ten years plus had done nothing to dampen my passion. I was loving it. I was back.

My game plan was straightforward and I executed it fully for 60 minutes until I had nothing left. I'd busted my arse, was totally spent, and given all I had. Replaced with 20 minutes to go in the first international for a while, I was exhausted. We won 49 -11 and I had another cap to my name (or to Mark Alun Jones' name), but if I was to get a chance to play against the Boks a few weeks later, I needed to improve my fitness or pace myself a bit. Easing up wasn't an option, I was playing for my country and I'd never consider that, so I needed to put some extra work in to last the whole match. Subs weren't used like they are now. Tactical changes were in their infancy so players were expected to last 80 minutes. There was a good hour in me but that was it at this level. I was under no illusions.

The next game was against the Emerging Springboks on 16 June in Secundar, 1,600 metres above sea level in what was then Eastern Transvsaal. The highest point on the heads of the valleys near Tredegar is 410 metres, so this was very different, and much hotter. Playing at such a high altitude caused problems for the boys, who were struggling to breathe and fill their lungs with enough air to function. There had been a few casualties in the Zimbabwe game and replacements were being flown in. Sometimes a big hit can raise the spirits amongst the players. The one I attempted in this match had no effect at all. At that point I knew the team was shot. It was also clear that I was only good for 30 minutes at that level. I hoped it would be enough for a spot in the Test side – I was desperate to face the Boks – but in the week before the first Test disaster struck.

We'd travelled back to Pretoria to prepare for the first Test and I'd gone to bed, completely exhausted, but woke up during the night with a drawing pain at the bottom of my spine. It was pulsing and red hot. I couldn't sleep. I couldn't get comfortable. I had to lie on my front and pray for morning. I made it down for breakfast, walking like John Wayne after riding his horse across America wearing only underpants. A doctor examined me and I could tell by his expression that something wasn't right. The diagnosis was an abscess on my coccyx and I was whisked away immediately to the hospital where I had the operation the following morning. Anyone who has had one of these will know it's not a nice experience.

When I came round, I was on my stomach with the back of my gown open exposing my arse. In walked the nurse who was the image of Stuart Evans, but uglier and with bigger muscles. She looked at me, looked at my arse, pulled my cheeks apart with her huge hands then scrunched up her face with an, 'ah well here goes,' expression as she grabbed the dressing which I later learned had been packed into the wound after the removal of the abscess.

The dressing had been in there for two or three hours and the blood had congealed. She whipped it out of my back passage like she was swishing back the curtains in her front room. I didn't have time to scream. All I felt was a searing, white heat and the world went dayglow. I almost passed out. As the pain eased, I saw her stuff a huge wadge of bloody cotton into a medical waste bag before leaving as quickly as she'd arrived. Minutes later, she was replaced by a younger, more feminine-looking colleague who proceeded to bathe and dress my wound. This tortuous procedure happened four more times in the following 24 hours and I couldn't wait to be discharged and back at the team hotel.

While recuperating from the operation it seemed as if hundreds of new players were being flown in, as fast as injured players were being flown home. Eventually it was my turn to head home and I was flown back, business class. The tour continued, with tough games coming thick and fast. We lost to the Border Bulldogs (24-8), the Natal Sharks (30-23) and the Falcons (39-37) before the Test match in Loftus Versfeld in Pretoria, which was an utter annihilation – an embarrassing, 96-13 record defeat.

The tour was in trouble the minute the squad was announced, and players started pulling out because they weren't getting paid enough. They believed they were on a hiding to nothing. Yes, the game had gone professional, but not all the players were full-time professionals! There were a few guys who really showed their mettle on that tour. In my opinion, Colin Charvis, Bryon Hayward and Ian Gough all came home with stripes. There were some positives.

After that disaster of a tour, and a national humiliation in Pretoria. Wales headhunted Graham Henry to start the revival of Welsh rugby, and his first game in charge was against the Springboks at Wembley, the opening match of the autumn internationals. Henry named me in his first squad. I don't think that was a hard choice because, after coming over and watching a few club games he picked a squad of about 60. We all turned up for squad sessions which consisted of fitness tests and mini games. This went on for a few weeks and the squad was whittled down. During the sessions I could see which way he wanted to go. Welsh rugby at the time was in a bit of a mess at international level. The players were there but the team had no structure and no direction. We had been smashed in South Africa weeks earlier, not that I'm really entitled to say 'we' because I wasn't there when the points started to pile up. However, I was part of the initial squad so 'we' it has to be.

Graham introduced us to the pod system. It consisted of getting four players working together in units. This had the effect of not leaving us short of numbers at rucks, and gave us a good opportunity to recycle the ball. He told us to keep the ball for as long as possible. To play in certain areas and to maintain a good defensive line. Pretty basic stuff, you would have thought, but at that time Wales had none of that structure and this approach made a massive difference to the performance of the team.

Graham Henry laid the foundations and singlehandedly rebuilt Welsh rugby. He was called the Great Redeemer, and his approach is still used by hundreds of coaches worldwide. In the late 1990s and early 2000s, we all played this way in Wales and some of those former players are now coaching the same way. He later went on the coach the All Blacks and dominated world rugby for almost a decade.

Alongside Graham, Shaun Edwards also deserves huge credit for his work with the Wales national team. In my opinion, Shaun has had the biggest influence on rugby by implementing the defensive systems and mindset from rugby league, and was responsible for masterminding Wales' successful era under Warren Gatland. His very regimented approach, of not allowing players options in defence, is the key. It's human nature to take the soft option but Shaun eradicated that with his no-nonsense approach of, 'If you're not dead, then get back in the line and get ready to tackle again.' This is the foundation upon which the defence ethos of rugby league has been built. I can only imagine how this 'no excuses' regime was initially received by some union players who were used to a lower intensity game and had opportunities to go AWOL during matches. Watching him lay down the law to players would have been entertaining for us rugby league converts. You're a top man, Shaun. You really put Wales back on the map!

As Graham prepared for the autumn matches, a full list of fixtures was going on at club level and players were being viewed weekly by Graham and his support staff. It was a big job for him to identify the best players and mould them into a team in such a short time. At that time Ebbw Vale were doing well, and we had a few players in the initial squad. I was still in the mix by the time the training squad of 35 was announced, which I was more than made up about. I really thought I had an outside chance of making the matchday 22-man squad, until I had a brain meltdown on a Wednesday night at the end of a game against Pontypridd.

It was a home game with a great atmosphere. With 10 minutes to go we were leading and the game was ours to lose. A lineout was called, about 35 metres from the Pontypridd try line, and their hooker threw the ball towards Ian Gough. It never got to him. Our player, the brilliant, Kuli Faletau (the father of Wales and British Lions forward, Taulupe Faletau) intercepted the throw and tapped it down to our scrum-half. Frustrated and angry for losing a lineout on their throw, Goughy started to throw a few punches at Kuli, who wasn't a fighter. Kuli was one of the fairest and nicest guys to ever lace up a pair of rugby boots, just like his son.

Seeing this attack on my teammate, the red shutters came down. I instinctively landed a haymaker which connected squarely with Goughey's cheekbone. The intake of breath from the crowd was audible as he instantly went down. The mist started to clear a little as I stared down at him. Derek Bevan, the Welsh international ref didn't have any option but to give me my marching orders. 'What the hell have I done?' I thought as I trudged off the pitch.

For the first time ever, I felt total remorse for my actions. Goughey was in the national squad with me. I liked him and we got on well together. I knew I was out of order for doing what I did.

Immediately regretting what I'd done, the guilt that began to overwhelm me as I walked off was something new. I felt a need to do something, so headed to the away team changing room to apologise to Goughey. My head was still spinning as I heard a voice say, 'Fuck off, Scoob. That was way out of order.'

I didn't hang around. I went back to the showers feeling totally ashamed and disturbed by what I had done. Sitting in the corner, shaking, I could hardly breathe. Even my own teammates, who soon trooped in after the final whistle, gave me a 'That was bad, Scoob' kind of look. There was no tapping me on the back and trying to console me. The silence was deafening as teammates were now avoiding my glances.

I really can't remember the details of the next few days. The incident was shown over and over again on the TV. It was talked about on the news and on radio shows. Ian had surgery to repair his broken eye socket and I was public enemy number one, two and three. There was talk of a prosecution, and prison if convicted. I didn't want to see anyone and withdrew into myself, sitting in my front room with the curtains drawn – wrestling with my thoughts and fighting my demons.

There was a Welsh squad session that the week. As soon as I'd arrived at the Arms Park, I was told not to go training but go directly to Graham's office. I felt like a naughty schoolboy getting sent to see the headmaster. Graham had been a headmaster in Auckland before becoming a professional rugby coach, but I knew he would be giving me a lot more than 'six of the best'.

'Come in,' he said, as I knocked quietly on the door. The boss was sitting behind his desk, and Steve Black, the conditioning and mental health coach, was sat in an adjacent chair. My heart was beating so wildly in my chest I thought they could hear it. My guts were churning and my stammer was out of control. What was going to happen to me? I had no idea where this was going. Had I blown my chance to play for one of the best and most respected coaches in world rugby?

After the initial, informal, introductions and greetings, I sat down and was asked to go through my version of events. My mind went back to the interview room in the cop shop when I was locked up for fighting at 18. Was this going to be another 'good cop, bad cop' experience, and which one was which?

'I... I... I...' I started to explain. As you can imagine, it took me about 30 minutes or longer to go through the incident. It should have taken me about three at best. All the time, Graham was taking notes and asking me questions. How had I felt after it happened? How was I feeling now? What made me react like that? Would I do it again? What do I think are the consequences? Did I think about consequences? Why did it happen? He was very calm and measured.

I told him I was ashamed of my actions, and I was. I really was and still am to this day. I don't know why I did it. Well, I did know why. It was a total brain meltdown but I was full of regret and remorse.

He continued taking notes. I could tell he was once an experienced teacher.

Next, Blackie entered the interrogation. Steve was as much a coach of the mind as the body, an expert motivator and someone who was ahead of his time in terms of sports psychology. His questions to me were all about what was going on inside my mind. Why did I get so angry? What triggered my anger? Who did I get angry at? At the time I didn't realise I had an issue. I just put it down to growing up in a violent place, in a violent time and playing a violent sport. I didn't know it was something deep-rooted inside me. I do now, and during that meeting in Graham's office I began to see what my main problem was and where it all stemmed from. It was as if I'd gone to an AA meeting and stood up in front of a crowd and blurted out, 'My name is Mark Jones, and I have anger management issues.'

My problems were obvious and I wanted to resolve them. I was desperate to move away from the person I was and find the person I knew I could be. He was in there somewhere, trying his best to claw his way out. When Blackie suggested counselling, I agreed straight away.

Graham sat, stony-faced, still writing all of it down. We talked some more, openly and freely, although I was really struggling to communicate. I don't know if they knew why. If they could see straight through me, to the real me trying to escape to freedom.

'Is your speech an issue for you Mark?' Blackie asked.

There was a short pause before I gave my usual reply of 'No way'. Followed by, 'I can get through life great. I have problems sometimes but it doesn't affect me.' What a lie! I think, or I knew, they could see straight through it. My battle with speech owned me. It had an impact on every aspect of my life. I hated it, and I hated talking about it. I sat in my chair, staring at the floor.

At the end of the interview, I was asked to leave the room and wait outside. I didn't know what they were going to do with me. 'They are going to kick me out of the squad,' was the only thought rushing around my head. Within 15 minutes I was called back in and walked the 'green mile' into Graham's office. A letter was placed in front of me. I read it. It was everything I had said in the previous hour's conversation, but presented in a way that could be understood and in a way that was a million times better than I could have written it. It expressed my remorse and shame, my regret and my desire to move forward. It stated that I accepted fully my anger issues and I expressed a willingness to change. It contained everything we had discussed and I had tried to express in the interview.

Anger management sessions with Steve Black were quickly organised, beginning with an informal chat between the two of us, but soon expanded into something I didn't like. If you have ever had counselling, you will know what I mean. It's a process which feels as if you are peeling off your outer skin and forced to strip back layers of your persona, to reach your core and identify the real issue. Once that is done, the painful process of trying to rebuild, from the inside out, begins. The real issue was my stammer but I didn't want to admit it. Fighting reality was getting me nowhere but I just couldn't bring myself to accept it. There was, however, no escaping the truth and it got to the point where I had to acknowledge it. I didn't let much out to Blackie, but when I went home I tore myself to shreds. My ex-wife saw none of this. I would just go off on my own and deal with it my own way. To the outside world I was handling the process normally, but deep inside, especially when I was alone, it was another matter. I felt I had no one to speak to, but probably wouldn't have opened up even if I did have someone to talk to.

I owe a lot to Graham Henry. He may not think so. He may not even remember the incident or he may remember it differently to me. The stark truth is that if Graham and Steve hadn't taken an interest in my wellbeing, got involved, and spent time and effort giving me the benefit of their experience and expertise, my life could have been so very different. My heartfelt thanks to them both.

Unsurprisingly, my time in the Wales squad had come to an abrupt end, justifiably most would say. So, I went about my daily business of travelling from my home in Neath to Ebbw, where I would be training every day and playing on Saturdays. Osian was going to nursery and pre-school so I'd drop him off on my way then drive up the Heads of the Valleys to Ebbw, which was convenient and gave me more time with him. I knew I was lucky.

Rugby was still my total focus, Ebbw were going great guns and Manon, my first daughter, was born in early November 1998, during the autumn internationals. Being outside the Wales set up gave me the leeway to do all the dad things when having a child in the house. Daughters are different to sons. You love them both the same but from different angles. A baby gives you a sense of peace, when nothing else matters and they are your total focus. Considering my mental state at the time, it was just what I needed.

As with Osian, I thought I was father of the year. Nappies, bath time, bedtime, feeding, walks, shopping, but then, I had the escape to rugby, the recharging of my batteries, my other world. Which was a definite distraction.

Those sessions with Blackie helped me look at what I was doing. Until now, while writing this book, I've tried to paint a picture of me as a victim of circumstance, saying that having a stammer forced me up a road, forced me into actions that I had no control over.

To try and explain: this was true, for the first 20 minutes of the game. In that time, I would flagellate myself of all the self-loathing, all the hate and all the embarrassment I felt because of my stammer, which had built up that week. I would charge into kick offs blindly and race around hitting rucks with no regard for anyone, my mantra was 'just hit anything'.

After this period of blind rage, the rugby sociopath would take over. Looking back, this character reared his ugly head after I won my first cap. I was so desperate to play for Wales again I would do anything to regain that shirt. I needed to be the best number eight in Wales. More than that, I needed to be the best number eight on the field when I played. I needed the selectors to know they couldn't pick anyone else, except me. If I didn't have the skill set to outplay my opposite number, I needed to find another way of dominating him, and this is when the idiocy kicked in. Ron Waldron often said, 'There's more than one way to pluck a chicken.' He was so right.

I did target players. I had learned how to, while coming through the ranks at Tred and Neath. I had learned how to disguise my actions, to wait and wait until an opportunity occurred. The key was spotting the moment, then getting it done. Rucks, mauls and kick offs were free-for-alls and by far the best opportunities to impose yourself. The target would have my total focus until he folded. Today I would have been sent off, but then you could get away with so much – a punch, a shoulder charge, ruthless rucking, all outlawed in the modern game.

The one thing I didn't do was hit any backs, I left them well alone. Firstly, because I couldn't catch them, and secondly, for fear of potential embarrassment. Imagine how it would look if you hit a back and he turned round and peppered you. There were some right hard nuts in the backs let me tell you. I did flatten Mark Ring once when Neath played Cardiff, but that was just because he was standing in the wrong place at the wrong time and he was their danger man. Sorry Mark. I only remember that incident because I saw it on *You Tube*.

Forwards, however, were fair game. Once, with Ebbw, we played Aberavon at the Talbot Athletic ground. Their eight, Steve Reece, was a big lad, a good ball carrier, and was doing well. He scored. That triggered me and I had to do something about it. At the kick off, I told Byron to put it high and straight to Steve.

Byron knew the score and dually obliged. The kick was perfect. Just as he was catching the ball I came through. He spun in the air like a Catherine wheel and didn't land very safely. The medics rushed on. As he was being treated, the ref called me over. He also called for our captain, Kingsley, and Colin Laity, the Aberavon captain, who knew me well from when we both played for Neath.

'Be careful, Mark,' said the ref. 'I can see that your run was mistimed. Don't mistime it again!'

'That wasn't mistimed,' Colin chirped. 'He bloody timed that perfectly, the dirty bastard.'

My run-ins with referees over the years have been interesting, to say the least, but as Huw Watkins, the WRU referee and Rugby World Cup touch judge, comments below, I've generally had a good relationship with the men in the middle:

> *'I first refereed Mark in the very late 1990s and he came with a reputation. As 'Scooby' was well known for being a tough player, younger players would push their luck and try and wind him up. As a referee you would always have your good eye on Mark and the other eye on the game. I fondly remember one game at Pontypool Park where Ebbw Vale were playing Pooler in a live televised game. Mark was captain of Ebbw Vale and during my boot check with the Ebbw team, Mark asked me to clear the tackle area as, according to Mark, Pontypool were renowned for loitering there. So, 10 minutes into the game, Pontypool were close to the Ebbw Vale try line and Mark was lying all over the player and taking a bit of shoeing. I blew the whistle and said: 'Mark, I've done exactly what you asked me to do and cleared the tackle area, now go for 10 mins.' He looked at me and grinned, gave a little wink and off he went. After the game he was first to have a drink with you and a great player to referee. A good uncompromising player, but great off the field as well.'*

There has always been a fierce rivalry in Gwent between Ebbw and Newport–Townies v Valley Commandos. Ebbw were in the ascendency but, out of the blue, Newport signed the brilliant Springbok number eight, Gary Teichmann, and we played them at home just days after he'd arrived in Wales. The hype surrounding the game was massive. He was brought in to put Newport back on the map and, for me, he had a target on his back. Within minutes, his class was obvious. To be fair, he was a former South African captain who had done almost everything in the game, but he had never played in Ebbw Vale with the rain and the wind howling across the field.

At a re-start I decided to make my move and gave my usual call, 'Put it on him, Byron.' Again, our outside half didn't disappoint – the kick was perfect. Hitting and engulfing Gary as he caught the ball, the Springbok hit the turf, closely followed by an 18 and a half stone Tred boy. I felt the air come out of Gary like a busted air bed. As I peeled myself off him, I rubbed his head into the mud and gave him a load of verbals. For 60 minutes I made sure he knew I was around, but fair dos to the fella, he got back to his feet every time, dusted himself off and got on with the game. Then Newport took him off. He'd taken enough of a Eugene Cross Park battering from us. The following day he appeared, looking a bit worse for wear, as a special guest on the BBC's *Scrum V*.

After that, Newport continued their re-build with Teichmann orchestrating the team. By the time we played the return fixture at Rodney Parade later in the season, he had definitely found his feet because there was no repeat of the previous encounter. We went ahead in the first half after I scored a try. It felt like it was a 30-metre screamer, with five defenders hanging on my back, but was probably about three metres in total. We wore ourselves out but couldn't put them away when we had our chances, and they just snook it at the end. Teichmann was a great signing who had given Newport the steel they'd been missing. Towards the end of the season we played Newport again in the Welsh Cup semi-final, a double header at the Millennium Stadium. By then Newport had spent big on new players. Shane Howarth, Simon Roweli, Andy Marinos and Jason Jones Hughes had joined the club and Teichmann had well and truly put his mark on the team. They were a really good outfit and they beat us well. So, I've got big respect for the guy. He was a top player.

Although my Wales days were well and truly over, I was still ambitious and enjoyed the European cup competitions Ebbw had qualified for. In the 1999-2000 season we reached the quarter-finals of the European Shield, when we played London Irish at home. They were a big-spending glamour team at the time, had an army of top-class players, and the game was scheduled for prime time viewing on a Saturday afternoon. This was the big time for us. The match had been hyped in the media all week and the eyes of the northern hemisphere were watching. It was tight, very tight. We scored, they scored, we scored again, and on the two teams went. They were good mind, but so were we, and both teams punched themselves to a standstill. We were both out on our feet. It was a brutal, physical encounter.

With about four minutes to go, we were ahead and I was thinking, 'Yes, yes, we can do this.' I could sense the anticipation and the crowd were willing us on but then there was a sharp blow on the whistle. A penalty was awarded against us. Up stepped their kicker. We all held our breath but he sent the ball straight through the posts. They shut up shop for the remaining few minutes and we were out. At that moment of defeat, dejected and frustrated, I looked to the sky and bellowed, 'Fuuuuuccccckkkk! Then hands were shaken, backs were patted and we walked dejectedly back to the dressing room, totally gutted. It was one of the big disappointments I've had playing rugby. There was no massive debrief, just sighs and lots of head shaking.

As we were all getting showered and changed, lads were turning on their mobile phones. Messages were coming in thick and fast. Some of the phones were the all singing and dancing types, but mine was an old black Nokia that cost a tenner but did the trick. I never usually turned it on, but I did that day. As I sat there in my pink leopard skin print jockstrap, licking my wounds, it rang.

It was Mam. My heart skipped a beat. What did she want? She never rang. I knew she would have been watching. She watched and taped everything. I've still got, somewhere, over 200 VHS tapes of games I'd playing in.

'What's up, Mam? Are you okay?'

'Am I okay?' she replied. 'I'm ashamed ... ashamed I am.'

'What have I done?' I thought. I'd stayed on all game, gave away a few penalties for some off-the-ball stuff but nothing major.

'Why Mam?' I asked, confused.

'Mark, you swore on the telly. You said the 'f' word. Plain as day it was. I'm ashamed. How can I go down the day room now?' Mam was living in sheltered accommodation by then. My old junior school in Earl Street had been demolished and rebuilt as an OAP unit.

'Everyone would have seen it,' she added. 'What will they say about me? Ashamed I am.'

'Mam c'mon,' I felt like bursting out laughing

'Right at the end it was. Full screen and all. The camera was on you, just you and you said that.'

'C'mon Mam, leave it there. It's not as if I hit anyone or got sent off.' Maybe she would have found that acceptable.

'I know, Mark, but everyone thinks you are so nice when you come and see me. I can't go out now.'

'Mam, mun, chill now. I'll come and see you tomorrow, okay?'

'I'm alright,' she said. 'Will you bring the children to see me?'

'Yes Mam. Of course. now chill. Bye Mam.'

Can you believe it. There I was, a 35-year-old man still getting a bollocking off Mam for swearing on live TV. Superb!

Mike Ruddock came in as coach for Ebbw after Leigh Jones moved on. I knew Mike from years before and he was a big name in the valleys. He'd had to end his promising rugby career early because of an accident in work. He was widely liked and respected and had big kudos among rugby people. A good coach then, and a good coach now. He was really professional in his approach and his own ideas shone brightly. Very approachable and always straight, I didn't forget that he'd given me my final cap three years previously.

I was 36 by now and still playing good rugby, if you could call what I did good rugby. My fitness was unquestioned and I wanted another two years to see my time out at Ebbw. I envisaged playing 15 games a year, be it back row or second row, while helping to pull the next generation through. I would have been happy with that but I knew things were on the wane for me. We had a good young squad with players like Nathan Budgett, Chay Billen, and Gareth Green, while I was the last one left from the old crew. Byron, Kingsley and Dai had all moved on.

Rudd pulled me aside and asked would I fill in for him as player-coach when he couldn't make it to training. He had a lot going on at the time and wanted me to front some conditioning skills sessions. The main sessions were always done by him. When these conversations happen, players know they're considered an elder and their time as a player is running out. In March, he pulled me in again. I knew the subject of my contract would be broached, as a few others had gone already. I thought I was next. Mike was matter of fact and totally up front. He didn't want to sign me as a player for the next season. It was time to bring the new group through which meant I wasn't part of it. This wasn't what I wanted to hear and I gave my view that I still had a lot to offer and brought a lot to the table. My pleas made no difference, he'd made up his mind and I knew the economics of the situation. Rather than pay me, an aging former international, a £30k salary, we both knew he could sign two young, aspiring internationals for roughly the same money. It made sense but there had to be another solution. Mike told me he wanted me to stay around the squad and what he could offer me to be team manager, and use my experience to mentor and assist the new generation. Paul Russell had come up with this idea and was prepared to subsidise it, which made me feel valued. Thanks Paul.

I was making strides with my speech through therapy, continual rehearsal, relaxation and breathing techniques so with a bit of understanding from the boys I could handle the role of manager, the phone calls and the communication. I wasn't ready to finish playing, though. I wanted to play rugby forever.

It was clear, however, that my full-time professional playing career was over. It had started with Ray Griffiths in 1988. Now, in 2001, a new life beckoned for Scooby. Finding a job that would cover my financial commitments was tough. There were offers to be a player-coach in Ireland, which would have earned the money I was looking for, but it would have meant being away from home for weeks on end. That would never have worked.

Then there was the psychological factor – how was I going to cope? For 13 years, from the age of 18, all I'd known was rugby. Being around rugby players, training every day for matches on weekends and then back to training on Monday. I'd become institutionalised. I was an unemployed former player.

This was going to be a challenge.

16

(Pooler) Über Alles

'The facts speak for themselves. A north Gwent boy stars for Neath and Wales in union, then Hull, Warrington, Wales and Great Britain in rugby league. That's a remarkable career in any era. I was honoured to 'coach' Mark towards the end of his club career whilst at Ebbw Vale. Always great company.'

Mike Ruddock

Bob Jude had other plans for me. He had taken over at Pontypool RFC, injecting his own money and devising a plan to win the Division One title and see Pooler promoted back to the Premiership, the big time. All the players Mike had dispensed with at Ebbw that summer signed with Pooler, plus Byron Hayward had come back from Llanelli. It was an offer too good to reject.

As part of the deal that took me to Pontypool, I started working for Bob as a sales rep for his flooring company, Bob Jude Flooring. I was made up. The job gave me a massive lift It made all the stress of speech therapy worth it. I was doing a normal job, doing standard things like making calls and meeting customers, things that everyone else took for granted.

Before the new season at Pontypool started, the whole family went to Australia for 10 weeks. I had landed a player-coach role on the gold coast at Currumbin (known as the Alley Gators) through a mate, Taffy Longman. The rugby was a great experience but the trip highlighted major issues in our marriage. We were together but had been functioning separately and now we had to spend ten weeks in each other's company. It was strained, but the children came first and we made sure they had a great time. By the time we returned home, however, I knew big changes were coming.

Back in Wales, I got back into work with Bob and playing for Pooler – leaving home at 8.30am, after I'd taken Osian and Manon to school, and often not coming back until 10pm.

We had a top-quality squad that went on that season to be pipped by Aberavon for the title, and we won it by a country mile the following year. The rugby was a lot more earthy in Division One, with many old school guys, who would mix it up if needed. If you bashed someone, they had no qualms about giving it back. I got clipped a few times. In one game against Tondu I left my head hanging out the side of a maul after I'd cleared a few rucks and Kevin Sadd took full advantage. He definitely rang my bell! It was one hell of a hit but I shook it off and played on.

Then there was a hooker for Glamorgan Wanderers. I don't know him to this day. Roughly the same thing happened. I should have learned to tuck my head in when driving in a maul after the smack from the Tondu bell-ringer, but arrogance got the better of me and the guy dropped me to one knee. I went off for five minutes but returned after the ice-pack had done its job and my head had cleared.

I'd taken two big hits in my first season in Division One. At Ebbw I'd only been clipped like that once in five years, courtesy of Newport's Rod Snow. I'd wiped him out at a ruck at Eugene Cross Park then, on the recoil, he swung a roundhouse right, that caught me right on the button. Down on one knee I went. Respect to all three of them.

I was still training hard and still playing as hard as I could. After games I continued going out with the boys and getting hammered on the weekend, just as a lot of rugby players did back then. I just immersed myself in rugby and being that person. The normal family things with my kids came top of the list when I wasn't training. From the school runs to DIY to playing computer games I was wearing that mask. The rest of the time I was 'Rugby Mark'.

Over the coming months it started to take its toll. Family, work and rugby was hectic and I was concerned that the fatigue was affecting my rugby. One idea was to stay with Bob in Cwmbran on training nights so I could go into work from there. This didn't work. It was around this time I first bumped into Julia in a pub in Neath. From Ystradgynlais but working in Ascot, Julia and I began chatting. We immediately clicked. In fact, she made me feel so relaxed in her company that I spilled the beans about my stammer. It turned into a bit of a counselling session. This was the first time I had ever admitted it to anyone outside my professional counselling. It surprised me that

I'd opened up to anyone, let alone a stranger. The reason was obvious – Julia had the wow factor, big time, but we also had a lot of mutual friends and our backgrounds were similar. Her dad was a collier and she was also an international athlete – a swimmer who had competed for Wales – but there was something else, she was someone who actually wanted to listen and didn't judge me. She didn't laugh at me – we laughed together, and I felt comfortable enough to share my biggest insecurity.

Living in Neath but working for Bob in Gwent and playing rugby for Pontypool wasn't good for my marriage, and by April the following year divorce was inevitable. It was the most traumatic time of my life, and leaving my kids when I left the family home nearly killed me. The impact it had on my children has been horrendous, which is incredibly sad and still haunts me.

When I called Mam, to give her the news that I had moved out of the family home and was getting divorced, she didn't say much. Her priority was that I and her grandchildren were okay, and that I had somewhere to stay. All the practical stuff. I reckon Mam knew it was coming and had seen the signs for a while. We rarely visited her as a family and when we did it was either me alone or me and the kids.

When I visited Mam in Tredegar the following day, I reassured her that things were good for me and that the kids were fine. I gave her a cwtch and a kiss. I always kissed Mam. I turned and waved ta-ra at the door and told her I would be up on the weekend with the kids. Then off I went to Pontypool for training.

That was the last time I saw her. Sandra called me two days later to tell me that Mam had died from a heart attack, in the day room while having a cup of tea with her friends. Sandra said she'd been told that Mam was talking away, happy as Larry, and had just gone quietly. They tried to revive her but she had slipped away, peacefully.

I still don't think I've ever truly accepted it. Losing Mam during the emotional turmoil of a divorce meant I wasn't able to fully comprehend what had occurred. I don't believe I ever really grieved.

I beat myself up for a while, like with my father, thinking it was me who had caused her death. Had he died because of worry about me going north or had he gone because I was sorted? Had Mam gone with the worry or had she gone happy? The two most life-changing things that had happened to me, had been accompanied by a family tragedy.

I went to see Mam in the chapel of rest and Glyn kindly came to the funeral with me and that's about it. I really don't remember much. It may be because, sub-consciously I'd blocked it out. The pain of losing Mam at the same time as leaving my young children, aged just four and eight, in the family home was traumatic and I found it almost impossible to cope. By then, and for the next six months, I was spending half my time staying at the house of my mate, Bowen, in Cadoxton, almost next door to the Green Dragon, and in Cwmbran. Again, my friend, Stella, was my crutch.

I would see Osian and Manon most days but the relationship between me and their mother had deteriorated and become quite toxic. Trying to explain to your children that you love them so much but have to live somewhere else is heart-breaking. The whole thing was getting too much and it overwhelmed me in a home game at Pontypool Park.

After a scrum we had kicked ahead and I was chasing the ball up field. The other players raced away but I went into slow motion. While everyone else was running off, into the distance, all I could hear was silence, as if I had been transported, alone, to the summit of a mountain. I slowed to a stop and just stood there, oblivious to what was going on around me. My eyes welled up and I thought, 'What the hell am I doing this for?' After a few seconds, I began to come out of my mind-mist. The game had stopped and some of the players were looking back at me with puzzled looks. I had no idea what had happened, or what to do, so I just clutched at my hamstring, called for the medic and limped toward the touchline. Grabbing a bag of ice, I rushed down the steps to the changing rooms, knowing that I needed to get out of there before my head really went. A quick shower followed, then a sharp exit. I needed to sort my head out and get my life back on track. Easier said than done.

All the ups and downs of a divorce were so hard to handle. Staying with my mate solved a very short-term problem – Jon was another friend I leaned on at the time, and I'll always appreciate his support – but I desperately missed being with Manon and Osian. My decision was made, it was time to rent a place and have my children over to stay as often as possible. So that's what I did. I eased up on the booze, and my old friend Stella was relegated to an occasional acquaintance as I got the kids sorted and focused on my work. This really helped and the constant turbulence changed to a few bumps now and again. Seeing my children made all the difference. I was coping, not thriving, but the job was sound and Pooler were flying high. The good in my life was outweighing the bad ... just!

Julia had left Ascot and had gone to work in Malaysia, as head of PE in a private school. She stayed out there for 18 months so wasn't around much, but I was getting back on my feet and she was there for me emotionally, which was the important thing. We spent the school holidays together and during that time our relationship grew and we laid the foundations of what was to come.

Julia's mam and dad supported me throughout this time, like they were my own parents. I'm eternally grateful to them for that and the support they give us now, even though we live 6,000 miles away.

Pooler won the Division One championship in 2003-04 and then things went pear shaped. Bob Jude was forced to pull the plug on the club due to economic and political factors. I carried on working for him for six months, but then that ended too. The two years I spent at Pooler had coincided with some momentous changes in my life – I'd met Julia, lost Mam, and been through a divorce. They say things come in threes, that's certainly true for me.

My personal life improved when Julia returned to Wales to be with me. She found a job in Neath so we could be near Osian and Manon, and we bought a house at an auction, making sure we found a home in which the children could have a bedroom each when they came to stay. We also enjoyed a few caravan holidays with the children. Moving in together, our relationship flourished but my working life took a dip when my job with Bob Jude came to an end and I was unemployed for a while. Julia was wonderful and so supportive, financially and emotionally, encouraging me to face the issues I had and to keep looking for a new job. Equally important, she was also there to pick up the pieces when my job applications were rejected. Without her love I would never have been able to keep myself afloat.

Getting interviews wasn't that difficult, but converting them into paid employment was hard. For a while I was a debt collector, but that didn't go well. My speech had improved, but speaking to people in pressure situations wasn't for me so I went back into landscaping. The hours were also unsociable and I wanted to be with my children. I then applied to the prison service and made it through to the final assessment, but the role play scenarios in the interview exposed my speech issues so it wasn't for me.

Then the Neath connections came into my life yet again. I had worked as a fitter/turner for an engineering company in Port Talbot in 1989, courtesy of Brian Thomas, but the travelling from Tred each day, to work and then on to the Gnoll for training was too much at the time and I jacked it in. If I'd moved to the area, working in Port Talbot and playing for Neath, my life may have turned out differently. I would probably still be there now, turning, milling and grinding machine components. I'd noticed that the same company was advertising for a field sales engineer so 15 years after leaving, I called in to see Terry and Len and they kindly gave me the job. I cannot express how significant this was for me, and how it enabled me to be a part of the real world again.

With the new job, my personal jigsaw was complete. Earning decent money and being an equal partner, financially, with Julia was good for my self-esteem, and I was spending time with Osian and Manon which meant the world to me. Life was good, and I asked Julia to marry me.

I was now a different, and hopefully better, person that I'd been when I was first married. As a younger man, my demons were destroying my life and having a negative impact on others around me, that I was oblivious to. The acknowledgement that my stammer was the core reason for my unacceptable behaviour, and the benefits of the speech therapy had increased my self-esteem and made me a calmer man. The new me was ready for the life I'd always craved.

My reputation, however, was still not a positive one. When Julia first told her father that she'd met me and we were becoming an item, his initial comment was very understandable: 'Jul, you've met some 'eaders in your time but he's a prize one'. His views changed after meeting me and, as Julia reminds me:

> *'By the time of the wedding, those views had disappeared. My father loved Mark.'*

Julia's mother was also won over. Like all grooms, I was nervous about the wedding vows and determined not to make a mistake, but I was no longer the terrified tongue-tied young man: 'I could sense Mark's anxiety about his speech, but his vows flowed and my mother told me she'd never have to worry about me again.' How sweet!!

The perfect new life I had found got even better when we decided to start a family together, and the following year Izzy was born. When your first baby is born, you love them with all your heart, and would do anything for them. If you're lucky enough to have a second, you may ponder 'how can I love this one as much as the first?' but you can and you do. Whenever children come into your life you have the same feelings towards them as for your first-born. Your capacity to love grows with every child. It's never ending. Love is equal and unconditional.

As children grow up, family dynamics and personal circumstances change and there may be certain situations where relationships feel unbalanced, but the truth is parents have the same combination of love and worries for all their children. You love them equally and the pride felt when they succeed knows no bounds. They are your children and you love each one with all your heart.

Another positive development in my life was signing again for Neath in the semi-pro league. I was 38 and knew I couldn't go on forever but it felt great to pull the Maltese cross back on and run out at the Gnoll again. I had always been known as Mark Jones Neath and I reckon I always will be. I'm proud of that.

Rowland Phillips was coaching with Pat Horgan, but I often chipped in sporadically to pass on any applicable knowledge. The team were a mixture of young bucks and old bulls: myself, Andrew Howells and Paul Jones slowing down the young guys like James Hook, Simon Peters and Richard Carter. It was like the old proverb of two bulls in a field:

'Let's run down there and roger a few of those cows?' the young bull says. 'No, lets walk down and roger them all,' replies the old bull.

With so many characters blending together so well and so quickly, we had a great season in 2003-04 and won the Welsh Premier championship and the cup. I tried my hardest to be on my best behaviour while playing, however, there was an incident in the Welsh Cup final against Caerphilly, which saw me banned for 11 weeks. I was cited and really taken to task for what was, on the field, seen as an accidental clash of heads. When it was examined and pulled apart by video jury, and most of Wales, it was deemed as a deliberate head butt. I'll let you decide.

That was the end for me. I'd had a great innings and had gone out with a cup winners medal, and an 11-week ban. My career had run its course. The last dinosaur was forced into extinction that day. Things had evolved, most would say for the better – not me!

17

Holidays in the (Qatar) Sun

'As manager of the Wales RL team I got to know the man as well as the player and I have nothing but the highest respect for Mark. His stammer did not make life easy for him and challenged his mental health, but his immense strength of character saw him beat his demons and win his battles. Mark Jones is a giant of a man with a huge heart who has a great story to tell.'

Jim Mills

The big issue at the moment in rugby is concussion and head injuries, but it's not only the head that gets smashed. It's a tough old game and steps have been taken to make it safer. The shoulder charge has been outlawed, the wipe-out at the ruck is banned and the no-arm tackle is penalised. All three can see a lot of damage done at the contact zone. Back in the day, every forward had a broken nose or a cauliflower ear. They were worn like badges of honour not splurged over social media with an air of self-pity. The game was not as quick as it is now, but it was tough, dirtier and relatively unpoliced,

Since the 2000s, the players have become more athletic, quicker and more muscular, so the impacts had become bigger and more physical. Guys like 'Bakkies' Botha, Dale Macintosh and Jacques Berger could really do damage just by their sheer size and spectators witnessed some bad stuff – Rickie Evans getting hit by Olivier Merle, destroying both his legs, and career, were a prime example. All this highlights the dangers that rugby players expose themselves to, but players know the dangers when they take the field. The game was and is fraught with danger but that is why men and women choose to participate and choose to test themselves. The game was hard enough without the transgressions outside the laws of the game. No one wants to come away from a match injured. I realise this now.

I realise that the way I played was endangering other players and would simply not be tolerated now. Looking back, some of my actions make me feel ashamed. How could I react in that way? There was no excuse. I can only apologise for my transgressions.

I was a product of circumstance. I can't excuse it. I can only try to explain it.

Not that I've been diagnosed, I'm too afraid to be assessed, but reading about all the symptoms of brain trauma I would put a tenner on it that I'm suffering the effects of head knocks. I signed for Hull in 1990 and played rugby league for seven seasons. By the end of the fifth, sixth and seventh seasons, my speech had deteriorated that much, I couldn't put three words together. It reached a point where I would go to bed and regularly be woken in the early hours by a huge clanging and banging in my head. It was as if someone had hit my skull with a cricket bat. My head would pound for hours.

I never mentioned it to anyone but I knew that I had to get out of league. The head collisions had a major effect on me and my speech, and boiled over into my everyday life. I had mood swings and violent outbursts. I was totally frustrated, incredibly anxious, very angry. I could not control myself. I would play music at full volume when driving at 100 miles per hour along the motorway and just scream, with tears streaming down my face like some crazy bastard from a Mad Max movie. When I signed for Ebbw, there was the incident in the service station that Kingsley has already spoken about. Then another in the canteen at Ebbw Vale's training facility in Usk, not to mention all the other stuff on the field,

It was all a release from the frustration and anger I felt inside. I wanted to escape, wanted to get away from everything. When things got really bad in Hull, and I couldn't deal with it anymore, I'd drive to places like Bridlington late at night and just sit on a bench listening to the waves crashing over the pebbles on the shore. The sound was mesmerizing. The soothing sound of the pebbles ricocheting off each other as the waves threw them about took me to a different place.

When I came back to Wales I found other places, near running water, where I could escape to – walking my dog Charlie for hours along the banks of a mountain stream or along the coast. It was the sound that drew me in. It spirited me away, eased me, soothed me and helped empty my mind of the chaos going on inside. No other sound could do this. It engulfed me, flowed into my head and washed everything away.

I constantly wondered why I was acting like this. It wasn't just my stammer. It's not until recently I've made a connection, maybe it was concussion. Players are reporting symptoms of dementia and memory loss and are preparing claims against rugby's governing bodies, seeking compensation for injuries caused by neglect of personal safety and duty of care by the national unions and the global organisations. In my opinion, there has been no neglect by the governing bodies.

The implications of concussion are being discussed continually and when proven research has become available the powers that be have acted upon the available medical advice and introduced protocols to deal with the issue. For example, the introduction of the blood bin, the Head Injury Assessment (HIA) protocols and the rule changes designed to minimise head contact. I think the rule makers have acted responsibly and in full consideration of the players.

My friend gave me different information. He told me that players in New Zealand were requested to sign a waiver before they played. If correct, this would point to neglect in the northern unions.

The issue of concussion has been around for a lot longer than the current legal cases. I played senior rugby in Wales from 1984 to 1990, and was only concussed once in a club game, when I was clattered by Clive Burgess. When I played for Hull, it was a weekly occurrence. It happened far more often in rugby league than in rugby union. You only have to watch one game of National Rugby League (NRL) in Australia to see the difference. You get more HIAs in one game of NRL than you get in 20 games of rugby union. Yet not one of those players are submitting legal claims. Numerous players in the NRL have recently been forced into retirement due to complications linked to concussion, but not one law suit. Why is this? Are attitudes different in Australia?

Is there a link between concussion and neurological disease such as motor neuron disease? Absolutely yes. You only have to look at the high-profile cases of Mike Gregory, Rob Burrow, Joost van der Westhuizen and Doddie Weir to know it's happened. Superb players all, cut down in their prime.

I can only relate to my own experiences. All I can say is that my speech was really affected. I could provide a list of symptoms which many would consider as 'normal' and things that happen to everyone, but for me, it's the frequency of these occurrences that are concerning. What really made me sit up and take notice was when, for my current role, I began to study A level physics as part of my professional development. What I learned today would be gone tomorrow. My short-term retention of information is nonexistent. That's where I am. Others will be further down the line.

The principle here, however, is different. No one puts gun to your head and forces you to play rugby. When you walk across the whitewash you know what could happen. You know you could get smashed in the head. We all knew the risks but chose to forgo the consequence. I find it very hypocritical that there are thousands of players out there, the current group of claimers included, who were and are abrasive players. They enjoyed the smash. They enjoyed displaying brute force. That's why people play rugby – the physical confrontation, the physical dominance gave me and many others a buzz. A number of these players have done as much damage to others as they have incurred themselves.

If you were to ask any of the former players involved, 'Did you ever get a buzz from putting a big hit on someone?' and they answered 'No', they would be lying. It's what we did!

We definitely have to protect the integrity of the game, eradicate dirty play and introduce – based on the latest medical research – protocols to protect players, but we also need to protect the game. In my opinion, some will jump on the band wagon just for the chance of a pay-out.

As players, we've all taken the accolades, loved the kudos, enjoyed the applause and received the pats on the back, but everything has a price. For every Ying there comes a Yang.

We shouldn't forget how lucky and privileged we have been, to have a gift that allowed us to compete at the highest level in sport we love, and get paid well for doing so. We all need to give something back, help the players of the future and help ensure they aren't exposed to the same risks we were. Funding needs to be made available for research and care, absolutely, but not to pay off someone's mortgage. We also need to take steps to ensure the game we played is not destroyed. It should be put on even firmer financial foundations, starting at the grassroots community clubs and taken around the world to nations struggling to promote the game. Our duty is to help rugby give others the chance to experience what we had.

Back off my soapbox and back to the story.

The Lions headed to New Zealand in 2005 and I had just turned 40. Out the blue I was called by Phil Kingsley Jones (Kingsley's father), who asked if I fancied a free trip to the Land of the Long White Cloud, plus expenses. Of course I did, who wouldn't? There was, however, one condition.

'You've got to box, Mark.'

'Box! I can't box kippers,' I replied.

He went on to explain it was for a meningitis charity. The great Keiron Gregory, who I respected and admired, had died from meningitis, so I agreed to get involved. The trip including spouses and children, so Julia and Izzy, who was only six months old, could also travel with me. Visiting New Zealand was too good an opportunity to miss and the boxing would only be a charity thing, so no one would get hurt. Not wanting to let myself down, I started training and did a little bit of sparring. It wasn't enough, nowhere near enough. Richard Webster, Byron Hayward were the other Welsh lads on the trip. Facing us were the formidable Kiwis Frano Botica and Frank Bunce, and I'd be going into the ring against Mutua Parkinson, a 6'1, 16 stone openside flanker, and 10 years younger than me. I should have read the signs which were, quite frankly, staring me in the face.

It was a fantastic trip. Joe Frazer was the guest of honour. What a guy. He held Izzy in the palm of his giant hand. It was totally humbling to be in the presence of such a gracious human being. A treasured memory.

As the bout loomed I devised a plan. 'Failing to prepare is to prepare for failure' is that well-known phrase. Mike Tyson's comment was, though, a lot more pertinent: 'Everyone has a plan until they're punched in the face.'

My plan was to use my left jab to keep him at bay and then pick him off with the right. It didn't quite work out like that. The bell rang and off we went. I was jabbing and keeping out of the way. He was a mean looking hombre. After only 30 seconds he moved to his right and came straight over the top with a bomb of a right hand. He hit me straight in the face. Like cartoon characters being slammed with an anvil.

I'm not a great dancer but I automatically started doing the moon walk! It was another Olivier Roumat moment, but Mike Budd wasn't there to lean on. I dropped one knee. The crowd were cheering and I was panicking, desperately working out what I was going to do next. What was my Plan B? By the count of six my head had cleared and the referee signalled I could continue.

If he hit me again it would be curtains. I'd have gone straight down on my arse. A sharp exit from the ring wasn't an option, even though I knew I should get the hell out of there. Back to my feet, I just remember trying to get through the next minute until the end of the round. How I managed to fend him off, as he came in for the kill and the crowd roared him on, I will never know. It was pure self-preservation. The bell rang and I lurched over to the corner.

'Jab, Mark,' said the trainer, trying to encourage me. Throw the right, and move.'

'You fucking jab, throw the right and move ... the bloke's a beast.' I thought.

I was desperately searching for ways not to get hit again, and decided to simply try and shut him down: 'If he can't swing, he can't hit me.' So that's what I did. I wrestled him for the next two, two-minute, rounds. I got hit a few times but no more bombs, just shrapnel. My face was battered and I had a nose like WC Fields. The crowd weren't happy, they wanted fireworks and I had given them a damp squib, but I didn't care. I was the one getting hit, not them. It was the hardest thing I'd ever done. It definitely felt like part-payback for what I'd dished out in the past: well-deserved karma to all those I'd battered. I was glad I hadn't gone down the boxing route when I was growing up, and those men and women who box have my utmost respect.

Before I rejoined Neath, I had been meeting Chris O' Callaghan at Aberavon RFC. Chris is a few years older than me and was finishing his career when I was coming through. He's old school, tough as they come, and has a great brain. There were a few around like him, such as Roger Powell of Newport. The fact that they were intelligent made them a lot more dangerous. They wouldn't react first-off. They would wait, pick their moment and then pounce. They were like the SAS – mess them about and they'd exact revenge on their own terms. I had big respect for him, so when it was over for me at Neath, I joined Aberavon as player-coach, working alongside Kevin Hopkins who'd been with me at Ebbw.

The history between Neath and Aberavon is legendary. It's a rivalry that goes back decades and, as I was about to discover, I wasn't the flavour of the month with the stalwarts of Aberavon. The owner, Andrew Vaughan John, was a top man and a total gent. He had a moral compass and was as straight as a dye. He divulged that there had been some stiff opposition to me joining the club from some die-hard Aberavon supporters. Their feelings ran so deep that many stopped coming to support the team because of my presence. This mirrored similar comments from the Baa Baa's dignitaries – that I wasn't the type of player the Baa Baas wanted to be associated with – passed on to me by Keith Harse, their physio in the 1980s. I received a comparable message from the great Terry Holmes when speaking to him about joining Cardiff when I was looking to come back from league. 'Mark,' he said. 'The boys upstairs said 'no way'.'

I knew I was an acquired taste!

All in all, I had a great 18 months in Aberavon. I captained the team on a few occasions but then leant towards the coaching side. I didn't see eye-to-eye with a few people but that's not an issue for me. We all have different ways of achieving our goals. Others aside, Andrew was always professional and I thank him for that.

The field sales job had also finished. After years of being told by companies I was being let go because of my speech issues, it was refreshing, but very sad, that it was purely a business decision – an unfortunate scaling back of commercial operations. I left with no issues and full of gratitude to the employers who took me back and gave me a chance.

After kicking my heels for a few weeks, I was interviewed for a job in Parc Prison in Bridgend, as a horticultural instructor. I'd never had an interest in gardening because of the gruelling hours I had spent as a kid digging over my dad's vegetable plot every spring. At Parc, I specialised in hard landscaping where I had some previous experience, mainly running away from human contact. The interview followed the familiar pattern of me controlling my stammer with deep breathing. A positive sign was that the nerves in my stomach were now reduced to a hand blender, not a cement mixer, a golf ball in my throat not a basketball, and a slight sweat not a full body drenching. It went well. I thought I'd spoken well and given a good account of myself.

Then came the final question, 'Mark, do you think your speech will have an effect on your delivery and effectiveness?' What? How can he ask that? I had done great I thought but now this felt like a massive insult and brought me straight back to earth. I laughed it off.

'No not at all, I can function very well,' I replied, without any blocks I must add. It made me realise what I think is good is not good to other people. Yet, I got the job and spent a cracking two years tutoring and taking lads on day-release into the community.

Julia was often asked, around that time, 'What's Mark doing now?'

'Oh, he's in Parc Prison.' Meaning I worked there.

People would look shocked and say, 'Oh no, are you coping ok? What did he do to get sent down? Was it something on the rugby field?'

Again, my reputation preceded me!

I liked it there. Hugh Williams-Jones tells a story of the day I met his wife in a shop in Cowbridge. She asked me what I was doing.

'I've got some prisoners outside cutting grass.' I replied.

'What if they run off?' She inquired, her face giving her thoughts away.

Apparently, I turned to her and growled, 'They won't run away because I've told them I would hunt them down and kill them if they did.' I then paid for my items and walked out.

After leaving Aberavon by mutual consent the following Christmas, I picked up another coaching role in Clevedon, near Bristol, thanks to Phil Kingsley Jones. I also did a stint with Mathew McCarthy at Dunvant, and those two positions saw me through to the end of the season.

Without a coaching position sorted for the following season I was lucky to land a job at the Port Talbot steel works – 12-hour shifts moving torps, vessels of molten iron, between the blast furnace and the steel making plant. This came at precisely the right time as I still needed to maintain a decent salary to pay the bills and raise my new family.

It could be a filthy, dirty job but the craic between the boys in the crew more than made up for the discomfort. After six months I'd passed the induction and the required training and was paired with Darren Phillips, a driver who had worked there for 20 years or more. He was, and is, a bit of a rebel with a full body tattoo. He loved showing it off, and other things, at shower time. Working shifts for 20 years had its effect on his outlook. He was very frank and said it as it was. His honesty was refreshing. One shift, we were moving iron and he was up in the cab, nice and warm. I had been out at 3am in the pouring rain and was soaked through. As I burst in through the door and took a brief interlude from the storm, he looked at me with disbelief in his eyes and, in the dim light cast by the 12-watt bulb in the cab, said: 'How the fuck is Mark Jones shunting rail on a shitty February morning?'

'What do you mean butt? I'm the same as you, a council estate boy,' I said.

'Fuck off, Mark, you know what I mean. You've done the lot in rugby. Big name an' all. How have you ended up in this shit hole?'

What I said next was the stark realisation of where I was in life. 'Because of my speech and because I need the money,' I told him.

This was huge for me. For once I hadn't tried to hide my stammer. I hadn't tried to ignore the fact. I hit it head on. Why I chose that moment to put it out there, or why I chose to own up to Darren, I don't know. It must have been that I knew he was non-judgemental and, to him, it would be no big thing. I also realised I'd come full circle. I had started my working life in the steel works, at 17, with a stammer and I was back there 30 years later, at 47, still with a stammer. My old man was right: 'You is what you is. You can't escape what you are. Life is not about the destination, it's about the journey.'

On my journey, from 17 to 47, I had done and seen things I could never have imagined, and this wasn't going to be the end of my journey. You are what you are, sure enough, but you're on that journey until they put you in the box, open the red velvet curtains and roll you through. It was then I started to realise that the person holding me back, was me, and that needed to come to an end. I was still on my own personal journey and there was still a long way to go.

With that infusion of reality, I felt invigorated and quickly put myself forward for a job as hot metal controller on the blast furnace. The job entailed me issuing directions to rail crews via radio links, who were transporting the molten iron on a 1km route from the blast furnace to the steel conversion plant. The controller is a vital link between departments and a very stressful role. There was so much going on that it was an intense role for any one, let alone a guy with a stammer. It meant I had to constantly employ my breathing techniques and de-stressing strategies to get through a shift, constantly aware of, and constantly focused on, my speech and the requirements of the job.

When things were quiet, I was comfortable, I could breathe and converse with the crews competently, but when things got hectic, which could mean speaking to three crews and answering the phone simultaneously, it stretched me to the limit, and a bit further sometimes. Even though I'd be exhausted by the end of it, the feeling of triumph and pride I got from that job was unbelievable.

'You've done it, you can speak,' I'd say to myself. 'You can do a job that anyone can do, you're normal.' It was the first time I'd felt normal in my life. I did the job for a few months and was then called in by the manager, who more than understood the issues I was facing. He asked me if I thought the job was suitable for me and if I'd consider a sideways move to another role in the department. It was a well angled question by Simon because we both knew I was struggling at times but I'd never have admitted it. It was the first time I had felt normal but knew that the job wasn't for me. I took the other role but left feeling proud of what I had achieved.

Another thing that happened around this time, that made me even prouder, was when Zara was born. By now I was 46 but was made up to have another daughter and looking forward to all the love, the cwtchs, and affection a girl can give you. It was unlikely we'd have any more children, so I wanted to enjoy every moment and make the most of this final opportunity of being a dad. We had moved by then and were now living about a mile from the steel works. I was working 12-hour shifts and spent the rest of the time doing baby and family stuff. I would cycle to work when it wasn't hammering down. I was certainly living the life of an industrial worker but I wouldn't have swapped it for anything.

After some difficult years, that succession of jobs helped me and moved me forward to where I am now. I was given opportunities to do those jobs because I was in control of my speech. I was far from perfect, but I could function. When I was younger, I wasn't in control and couldn't function, so grew my personality to cope. I had rugby as a release, then, and I've now dealt with it. Being open and talking about my journey is the final part for me. I feel free.

I still stammer but it doesn't encase me as it did. I can speak to an audience and ask for a ¼ of sherbert bonbons in the shop. It's not about me anymore. I don't want to be a champion of the oppressed or the leader of the Justice for Stammerers League. There just needs to be realisation within society that just because you can't see it when you first look at someone, that it doesn't exist. Stammerers don't want to talk about it. They want to hide it. They want to fit in. They want to be like you. What's insignificant to you is massive to us, a little smirk, or a whispered comment can grow like a cancer, into a massive, raging tumour full of self-loathing and humiliation. Living without confidence and getting laughed at by society is not a nice place to be. I dealt with my stammer by pulling on a rugby jersey releasing all my frustrations on everyone who stood in my way.

You can only kick a dog so many times before it bites, and when it does, who's the bad guy?

The opportunity with Ampthill happened around this time and I played at Twickers again. After this, I coached part time at Abercrave RFC. This was cracking. A little club with big ambition with loads of young local talent. I helped a few of them have a crack at the big time. I was working shifts and finding it tough to juggle rugby and work. Something had to give and sadly, that was where my rugby career finally finished.

It had been ten years since Julia came back from Malaysia. She had come back for me and was working in Neath. We had got married and had two girls, Izzy and Zara. From the very start Julia said, 'There's a world out there and I'm going to give our girls every opportunity.' Osian and Manon were well into their teens and focusing on their education so, if there was a good time to look for opportunities abroad, this was it. Now was time to realise the ambition.

There were months of job applications and offers but they just weren't right, but then Julia had a job offer in Qatar and we decided to give it a crack. Looking back, moving to the Middle East was difficult for me. Julia was born with travel in her blood and wings to fly. I wasn't. I was used to knowing everyone in Tredegar, Neath, Ystradgynlais, Ebbw Vale and Wales and, more importantly, them knowing me.

Arriving in Qatar as a sponsored spouse with only the promise of a job, leaving Manon and Osian in Wales, was tough even with a pool and the sun shining

I missed being recognised and being stopped by rugby fans in supermarkets. Those interactions boosted my feeling of self-worth and pumped up my ego on a daily basis. Slowly, though, the pressure began to lift and I realised I didn't have to be Mark Jones, the number eight, anymore. I could relax. My speech started flowing and I started work. I studied physics A level and became part of the Qatar Rugby coaching set up. I was now just Mark Jones, not Mark Jones 'the stammerer'.

The sun shines 95% of the time – in all sorts of ways. We are blessed. The country is safe, the company have been amazing to us and literally Qatar has given us a great life.

The rugby in Qatar is a little sporadic, but my daughter's swimming career is taking off, so that needs constant attention. I had never considered what it takes to be successful in other sports until I became involved indirectly in swimming. My wife swam at the Commonwealth Games in 1990 and Izzy swims competitively.

She recently won her first Welsh cap in Ireland. I was so proud. The number of hours she puts in is unbelievable. She's in the water for over 20 hours a week, then there's the gym and flexibility exercises, which takes her swimming training to over 24 plus hours every week. That's far more than any other amateur sport, and most other sports. It's not just a sport, it's a lifestyle.

Zara is now 11. She is the free spirit of the family. All she wants to do is dance and perform – the polar opposite to Izzy. Zara hasn't realised it yet, but she has a real talent for swimming. The girl just loves life. I just want to give her the freedom to express herself and not to worry about mundane things.

I know I've changed and Julia can see that as well. When asked about the new Mark, the Mark she shares her life with, she wrote this:

> *Mark is the kindest, most helpful person you could ever wish to meet. He still thinks he is 36 and is a very lateral thinker. I have learnt how to ask and when to ask and guide him. If you ask him to get a cooked chicken from Tesco, be prepared for him to have eaten it before he comes home. Give Mark a beer and he loves a story and a song. He could definitely perform as an Elvis impersonator. He is very entertaining and a real gentle giant. I would in a heartbeat choose him again and again.*

A lot has happened in the time I've been in Qatar. I now have two gorgeous granddaughters, Mali and Etta, but due to Covid I haven't had the opportunity to see a lot of them. I hope that when the world settles down, I'm able to travel back a bit more and get to know them a bit better. This time I'm certainly looking forward to reading them bed time stories.

I'm going to finish things off now. I've said all I can and I just want to put things in perspective to all the people who may not still understand: 'He's got a stammer, so what?'

Having a stammer is debilitating. It can destroy you from the inside. It's like one of those old films where a kid wets his pants in class and he's made to stand up, humiliated, with all the other kids in the class pointing and laughing. The camera zooms in and out, showing him ashamed and alone. I was that kid every time, being made to feel worthless and told to man up and just get on with it. Swallowing your pride a few times in your life is not always a bad thing, but being forced to swallow your pride every day leaves you with zero self-esteem.

After a while it gets to you, and it put me in a place I didn't want to be. I admit, the inner torment twisted me, hurt me, and drove me in all directions, so I hope my words can help you understand why my mindset was different to 95% of the other players and why I did what I did. It was, simply, to survive.

Writing this book has raked over a myriad of buried emotions. It's been disturbing and enlightening. It's been painful beyond compare. All the trauma I had previously disposed of, and all the emotions I have buried deep inside me have been printed here for you all to see. The process of working on this book has made me realise that they were buried for a reason, but I have now opened Pandora's Box and I can't close it again.

I know I'm putting myself in the firing line, I know I'm likely to cop a bit of flak from certain quarters. Like the keyboard warrior who hides behind his screen anonymously ripping other people to bits to hide their own inadequacies, safe in the knowledge that there will be no consequences for their stinging remarks. I know the score. I was the one hiding my own inadequacies with verbal and physical outbursts.

I'm expecting some people to think, 'Scooby! Book! I hope it takes him a shorter time to write it than it would to say it, hahahahaha.' I'm well used to that. It drove me insane 30 years ago, now not so much.

It's the same as when you had a poor game, the critics can't wait to rip you apart. It comes with the territory. Everyone is entitled to an opinion and now social media gives a platform to this type of criticism. It's always been there but previously it was kept to the pub and the carpark. Now the slagging goes viral. Some players and partners get offended by it, but that's where we are. The simplest and easiest way to stop the verbals 30 years ago was a sharp left jab to the nose. That was the consequence of abusing someone. Now, there's no real consequence. Were the old ways the best?

In Tred, when I was growing up, there was a guy called Freddie Vaughan. He had the most severe stammer you had ever imagine. He couldn't say a word. It was pitiful. Although he lived among us, he operated outside every day society – his one release was his singing, being able to sing like a bird without a single block. For everything else, his stammer was so severe, he wasn't living, he was existing. No one took the piss because it was that bad. He was looked upon as the stuttering fool – pitied but not helped. I didn't want to be looked upon like Freddie Vaughan. That's what drove me. To this day I hate it if anyone says, 'You can sing though. You don't stammer then.' Or if anyone finishes a sentence for me. Raking up my memories forced me to think about Freddie, and how he must have felt? What I've experienced pales into insignificance compared to him. There's always someone worse off than you.

I've been lucky to have been helped by so many strong characters throughout my life. My father was a huge influence and gave me my first pair of rugby boots. I owe him so much. Other father figures have been very influential and I owe them all so much: from Dai Chard for helping me get noticed in youth rugby, to Ron and Brian in Neath, Marcus and Paul Russell at Ebbw Vale, and finally Bob Jude. So many players, coaches, and club officials have tried to help and given me the time and the space to find my way in life. And then there's Mam – there are no words that could adequately describe what she did for me.

Through most of that time, I did my best to mess it all up. Arrested, sent off, banned and being obnoxious was what I did. I wanted and I needed a way to escape from being what and who I was. I sold my soul to get my name in the paper, and got the Welsh cap, but I still stammered. Being 'Rugby Mark' was the price I had to pay to achieve what I did. I grew the character. I lived it. I thrived on it. The more anger I had the further I got. It was self-fulfilling. Without it I would have never achieved what I did and it definitely compensated for any lack of skill I had.

When I first opened up about my stammer the media came knocking at my door, and I spoke honestly about my experiences. That was a therapeutic process in itself, during which more pieces of the jigsaw fell into place. I finally realised that all the fighting against it, all the stress to hide it, and all the fear of stammering was actually allowing it to grow. Actively forcing it to grow. It was feeding off all the negative energy I was generating.

The moment I exposed it, I felt the grip it had on me loosening. I could feel it fading away, leaving me like burning embers blowing away. The burden had gone. I felt lighter. I could breathe again and I finally felt at peace, because I had exposed it and spoken about it. It was an epiphany, a total revelation. It's my resurrection.

Some may think, 'What the hell is he talking about. He's off his head.' I'm certainly not the finished article and there is more road to travel down on my journey to redemption but opening up feels like I've been cleansed. I've been blown away by how positive it is making me feel. There was a time when I would tell people I had a twin brother. Now I just say he's emigrated.

The only other person I have spoken to in any depth about this is my wife, Julia, who has given me the strength and focus to learn to cope with it. Without her I'd still be standing at the bar.

As an adult you're going to have disagreements with people. You are going to have to stand up verbally when you think you've been ripped off or wronged, but how can you argue your point when you can't speak? You either argue and get aggressive because you're trying to make a point, while fighting the stammer, or you just say, 'Yes, okay' and walk away. That's why I avoided verbal confrontation like the plague. I used to get totally wound up and I just would not put myself through that hurt in a situation where I could lose control.

It would have been easy to shut the door and never go out, and it has definitely challenged my mental health on a daily basis. I refused to do that and just kept fighting. Picking your battles is important, though. I'd fought for 50 years and lost every time until I realised putting the stammer out there, accepting it, is the best way to overcome it. When you tell people it exists, its power over you subsides and you can start taking control. That's the first step to owning it, not it owning you.

Just remember, we are all dealt a hand of cards in life, but the difference between success and failure is how we play those cards.

Pre-pandemic, in August 2019, I had lined up a cameo performance in Paul James' testimonial game at the Gnoll. I was on holiday in Tenerife but was scheduled to be back in Wales the day of the match, a few hours before kick off. I wanted to see all the boys and this was an opportunity to relive past glories and get cheered by the crowds again. All past players love this sort of stuff. It's one of the reasons we played the game in the first place.

As it happened, I was delayed and didn't reach Neath until 6.30 pm. The game was done but the craic was still happening. The club was bouncing. And numerous stars, like Chris Wyatt, Shane Williams, Mike Richards, Carl Gnojek, Phil Pugh and Leigh Davies had stayed after the match to have some fun with Paul.

All the old stories were being retold, of when we were all two yards faster and could jump two feet higher. Proper fishermen's tales but rugby style. After a few drinks we left the club and visited all the old establishments in Neath town centre. It was now around 10.30 pm and I was ready for home but I bumped into Mal Langford in one of the pubs. I was with a different crowd adjacent to his group and we were all conversing, laughing and joking. After about five minutes, I could feel him staring at me with a quizzical look on his face. He gestured me to come over and I leant in to hear what he had to say. 'Mark, I've been listening and I can't believe it's you. Where's your stammer gone?'

I didn't expect such an upfront comment but I was bursting inside with pride. I looked at him, just managing to control my eyes from welling up, and said, 'I'm just not angry anymore.'

And for me that's it. I'm not sure if speech was the cause or if anger was the catalyst but I know they work hand-in-hand. One fed off the other. I still stammer but now I realise ... does it really matter?

Epilogue

On a side note, on all the programmes and official documents from my time playing for Wales, I am listed as Mark Alun Jones. This is incorrect. I'm just plain Mark Jones. I have looked into this and have come up with an explanation, I think. The year before I was first selected for Wales Youth, around 1982, there was a player named Mark Alan Jones from Rhymney in Gwent. I believe he was also a number eight and who also got capped by Wales Youth. After that youth cap, he went off the radar and didn't progress into senior rugby. Then a year later I came along, Mark Jones, also from Gwent. This must have caused some confusion among the administrators at the WRU. What's the chances of two number eights with same name, roughly the same age and from the same area? They must be the same guy. Wrong! If you have ever been to the valleys you will know. There were three boys called Mark Jones in my school, it's a pretty popular name. The WRU got his name wrong, and linked it to mine!

I remember telling the team bosses that I wasn't Mark Alun Jones, just Mark Jones, but my protests fell on deaf years. To this day, over 30 years later, I'm still officially known as Mark Alun Jones in those programmes and official publications. There was no Mark Alun Jones, just a Mark Jones and a Mark Alan Jones.

If anyone knows someone at the WRU, please give them a nudge!

Playing Career Statistics

Rugby Union - Club		Appearances	Points
1984-85	Tredegar	23	20 (5T)
1985-90	Neath	168	244 (61T)
1997-02	Ebbw Vale	107	70 (14T)
2002-04	Pontypool	48	25 (5T)
2004-05	Neath	22	5 (1T)
2005-06	Aberavon	13	-
Rugby Union - International			
1983-85	Wales Youth	4	4 (1T)
1985-88	Wales B	5	8 (2T)
1987-90	Wales	15	8 (2T)
Rugby League - Club			
1990-95	Hull FC	68	20 (5T)
1995-97	Warrington	38	8 (2T)
Rugby League - International			
1991-96	Wales	11	16 (4T)
1992	Great Britain	1	-

Mark on Bunko

Amongst the madness that was Dowlais Rugby Club, there was always a safe haven, somewhere to talk sense and find respite from the insanity. When you had reached saturation point, I would gravitate towards Bunko who would always offer his ear and a sensible answer. He was, and is, a great observer of human behaviour as is reflected in his writing. His books and plays are about people and incidents that have occurred. His play, Knuckles is a pastiche of a number of characters, all of which he grew up with or around. He's not imagining, it's all true.

So, when Ashley suggested I work with Anthony, I was landed, as I knew he was on the same wavelength, had the same background and appreciated the same things as myself. I spent a fair chunk of time around Bunko, drinking, talking, laughing and carousing. There was always a story flying about who was the hardest in Merthyr, and who had done what that weekend. Good 'lad' stuff. Relating to each other has really helped to convey my story. He has a talent for putting the icing on the cake and he really gets where I'm coming from. I can reinforce a point and an angle, and he gets it.

It's been a pleasure working with you.

Thanks, butt.
Mark

Bunko on Mark

Out of all the autobiographies I have worked on over the years, Mark's book is the one I've enjoyed writing the most. I knew Mark back in the days when he played for Wales, when the late and great Steve Fealey brought Mark back to Dowlais Rugby Club when they played together. Along with a few others, I became good friends with the giant from Tredegar, but lost contact with him until a few years back when we bumped into each other in Swansea. Mark, who was then living in Qatar, was surprised to learn I was writing books and plays and other stuff.

'You'll have to write my life story one day,' he quipped. 'I would love too,' I replied, but we both left it at that. Fast forward a year or two, when out of the blue, Ashley Drake, who'd published the books I'd co-written with Spikey Watkins and Phil Steele, called me and asked if I knew Mark, because he had seen him in I Can't Say My Name, the BBC documentary about stammering, which had also featured his niece. He said he would love to sign him up to publish his story, and the rest, as they say, is history....

Although I was mates with Mark back in the 1980s and 1990s, I didn't really know or understand or appreciate, at that time, the pain and suffering he was going through growing up. To me, he was just one of the gang. I must admit I shed a tear or two when we were writing his story together. I have always respected him for what he did on the field and his friendship off it but after this, my respect for him is probably higher than anyone else I've ever known. I luvs you, Mark.

Stay free
Bunko xx

ST DAVID'S PRESS

NERVES OF STEELE

The Phil Steele Story

'I've been lucky enough to get to know Phil during my time as Wales coach. He is an excellent broadcaster who genuinely wants Wales and Welsh players to excel and I respect his friendly and personal approach. I also admire the fact that he has been able to do this while facing personal and life changing challenges.'
Warren Gatland

'Phil Steele embodies all that is great about the culture of Welsh rugby. His strength of character and sense of fun are all the more impressive given some of the dark and devastating times he has endured.'
Caroline Hitt

Known to thousands of rugby fans as a knowledgeable, passionate and witty broadcaster, and as an entertaining and popular after-dinner speaker, Phil Steele's confident demeanour and humorous disposition mask a life-long battle against depression and anxiety heightened by heartbreak and tragedy in his personal life. *Nerves of Steele* is a remarkable story and reveals the real Phil Steele, a man known only by his very closest friends and family.

978-1-902719-50-4 208pp £13.99 PB
978-1-902719-53-5 208pp £9.99 eBook

SPIKEY: 2 HARD TO HANDLE

The Autobiography of Mike 'Spikey' Watkins

'One of the most inspirational leaders that Welsh rugby has ever produced' **Mike Ruddock**

'A great friend...also a great inspiration...he led from the front and his team mates could always rely on him when things got a bit rough, even though he'd probably started it!!' **Paul Turner**

'No one trained harder, no one played harder...heart of a lion' **Terry Holmes**

One of the most colourful and controversial characters in Welsh rugby history, Mike 'Spikey' Watkins remains the only player since 1882 to captain Wales on his debut, and win.

978-1-902719-40-5 251pp £18.99 PB

NO REGRETS

Welsh Rugby's Plan To Conquer the World

'Matt is an honest, trustworthy journalist. I hope you enjoy the book and his account of the last few years!'
Warren Gatland

'Having followed Wales' every move over recent years, few journalists are better-placed to chronicle the team's journey over that period of time than Matt.' **Martyn Williams**

In *No Regrets - Welsh Rugby's Plan to Conquer the World*, acclaimed *Western Mail* rugby correspondent Matthew Southcombe reveals how the masterplan led to the 2017 tour success in Argentina, a clean sweep in the 2018 autumn internationals and, in 2019, a Six Nations Grand Slam, a record 14-game unbeaten run and a World Rugby #1 ranking. Hopes were high, amongst the squad and the nation, as the team headed to Japan with a genuine expectation winning the tournament.

978-1-902719-81-8 176pp £13.99 PB

ST DAVID'S PRESS

'this rugby spellbound people'

The Birth of Rugby in Cardiff and Wales

Gwyn Prescott

"...scrupulously researched [and] well written...Gwyn Prescott has given [rugby in Wales] a history to be proud of." **Huw Richards, *scrum.com***

"Prescott paints a meticulous picture of Welsh rugby's growth in Victorian Britain" **Rugby World**

"...a fascinating piece of research and a major contribution to the history of rugby." **Tony Collins**

The Birth of Rugby in Cardiff and Wales is the essential guide to the importance of rugby in Cardiff and to the significance of Cardiff to the development of Welsh rugby in the nineteenth century.

978-1-902719-43-6 304pp £16.99 PB

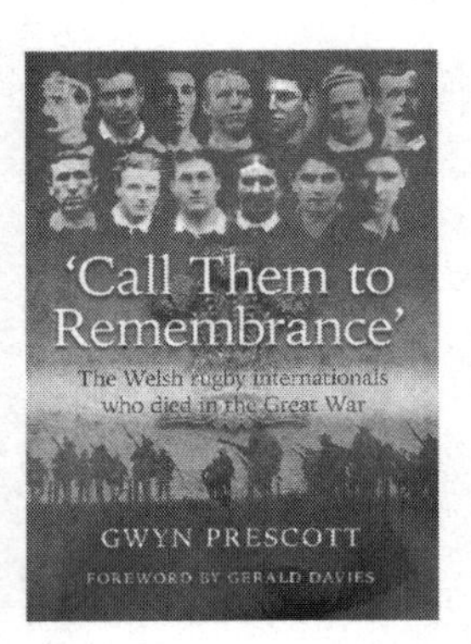

'Call Them to Remembrance'

The Welsh Rugby Internationals Who Died in the Great War (Second Edition)

Gwyn Prescott

'These pages contain an unexplored and untold tale which, from the deepest anguish of the suffering born of their unquestioning bravery, pierces the heart...This book is [an] acknowledgment of the sacrifice made by 13 Welshmen....Theirs was a sacrifice which needs to be told....Gwyn Prescott, with meticulous and sympathetic attention to detail, tells the story. This narrative is an essential record'. **Gerald Davies, from the Foreword**

It is estimated that the First World War claimed the lives of 40,000 Welshmen, all of them heroes whose sacrifice is acknowledged by a grateful nation. *'Call Them to Remembrance'*, which includes over 120 illustrations and maps, tells the stories of 13 fallen heroes who shared the common bond of having worn the famous red jersey of the Welsh international rugby team.

978-1-902719-82-5 PB 180pp £19.99
978-1-902719-90-0 eBook 180pp £19.99

ST DAVID'S PRESS

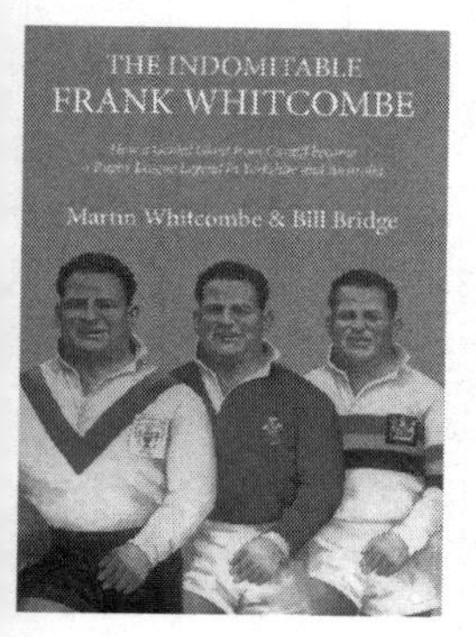

THE INDOMITABLE FRANK WHITCOMBE

How a Genial Giant from Cardiff became a Rugby League Legend in Yorkshire and Australia

'Frank Whitcombe was a rugby league cult hero in the days before there were cult heroes. An eighteen-stone battle tank of a prop forward, he graduated from Welsh rugby union to become a pillar of the great Bradford pack of the 1940s. In the process, he became the first forward to win the Lance Todd Trophy, a member of the 1946 'Indomitable' Lions touring team to Australasia and had even driven the team bus to Wembley when Bradford won the 1947 Challenge Cup Final. This book is his story - it is essential reading for anyone interested in the history of rugby and the amazing men who made the game.'

Prof. Tony Collins

'Frank Whitcombe became a Welsh international and a Great Britain tourist. He is widely regarded as an all-time great of rugby league.'

Fran Cotton

978-1-902719-47-4 256pp £19.99 PB
978-1-902719-59-7 256pp £9.99 eBook

THE INDOMITABLES

Rugby League's Greatest Tour
The 1946 'Great Britain' Tour to Australia & New Zealand

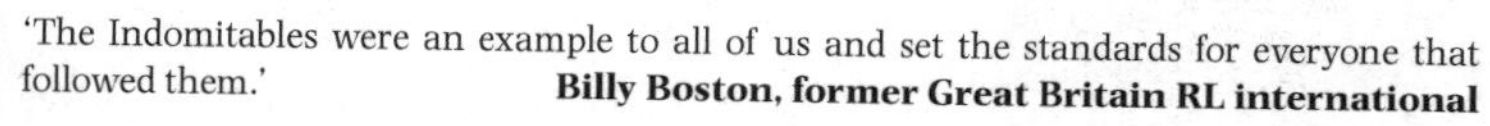

'The Indomitables were an example to all of us and set the standards for everyone that followed them.' **Billy Boston, former Great Britain RL international**

'Australians admire the best in sports and the Indomitables showed they were the best. Fans were fully engaged in every match and all the revelry that surrounded it. The papers were filled with news of the British players - they were celebrities and they seemed to relish that role. They were outstanding representatives of Britain, on and off the field.'

Pat Devery, former Australia RL international

Named after the aircraft carrier that took the 26 rugby players from Britain to Australia in 1946, the Indomitables won two Test matches and drew the third to become the most successful tourists in British rugby league history - a feat that has never been beaten.

These were ***The Indomitables*** – and this is their story.

978-1-902719-702 256pp £19.99 PB
978-1-902719-993 256pp £19.99 eBook

St David's Press

WAR GAMES

Rugby Union during the Second World War

Howard Evans & Phil Atkinson

Dedicated to 'all those in rugby who did - and who didn't - make it through those troubled times', *War Games* is a comprehensive and highly illustrated commemoration, packed with stories and statistics that for the first time chronicles the history of rugby - the men and the matches, from 'scratch' to international - during the Second World War.

Essential and entertaining reading for followers of rugby and military historians alike, respected rugby authors Howard Evans and Phil Atkinson tell the tale - meticulously and with great affection for the game they love - of those men who played for fun but who, on too many occasions, lost more than a rugby game.

978-1-902719-67-2 302pp £25.00 PB

THE WIZARDS

Aberavon Rugby 1876-2017

Howard Evans & Phil Atkinson

'I would rather have played rugby for Wales than Hamlet at the Old Vic. To that town, Aberavon and its rugby team, I pledge my continuing allegiance, until death.' **Richard Burton**

One of the traditional powerhouses of Welsh first class rugby, Aberavon RFC has a long proud and illustrious history, with 50 of its players being capped for Wales, the club winning many league titles and domestic cups, and - with Neath RFC - facing the might of South Africa, Australia and New Zealand. Aberavon RFC is a great rugby club and this is its story.

978-1-902719-66-5 256pp £19.99 PB

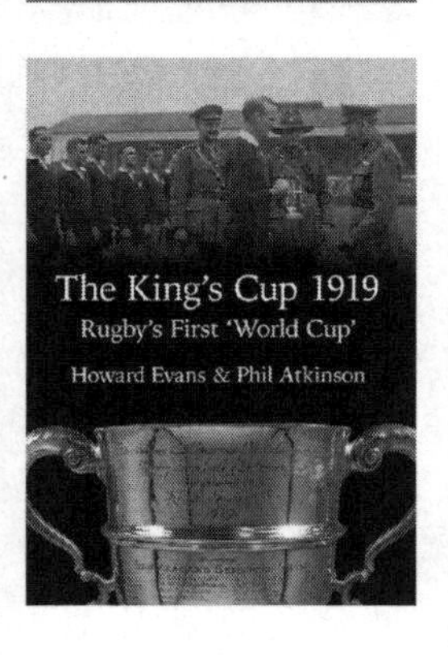

THE KING'S CUP 1919

Rugby's First World Cup

Howard Evans & Phil Atkinson

'An intriguing retelling of a significant but largely forgotten chapter of rugby union history, superbly illustrated.' **Huw Richards**

'Howard is an authority on rugby's history and meticulous in his research' ***Western Mail***

After the Armistice in November 1918 – with the forces of the world's rugby-playing nations and many of their stars still stationed in Britain – and with the public desperate to see competitive rugby played again, an inter-military tournament was organised. King George V was so enthused by the proposed competition that he agreed to have the tournament named after him, and so The King's Cup was born.

The King's Cup 1919 is the first book to tell the full story of rugby's first 'World Cup' and is essential reading for all rugby enthusiasts and military historians.

978-1-902719-44-3 192pp £14.99 PB

ST DAVID'S PRESS

THE BOXERS OF WALES
SWANSEA & LLANELLI

'My co-commentator, Enzo Maccarinelli, keeps telling me what a great fight town Swansea is. And here's the evidence. It's not just about the big names, like Colin Jones, Ronnie James and the Curvises - here you can learn of the only Welsh-speaker ever to win a Scottish title and the Llanelli girl who took on Germany's boxing queen. A great read!' **John Rawling, Commentator, *BoxNation***

'This book is a must for all serious boxing fans.'
Graham Houston, Editor, *Boxing Monthly*

978-1-902719-450 176pp £14.99 PB

THE BOXERS OF WALES
NEWPORT
THE GWENT VALLEYS AND MONMOUTHSHIRE

'Nobody knows Welsh boxing with quite the depth, understanding and empathy of Gareth Jones.' **Kevin Mitchell, *The Observer***

'Gareth Jones is THE authority on Welsh boxing, and always a joy to read. His exhaustive research uncovers wonderful stories that should not be missed.'
Matt Christie, Editor, Boxing News

978-1-902719-634 192pp £14.99 PB

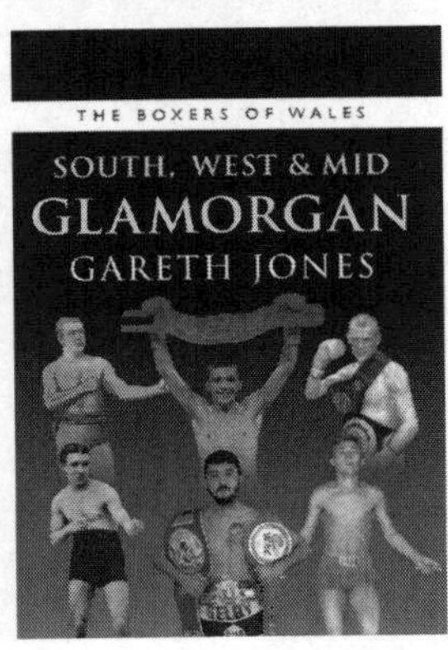

THE BOXERS OF WALES
SOUTH, WEST & MID
GLAMORGAN

'If I want to know anything about the history of Welsh boxing, Gareth Jones is my man. Delighted he has produced another book in his Boxers of Wales series - particularly as it includes someone I will always have a soft spot for, Lennie 'The Lion' Williams, who had two epic battles in the 1960s with Frankie Taylor and Howard Winstone.' ***Colin Hart***

'The Selby boys are here. Amateur glory, world title, so much talent. But once again it is a fighter that only the purest of fans can recall who catches the eye. This time it is Wee Willie Davies, a world-class flyweight, born near Maesteg, who moved to America as a child and met nine world champions. Welsh boxing, British boxing and even world boxing owes Gareth a great debt.' **Steve Bunce**

978-1-902719-801 176pp £16.99 PB

St David's Press

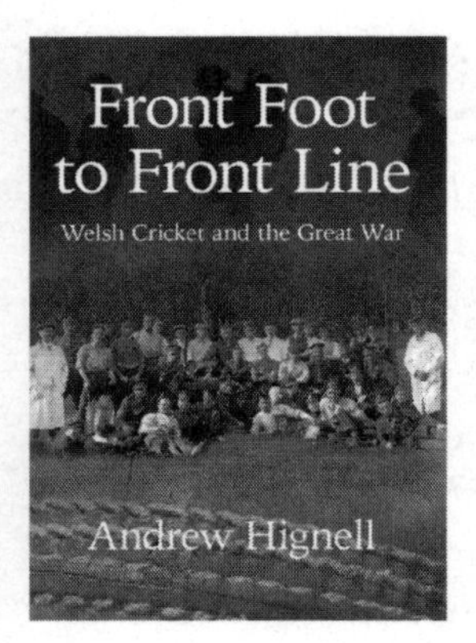

FRONT FOOT TO FRONT LINE

Welsh Cricket and the Great War

'recommended reading...nicely produced and well illustrated' **CricketWeb.net**

'this is a book that I have enjoyed more than any other on the subject of cricket and the Great War' **Association of Cricket Scorers**

'perceptive...absorbing...poignant...there is pride, excitement and amusement here - then grief again with more tales of fine, innocent, young cricketers whose luck ran out.' (4*) **David Frith, *The Cricketer***

Front Foot to Front Line commemorates Welsh cricket's contribution to the Great War by chronicling the lives of 55 professional and amateur cricketers who left the friendly rivalry of the crease for the brutality and horror of the trenches, and lost their lives as servicemen on the bloody battlefields of Europe.

978 1 902719 429 209pp £16.99 pb

BERNARD HEDGES

The Player From 'Ponty'

'Bernard was a true sportsman and played the game with an honesty and sense of fair play that stood out ... He was a good player but more than that, perhaps, he was a good bloke, easy company and willing to do anything for anyone.' **Don Shepherd, from his Foreword**

'As kids we grew up playing all sorts of sport in the street, including cricket and, when it was my turn to face the bowlers, I often chose to be Glamorgan's Bernard Hedges.' **Gareth Edwards**

The Player From 'Ponty' is the biography of Bernard Hedges, the talented sportsman from the valleys of south Wales. Hedges played rugby for Pontypridd and Swansea, represented a Great Britain side at football, and became a widely respected professional cricketer with Glamorgan between 1950 and 1967.

978 1 902719 566 224pp £19.99 pb